CONTENTS

Chapter 10: Positive Directions   203

Contributors   219

Chapter 1

FROM "JOBLESS RECOVERY" TO "JOB-LOSS RECOVERY"

BLACK JOB LOSS DÉJÀ VU

Think the typical job-loser in today's economy is a white computer programmer whose job has been outsourced to India? Think again.

Betsy Leondar-Wright
May/June 2004*

In July 2003, Mary Clark saw a notice posted by the time clock at the Pillowtex plant where she worked: the plant was closing down at the end of the month. The company would be laying off 4,000 workers. "They acted like we was nobody," she said; Pillowtex even canceled the workers' accrued vacation days. Clark had worked at the textile plant in Eden, North Carolina, for 11 years, inspecting, tagging, and bagging comforters. By 2003, she was earning more than $10 an hour.

Clark's unemployment benefits don't cover her bills. Because Pillowtex had sent her and her coworkers home frequently for lack of work in the final year, her unemployment checks are low, based on that last year's reduced earnings. She lost her health coverage, and now she needs dental work that she cannot afford.

It's happening again.

In the 1970s, a wave of plant closings hit African Americans hard. Two generations after the "Great Migration," when millions of black people had left the South to take factory jobs in Northern and Midwestern cities, the U.S. economy began to deindustrialize and many of those jobs disappeared—in some cases shifted to the low-wage, nonunion South.

The recession of 2001—and the historically inadequate "recovery" since—has again brought about a catastrophic loss of jobs, especially in manufacturing, and once again African Americans have lost out disproportionately. Jobs that moved to the

---

* Dates denote when the article appeared in *Dollars & Sense* magazine.

South during the earlier era of deindustrialization are now leaving the country entirely or simply disappearing in the wake of technological change and rising productivity.

Media coverage of today's unemployment crisis often showcases white men who have lost high-paying industrial or information-technology jobs. But Mary Clark is actually a more typical victim. Recent job losses have hit black workers harder than white workers: black unemployment rose twice as fast as white unemployment in the last recession. Once again, African Americans are getting harder hit, and once again, they face a downturn with fewer of the resources and assets that tide families over during hard times.

Last Hired, First Fired

The tight labor market of the late 1990s was very beneficial for African Americans. The black unemployment rate fell from 18% in the 1981-82 recession, to around 13% in the early 1990s, to below 7% in 1999 and 2000, the lowest black unemployment rate on record. But the 2001 recession (and the job-loss recovery since then) has robbed African Americans of much of those gains.

"The last recession has had a severe and disproportionate impact on African Americans and minority communities," according to Marc H. Morial, president of the National Urban League. In its January 2004 report on black unemployment, the Urban League found that the double-digit unemployment rates in the 14 months from late 2002 through 2003 were the worst labor market for African Americans in 20 years.

The 2001 recession was hard on African American workers both in relation to earlier recessions and in relation to white workers. Unemployment for adult black workers rose by 2.9 percentage points in the recession of the early 1980s, but by 3.5 in the 2001 recession. White unemployment, in contrast, rose by only 1.4 percentage points in the early-1980s recession and by 1.7 in the recent downturn. The median income of black families fell 3% from 2001 to 2003, while white families lost just 1.7%. Today, black unemployment has remained above 10% for over three years.

Official unemployment figures, of course, greatly understate the actual number of adults without jobs. The definition doesn't include discouraged people who have stopped looking for work, underemployed part-timers, students, or those in prison or other institutions. In New York City, scarcely half of African-American men between 16 and 65 had jobs in 2003, according to the Bureau of Labor Statistics' employment-to-population ratios for the city. The BLS ratios, which include discouraged workers and others the official unemployment statistics leave out, were 51.8% for black men, 57.1% for black women, 75.7% for white men, and 65.7% for Latino men. The figure for black men was the lowest on record (since 1979).

Manufacturing job losses in particular have hit black workers harder than white workers. In 2000, there were 2 million African Americans working in factory jobs. Blacks comprised 10.1% of all manufacturing workers, about the same as the black share of the overall workforce. Then 300,000 of those jobs, or 15%, disappeared.

White workers lost 1.7 million factory jobs, but that was just 10% of the number they held before the recession. By the end of 2003, the share of all factory jobs held by African Americans had fallen to 9.6%. "Half a percentage point may not sound like much, but to lose that much in such an important sector over a relatively short period, that is going to be hard to recover," said Jared Bernstein of the Economic Policy Institute, a progressive economics think tank. Latino workers increased their share of manufacturing jobs in 2002 and 2003 slightly, though their unemployment rate overall rose.

Some of the largest layoffs have occurred in areas with large African-American populations—just this April, for example, 1,000 jobs were cut at a Ford plant in St. Louis and 300 at a Boeing plant in San Antonio. Textile plants with mostly black employees have closed in Roanoke Rapids, N.C., Columbus, Ga., and Martinsville, Va. The states with the greatest number of layoffs of 50 workers or more are black strongholds New York and Georgia.

When Autoliv closed its seat belt plant in Indianapolis in 2003, more than 75% of the laid-off workers were African Americans. Many of these workers are young adults who got their jobs during the labor shortage of the late 1990s even without a high school diploma; now they have few options. "They were taken from the street into decent-paying jobs; they were making $12 to $13 an hour. These young men started families, dug in, took apartments, purchased vehicles. It was an up-from-the-street experience for them, and now they are being returned to their old environment," said Michael Barnes, director of an Indiana AFL-CIO training program for laid-off workers.

U.S. Chamber of Commerce executive vice president Bruce Josten isn't too worried about layoffs: "We're talking about transformational evolution—successful companies remaking their own operations so they're able to better focus on what their core mission is. It's not a deal where everyone gains instantly. At a micro level, there's always going to be a community that's hurt." The communities that are hurt come in all colors, but several factors make the micro level pain more severe in communities of color.

Hard Times Hit Blacks Harder

Prolonged unemployment is scary for most families, but it puts the typical African-American family in deeper peril, and faster. The median white family has more than $120,000 in net worth (assets minus debts). The median black family has less than $20,000, a far smaller cushion in tough times.

Laid-off workers often turn to family members for help, but with almost a quarter of black families under the poverty line, and one in nine black workers unemployed, it's less likely that unemployed African Americans have family members with anything to spare. Black per capita income was only 57 cents for every white dollar in 2001.

When homeowners face prolonged unemployment, they can take out a home equity loan or second mortgage to tide them over. But while three-quarters of white families are homeowners, less than half of black families own their own homes.

And thanks to continuing segregation and discrimination in housing, it's more difficult for black families to relocate to find work. New jobs are concentrated in mostly white suburbs with little public transportation.

History Repeats Itself

The term "deindustrialization" came into everyday use in the 1970s, when a wave of plant closings changed the employment landscape. From 1966 to 1973, corporations moved over a million American jobs to other countries. Even more jobs moved from the Northeast and Midwest to the South, where unions were scarce and wages lower. New York City alone lost 600,000 manufacturing jobs in the 1960s.

As today, the workers laid off in the 1960s and 70s were disproportionately African-American. The U.S. Commission on Civil Rights found that during the recession of 1973 to 1974, 60% to 70% of laid-off workers were African-American in areas where they were only 10% to 12% of the workforce. In five cities in the Great Lakes region, the majority of black men employed in manufacturing lost their jobs between 1979 and 1984. A major reason was seniority: white workers had been in their jobs longer, and so were more likely to keep them during cutbacks.

Another reason was geography. The Northern cities that lost the most jobs were some of those with the largest populations of people of color, and those inner-city areas sank deep into poverty and chronically high unemployment as few heavily white areas did.

The race and class politics of deindustrialization are also part of the story. The pro-business loyalties of the federal government dictated policies that encouraged plant closings and did very little to mitigate their effects. Tax credits for foreign investment and for foreign tax payments encouraged companies to move plants overseas. While Northern cities were suffering from deindustrialization, the federal government spent more in the Southern states than in the affected areas: Northeast and Midwest states averaged 81 cents in federal spending for each tax dollar they sent to Washington in the 1970s, while Southern states averaged $1.25. Laid-off black factory workers had no clout, so politicians faced little pressure to address their needs.

As dramatic as the movement of jobs from the North to the South and overseas was the shift from city to suburb. The majority of new manufacturing jobs in the 1970s were located in suburban areas, while manufacturing employment fell almost 10% in center cities. In the Los Angeles area, for example, older plants were closing in the city while new ones opened in the San Fernando Valley and Orange County.

The new suburban jobs were usually inaccessible for African Americans and other people of color because of housing costs, job and housing discrimination, lack of public transportation, and lack of informal social networks with suburban employers. In a study of Illinois firms that moved to the suburbs from the central cities between 1975 and 1978, black employment in the affected areas fell 24%, while white employment fell less than 10%. In another study, some employers admitted to locating facilities in part so as to avoid black workers. One study of the causes of black unemployment in 45 urban areas found that 25% to 50% resulted from jobs shifting to the suburbs. Even the federal government shifted jobs to the suburbs: although the number of federal civilian jobs grew by 26,558 from 1966 to 1973, federal jobs in central cities fell by 41,419. Over time, suburban white people gained a greater and greater geographic edge in job hunting.

Looking Forward

Mary Clark has been looking for work for nine months now without success. Stores get applications from hundreds of other laid-off workers; there aren't enough jobs for even a fraction of the unemployed. "It used to be that if one plant shut down, there'd be another one hiring. Now they're all laying off or closing," she says.

For years Clark had helped her grown daughter support her two small children. "Now the roles are reversed, and they help me." She has turned to charities to make ends meet, but some give aid only once a year, and others won't help a single woman without children at home. "It breaks your self-esteem to have to ask for help," Clark says.

Some of her former coworkers are in more desperate straits than she is. Some have lost their homes or gone into bankruptcy. Some people have found jobs far from home and commute for hours a day. Clark sees crime, divorce, and family violence all rising in the area.

What job growth there's been has been concentrated in the low-wage service sector, which pays less than the shrinking manufacturing sector. There's no law of nature that says service jobs are inevitably low paid and without benefits. Or that manufacturing can't revive in the United States. The recent wave of union organizing victories in heavily black industries such as health care represent one source of hope for creating more decent jobs for African Americans.

Dr. Martin Luther King Jr. said in 1968, "When there is massive unemployment in the black community, it is called a social problem. But when there is massive unemployment in the white community, it is called a depression." The New Deal response to the Great Depression included public works jobs and a strengthened safety net, most of which excluded people of color. Mary Clark clearly recognizes what happens when there is no New Deal for unemployed African Americans: "North Carolina has people who want to work, but we don't have anyone pushing work our way. We need the mills back. We're people used to working, and when you take the work away, what do you have left?"

Sources: Lori Aratani, "With jobs heading overseas, trade issues resonating with many," *Knight Ridder News Service,* 1/25/04; Louis Uchitelle, "Blacks Lose Better Jobs Faster As Middle-Class Work Drops," *New York Times,* 7/12/03; Dedrick Muhammad, Attieno Davis, Meizhu Lui, and Betsy Leondar-Wright, *The State of the Dream: Enduring Disparities in Black and White* (United for a Fair Economy, Jan. 2004); National Urban League, *The National Urban League's Jobs Report, Jan. 2004;* Janny Scott, "Nearly Half of Black Men Found Jobless," *New York Times,* 2/28/04; Arthur B. Kennickell, "A Rolling Tide: Changes in the Distribution of Wealth in the U.S.,

1989-2001," (Levy Economics Institute, Nov. 2003); Economic Policy Institute, *Snapshot, 2/11/04*; Gregory D. Squires, "Runaway Plants, Capital Mobility, and Black Economic Rights," in *Community and Capital in Conflict: Plant Closings and Job Loss*, John C. Raines et al., eds. (Temple Univ. Press, 1982); Lawrence H. Fuchs, *The American Kaleidoscope: Race, Ethnicity, and the Civic Culture* (Wesleyan Univ. Press, 1990); George Lipsitz, *The Possessive Investment in Whiteness: How White People Profit from Identity Politics* (Temple Univ. Press, 1998); Douglas S. Massey and Nancy A. Denton, *American Apartheid: Segregation and the Making of the Underclass* (Harvard Univ. Press, 1993); James H. Johnson, Jr. and Melvin L. Oliver, "Economic Restructuring and Black Male Joblessness in U.S. Metropolitan Areas," *Urban Geography* (Vol. 12, 1991).

HIGH AND DRY
The Economic Recovery Fails to Deliver
John Miller
March/April 2004

This economy is pumped. Boosted by economic stimulants—military spending, tax rebates, interest rate cuts, and a spate of mortgage refinancing—the U.S. economy expanded at an 8.2% annual rate in the third quarter of 2003, its fastest pace in nearly two decades, and at a respectable 4% rate in the fourth quarter. The Dow is back over 10,000. Corporate profits are up. Business investment is improving, and consumer confidence is holding.

Predictably, the *Wall Street Journal's* editors spent the winter holidays chortling about "the merry economy." The 55 blue-chip economists the Journal surveyed predict that economic growth will exceed 4% and that the economy will create 1.5 million jobs this year, just in time for George W. Bush's election campaign.

But despite this ginned-up sense of economic well-being, the specter of stagnation—that the United States could go the way of Japan and sink into a decade-long economic funk—continues to haunt the U.S. economy.

The current wave of frenetic economic activity has done nothing to solve the underlying flaws of the post-bubble economy. Overcapacity, especially the hangover from the collapse of manufacturing and the dot-coms, oppressive consumer debt burdens, an ever-widening trade deficit, burgeoning budget deficits, and unprecedented inequality—all are still with us. And even after a heavy dose of economic stimulants, job creation in this recovery remains the worst on record.

The Bush administration has expended a lot of fiscal firepower to stimulate this recovery. But the administration's stimulants of choice are not generating a cumulative and self-sustaining economic expansion. What's more, the prescription on many of them is about to expire. Future tax cuts will go ever more exclusively to the well-to-do, resulting in less new consumer spending. The Fed has little room left to cut short-term interest rates further. Higher long-term rates have already slowed mortgage refinancing. And that is to say nothing of the toxic side effects of the Bush team's economic antidepressants: they gut public-sector social spending and support an economic growth that does surprisingly little to improve the living standard of most people.

Eight Months Down, Three Years Sideways

Last July, the National Bureau of Economic Research (NBER)—the nation's official arbiter of the business cycle—declared that the recession that began in March 2001 had ended way back in November of that year, only eight months later. The 2001 recession was neither long nor deep. The average duration of post-World War II recessions is 11 months. And the output lost in the 2001 recession, measured by the decline in real Gross Domestic Product (GDP, the broadest single measure of economic output), was less than a third of the drop-off during the 1990-91 recession.

Why did it take the NBER's economists 20 months to recognize a recovery that was already underway? Because this recovery has been so weak that the NBER hesitated to declare the recession over. The economy fell for just eight months but it has crawled sideways for nearly three years. Real personal income (income of households adjusted for inflation) has grown much more slowly than in past recoveries, and the economy has continued to lose jobs long after a typical recovery would have returned to pre-recession job numbers.

Instead of a robust recovery, the economy has entered "a twilight zone—growing fast enough to avoid an official recession but not fast enough to create jobs," according to Paul Krugman, economist and *New York Times* columnist. Economic growth averaged just 2.6% from the official end of the recession in November 2001 through the second quarter of 2003. Economic journalist William Greider warned the U.S. economy was flirting with something far worse, "a low-grade depression." (See "The Japan Syndrome," page 8.)

Running on Fumes

At this January's World Economic Summit in Davos, Switzerland, Stephen Roach, chief economist at Morgan Stanley investment bank in New York, warned business leaders that "the main engine of the global economy, the … U.S., is right now running on fumes." Tax cuts, home sales and mortgage refinancing fueled by low interest rates, and Iraq-driven military spending—not self-sustaining job and wage growth—fueled the 2003 growth spurt. Each of those additives to the economic fuel tank will be less able to power future economic growth, either because it's now in short supply or because it has gummed up the economic engine.

Take monetary policy. Interest rate cuts were key to keeping the weak, post-bubble economy out of a deep recession: they helped underwrite last year's surge in consumer spending on durable goods, especially housing and automobiles.

But the Fed will be hard pressed to coax more spending out of the economy. With the federal funds rate at 1%, there is not much room left for further rate cuts. In addition, interest rates on home mortgages are already rising. This will slow the spate of mortgage refinancing that put money in consumers' pockets in 2002 and 2003: over the last two years, half of all U.S. homeowners refinanced $4.5 trillion in mortgage debt.

The Japan Syndrome: Could It Happen Here?

It isn't only left-leaning journalists sounding the alarm bells. Even the *Wall Street Journal* asked, "Is the U.S. economy at risk of emulating Japan's long swoon?"

During the 1980s, Japan enjoyed an economic boom as heady as the one the United States saw in the 1990s, complete with a soaring stock market and a red-hot housing market. But when the bubble burst, the Japanese economy sank into a decade-long economic slump. Japanese income growth slowed, falling behind the United States'. The Nikkei, Japan's major stock market index, lost three-quarters of its value from its peak in 1989. The Japanese real estate boom collapsed in 1991; in 2003 a house in Tokyo cost less than half of what it did in 1991. A tanking real estate sector and a slowing economy saddled Japanese banks with bad loans. Excess capacity, especially high for Japanese automakers, discouraged new investment and ensured that the slowdown would persist.

The 1990s boom in the United States came to a similar if less severe end. By 2000, the U.S. stock market bubble had burst. Broad measures of stock values lost about one-third of their peak values over the next two years. Manufacturing had already hit the skids. Industrial production fell steadily, contributing to a general excess of industrial capacity. Today, capacity utilization rates still hover at about 75%, and the manufacturing sector has shed jobs for some 42 straight months. The new economy fared no better. The NASDAQ, the high-tech stock index, melted down, losing nearly three-quarters of its value from March 2000 to July 2002, and gaggles of dot-com firms folded, putting plenty of white-collar workers out of work.

Only the continued strength of the U.S. real estate market, along with the willingness of debt-strapped U.S. consumers to spend, seemed to stand between the U.S. economy and Japan's fate. The Fed would add one more factor that insulated the U.S. economy

On top of that, consumers are up to their eyeballs in debt. Debt service now claims a record 13% of disposable income, despite the interest rate cuts. Three years of a bear market has put a real dent in people's net worth, and less mortgage refinancing will do nothing good for the value of their homes. With employment lower than three years ago and wages stagnant, consumers sooner or later will stop spending, as Roach warns. In fact, by the end of last year the surge in consumer spending, especially for automobiles, had already cooled.

Fed interest rate cuts never bolstered investment spending as much as consumer spending. Lingering excess productive capacity across the economy left businesses reluctant to make new investments. During much of the recovery, corporations have used the lower interest rates to pay down short-term debt and to buy back their own stock, not to add to capital spending.

Business investment did pick up considerably in the second half of 2003, posting its strongest gains since the first quarter of 2000. Robert Shapiro, economist with the centrist Progressive Policy Institute, says that "with consumer spending slowing, improved business fixed investment is now the strongest private sector support for the expansion in 2004." But even with the recent upswing in corporate spending, investment levels are quite modest. During the red-hot third quarter of last year, real against a Japan-style economic collapse: monetary policy. Ironically, it was the Fed's own repeated interest rate hikes in the second half of 1999 and the first half of 2000, along with the Clinton administration's downsizing of the federal government, that contributed mightily to bringing on the economic slowdown in the first place.

In the summer of 2002, the Fed devoted its annual retreat in Jackson Hole, Wyoming, to the threat of Japanese-style stagnation. Fed members and their boosters ended up assuring themselves that they had averted the threat by acting more quickly than Japanese central bankers had. While the Japanese central bank (CBJ) had waited nearly two years after the bubble burst to act, it then set about furiously cutting short-term interest rates, from 6% in 1991 to under 1% in 1995. The Fed did act more quickly than its Japanese counterpart, dropping the federal funds rate on overnight loans to commercial banks from 6.25% to 1.25% in just two years.

Has the Fed saved the day? That the U.S economy has muddled through the last three years with slow growth and is now in the midst of a growth spurt is enough for many to conclude that the threat of stagnation is behind us. But that would be a mistake. Japan's economy did not collapse into stagnation but slid gradually, as the Japanese bankers attending the Jackson Hole retreat emphasized. At the same time, economic forecasters repeatedly predicted that Japanese economic growth rates would soon pick up. Most ominously, Japan's real estate bubble burst a couple of years after its stock market bubble. If the housing market does fall apart, U.S. banks could end up in critical condition much as they did during the mid-1980s banking crisis that gripped much of the nation. And with U.S interest rates already close to zero, Pam Woodall, economics editor of the conservative British weekly the *Economist*, worries that "a housing bust might therefore nudge the economy into deflation."

business investment, as Shapiro himself emphasizes, was still 7% lower than it was in 2000 and even below its average level during the 2001 recession.

Fed interest-rate cuts were also supposed to fix another obstacle to sustained economic growth and job creation: the gaping U.S. trade deficit. But the fix hasn't worked too well. (See "That Pesky Trade Deficit," page 10.)

Fiscal Policy Misses the Mark

Fiscal policy, the manipulation of government spending and taxing policies, is just as problematic for sustaining economic growth as monetary policy. For the Bush administration, fiscal policy usually means just one thing: cutting taxes for the well-to-do. Three rounds of tax cuts for the rich, combined with last year's military spending for the Iraq war and its aftermath, have indeed shifted the government's fiscal status in a big way: the federal budget went from a $236 billion surplus in fiscal year 2000 to a $521 billion projected deficit in fiscal year 2004.

Such a powerful fiscal swing, the equivalent of about 7% of GDP, was sure to lift economic growth over the short term, almost regardless of the particulars. And Bush fiscal policy did goose economic growth rates in 2003. When the invasion of Iraq

That Pesky Trade Deficit

The U.S. trade balance has steadily worsened during this recovery, as imports rose rapidly while exports did not. U.S. exports are just now topping their pre-recession levels. At a comparable point following the 1990-91 recession, exports were up 18%. Last year, the U.S. current account deficit, the broadest measure of the balance of trade in goods and services, surpassed 5% of GDP—the level financial analysts traditionally use as sign of financial distress in a developing economy.

The Fed's interest rate cuts were supposed to help. By lowering interest rates, the Fed would bring down the value of the dollar, making U.S exports cheaper for foreign purchasers. The value of the dollar has indeed fallen by about 12% since early 2002, with the largest drop occurring against the euro, but we have yet to see any improvement in the current account deficit.

What's more, depreciating the dollar is tricky business. Lower interest rates make U.S. bonds less attractive to investors. But financing this record trade deficit depends on the willingness of foreign investors to accumulate dollar assets almost without limit. Foreigners already supply 42% of the funds borrowed by U.S. households, businesses, and government. For instance, in 2002, foreigners purchased 58% of new Treasury debt. And foreign lenders are likely to demand higher compensation as the value of their dollar-denominated assets declines, driving up interest rates. Alternatively, some large foreign creditors might dump their dollar holdings, triggering a full-blown dollar crisis that would cause interest rates to spike and the U.S. stock and bond markets to tumble. Either way, the current account deficit is sure to dampen U.S. economic growth.

gave rise to the biggest quarterly increase in military spending since the Korean War, GDP growth rates during the second quarter picked up from 2.0% to 3.1%, with economic analysts attributing three-quarters of the spike to government spending. Similarly, tax rebates over the summer added to the consumer spending that drove the third quarter GDP growth spurt.

But the limitations of the Bush team's attempt to punch up a sluggish economy for the election year have already begun to show. First off, future tax cuts will do less to add to consumer spending because they go ever more exclusively to the well-to-do, who spend a smaller share of their income than other taxpayers. Even in 2003, nearly one-half of taxpayers (49%) got $100 or less back in lower taxes, reports Citizens for Tax Justice. In 2005, that number rises to three-quarters of taxpayers, and it continues up from there. At the same time, nearly two-fifths of the Bush tax cut goes the richest 1%.

Second, the Bush stimulus package has done little or nothing to relieve the pressure on state and local budgets. With 30 states still facing between $39 and $41 billion in budget shortfalls in fiscal year 2005—the equivalent of 8% of their expenditures—more cutbacks in state spending are inevitable. Those state budget cuts are sapping the stimulative effect of any federal deficit spending. Nicholas Johnson, director of the State Fiscal Project at the Center on Budget and Policy Priorities, estimates that the state fiscal crisis is "taking at least half a percentage point out of the growth rate of the national economy."

The administration's failure to address the budget crisis in the states is not only trimming economic growth, it's also destroying critical programs. State budget cuts have hit working people and the poor especially hard. The federal government has shifted responsibility for social spending onto the states, and that is what's being cut. California, for instance, cut spending by $12 billion in the two years prior to last fall's recall election; schools there now go without computers, and public libraries are unable to purchase books. Nationwide, 34 states have cut programs such as Medicaid and the Children's Health Insurance Program that provide health care to low- and moderate-income families.

And while fiscal stimulus might be pumping up measured growth rates, the Bush administration is running large deficits likely to be sustained even if investment spending continues to improve and labor markets eventually tighten. Those long-term structural deficits, as economists call them, could provide the political justification for further cutbacks in social and infrastructure spending necessary to put economic growth on a more solid footing. In fact, if the Bush tax cuts are made permanent, there would be no room in the federal budget for any domestic discretionary spending in just eight years, according to a recent study by Eugene Steuerle, a senior fellow at the Urban Institute. By 2012, entitlements (Social Security, Medicare, and Medicaid), military spending, and interest on the growing government debt would have absorbed all remaining federal revenues, leaving not a dollar for education, job training, housing, environment, community development, energy, public infrastructure, or other domestic programs. That would be a disaster not only for working families and children, as the Urban Institute emphasizes, but for the productivity of the U.S. economy as well.

Jobless Recovery to Job-Loss Recovery

Whatever administration and Fed policies have done to produce an uptick in measured economic growth, they have done little to create jobs—the key to sustaining wage growth and a self-perpetuating economic expansion. And the Bush administration sure did promise new jobs. With the 2003 tax cut in place, the president's Council of Economic Advisors insisted, the economy would create 306,000 jobs a month from July 2003 to December 2004.

Hardly. When economic growth picked up in the final five months of 2003, the recovery finally stopped losing jobs. But the economy added a total of just 278,000 new jobs in those five months, with 80% of those job gains concentrated in temporary staffing, education, health care, and government. That is fewer jobs than the Bush team's promised monthly total.

Job creation in this recovery does not fall short just with respect to the administration's inflated promises, but by any reasonable measure. Even with those new jobs in the last five months of the year, the economy lost a net 331,000 jobs for 2003, on top of 1.5 million lost in 2002. The last time payroll employment declined for two consecutive years was in 1944 and 1945, as war production wound down. And that is a far cry from the average 300,000 new jobs per month the U.S. economy posted from 1995 to 2000.

Since the recession began 33 months ago, 2.4 million U.S. jobs have disappeared. Following every other post-World War II recession, jobs had fully recovered to their pre-recession levels within 31 months of the start of the recession. Worse yet, as a recent study by economists at the New York Federal Reserve Bank shows, a far larger share of recent layoffs have been permanent, rather than the temporary cyclical layoffs dominant in most previous recessions.

The current recovery can't even stack up to the only other "jobless" recovery on record, the 1991-92 recovery that cost Bush's father re-election. *Business Week* calculates that to equal the job creation record of the early 1990s rebound, the economy would need to have added 3 million more private sector jobs by now, including 1,547,000 more manufacturing jobs and 707,000 more information technology jobs.

Jesse Jackson warned the 2000 Democratic Convention to "Stay out of the Bushes"—advice that should be taken seriously by anyone concerned with holding onto a job or finding a new one. We have gone from a jobless recovery under the elder Bush to a job-loss recovery under the younger Bush.

Employers are unwilling to add new jobs because they remain unconvinced that the economic recovery is sustainable. Instead of hiring new workers, bosses are squeezing more out of the old ones. This, along with corporate restructuring and layoffs, has produced rapid increases in productivity—the economy's output per hour of labor input. For instance, during the last two years, the hourly output of U.S. workers has gone up at a 5.3% pace, exceeding the "new economy" productivity growth rate of 2.6% from 1996 to 2001. For the first time in a postwar recovery, productivity is growing far faster than the economy.

Manufacturing has been especially devastated. Factory productivity has gone up by 15%, versus a 9% rise in the comparable period in the early 1990s. That has helped produce the longest string of manufacturing layoffs since the Great Depression. Ohio, Michigan, and Pennsylvania have each lost 200,000 or more manufacturing jobs since January 2001.

Another drain on U.S. job creation is the increasing number of jobs lost to global outsourcing. Not only manufacturing jobs are going abroad, but also white collar work, from backroom office operations (bookkeeping, customer service, and marketing) to engineering and computer software design. Increased competition engendered by the Internet has allowed formerly non-tradable jobs to escape abroad, in this latest bout of corporate cost-cutting. How many jobs are being lost to this global arbitrage, as economists call it, is a matter of dispute. There are no official data, but estimates range from 500,000 to 995,000 jobs since March 2001, or somewhere between 15% and 35% of the total decline in employment. Gregory Mankiw, the politically tone-deaf chair of Bush's Council of Economic Advisors, recently assured Americans that outsourcing is "a plus for the economy in the long run"—cold comfort for those who have seen their jobs move offshore.

Stephen Roach puts IT-enabled "offshoring" at the top of his list of possible explanations for the inability of this recovery to create jobs. "In my discussions with a broad cross-section of business executives," reports Roach, "I was hard-pressed to find any who weren't contemplating white-collar offshoring."

Typically, economic stimulus policies activate "multiplier effects" that sustain economic growth over time. Higher government spending calls forth more output. Employers in turn hire more workers. New jobs put money in workers' pockets and empower workers who already have jobs to press for higher wages. And that fuels consumption. But without new jobs, that internally generated fuel is all but absent in the current upturn. Outsourcing and other trends are eroding the bargaining position of U.S. workers; predictably, wage and salary disbursements are currently running some $350 billion below the path of previous upturns. With cost-saving productivity gains and the offshoring of jobs showing no sign of abating, there is little reason to believe that this recovery will soon be able to run on its own steam. More likely, the economy will continue to grow slowly but create few new jobs.

Facing Up to our Economic Problems

This is no time to balance the budget. Dimitri Papadimitriou, president of the Levy Institute, a progressive economics think tank, estimates that the government sector as a whole (federal, state, and local) will have to run a deficit of 7% to 8% of GDP to keep the economy growing.

The public sector must both provide immediate economic stimulus and move to correct the economy's underlying problems through policies that will counteract economic stagnation and spread the benefits of economic growth more widely. Economic stimulus need not be toxic. Alternative policies are fully capable of jogging the economy back to life and at the same time creating jobs and making the economy stronger rather than weaker over the long haul.

Here is some of what has to happen. First, the Bush administration's pro-rich tax cuts, which provide less bang for the buck than more broad-based tax cuts, have to go. With 80% of taxpayers now paying more in payroll taxes than in income taxes, lowering payroll taxes would do more to boost consumer spending than cutting income taxes. But even payroll tax cuts, dollar for dollar, do less to stimulate economic growth than government spending. A one-dollar payroll tax cut adds just 90 cents to output in the following year, while a hike in unemployment benefits would generate $1 in output for each dollar the government spends, and one dollar in federal government spending to build up infrastructure would add an additional $1.80 in output over the next year, estimates David Wyss, chief economist at Standard & Poors.

There is still room for additional government outlays, especially if the Bush tax cuts for the super-rich are repealed. Relative to the size of the economy, the federal government is still no larger than its postwar average. And there is much to be done. To begin with, temporary federal unemployment benefits that were allowed to expire in December 2003 must be reinstated. Otherwise, by the middle of this year, an estimated two million unemployed people will see their benefits expire. The Bush budget proposal for FY2005 will cut another $6 billion in support for the states, but as much as an additional $100 billion in federal aid is needed to support cash-strapped states in the coming years.

Public investment, which has fallen to about one-half its levels during the 1960s and 1970s relative to the size of the economy, must be restored to maintain the nation's economic competitiveness. That means increased public investments in education, job training, and child care as well as in basic infrastructure, the environment, energy, and research and development. Many of these programs, especially spending on the environment and natural resources and on job training and employment services, have suffered deep cuts since 2000.

"In the end," as economist Anwar Shaikh points out, "government expenditures need to provide not only demand stimulus but also social stimulus." Otherwise, while GDP growth may be momentarily high(er), the well of sustained expansion and broad-based economic gains will stay dry.

Sources: "Jobless Recovery? Not in 2004, Economists Say," *WSJ*, 1/2/03; Jacob M. Schlesinger and Peter Landers, "Parallel Woes: Is the US Economy At Risk of Emulating Japan's Long Swoon?" *WSJ*, 11/07/01; Pam Woodall, "House of Cards," *The Economist*, 5/29/03; Nicholas Johnson and Bob Zahradnik, "State Budget Deficits Projected For FY2005," Center on Budget and Policy Priorities, 1/30/04; Louis Uchitelle, "Red Ink in States Beginning to Hurt Economic Recovery," *NYT*, 7/28/03; "The Hurting Heartland," Business Week, 12/15/03; "JobWatch," Economic Policy Institute, 1/04; Louis Uchitelle, "A Statistic That's Missing: Jobs That Moved Overseas," *NYT*, 10/5//03; James C. Cooper and Michael J. Mandel, "So Where Are The Jobs?" *Business Week*, 1/26/04; Jacob Schlesinger, "Bush's Early Electoral Edge: It's Not His Father's Economy," *WSJ*, 1/12/04; Stephen Roach, "False Recovery," Morgan Stanley Global Economic Forum, 1/12/04; Anwar Shaikh et al., "Deficits, Debts, and Growth: A Reprieve But Not a Pardon," Levy Economics Institute, 10/03; Randall Wray and Dimitri Papadimitriou, "Understanding Deflation: Treating The Disease, Not the Sympthoms," Levy Economics Institute, Winter 2004; Robert J. Shapiro, "Economic Recovery Remains Vulnerable to Setbacks," Center for American Progress, 12/22/03.

MISSING JOBS STILL LOST
John Miller
November/December 2004

"Missing Jobs Found"

... It turns out that this economic expansion is different from those in the past, but not in the way that many thought. New jobs are being created as usual, but they are different kinds of jobs. The U.S. economy is undergoing a structural change as more people become self-employed or form partnerships, rather than working for large corporations.

This transformation confounds the government's employment surveyors because they rely on the payroll data of about 400,000 existing companies ...

These [new] jobs show up in the "household survey." The government collects this data from workers rather than companies, and while it is more volatile month-to-month due to the smaller sample size (60,000 households), over the past three years it consistently told us that something unusual is happening. If you believe the payroll figures, the U.S. still has to create 700,000 more new jobs before it will return to the peak pre-recession level of 2001. But according to what individual Americans are saying, we've already surpassed that level by two million jobs.

In short, these are good times for most American workers ...

—*The Wall Street Journal*, October 11, 2004

The Bush administration may have struck out trying to find weapons of mass destruction in Iraq, but the *Wall Street Journal* editors say they have found the jobs that have gone missing during this jobless economic recovery.

Using the household survey of employment as their Geiger counter, the Journal's editors claim to have unearthed hundreds of thousands of new jobs overlooked by the traditional payroll survey of employment favored by the Bureau of Labor Statistics, the Congressional Budget Office, and most economists. With those extra jobs, the household survey has the Bush administration adding jobs to the economy, not losing them, and the recovery, as of September, creating 1,628,000 jobs on top of replacing the jobs lost since the last recession began, in March 2001. That picture is far more to the liking of the Journal's editors than the one painted by the payroll survey, which depicts the Bush administration as losing jobs and the recovery still down 940,000 jobs since the onset of the recession some three and a half years ago. Replacing the jobs lost to the recession is something the average postwar recovery managed to accomplish within two years.

But the truth is that, when used appropriately, the payroll and household employment surveys tell "the same (sad) story," in the words of Cleveland Federal Reserve Bank economists Mark Schweitzer and Guhan Venkatu. "Both surveys," they note, "show that employment has performed poorly in this recovery relative to the usual post-World War II experience." By historical standards, over four million jobs remain missing in today's economy.

Why the Payroll Survey Is More Accurate Than the Household Survey

Federal Reserve Board Chair Alan Greenspan feels the Journal editors' pain. Still, he can't bring himself to endorse using the household survey to measure monthly employment growth. Earlier this year, Greenspan told Congress, "Having looked at both sets of data ... it's our judgment that as much as we would like the household data to be the more accurate, regrettably that turns out not to be the case."

Why do Alan Greenspan, the Bureau of Labor Statistics (BLS) that conducts both surveys, and the nonpartisan Congressional Budget Office regard the payroll survey to be "the more accurate," to provide "more reliable information," and to "better reflect the state of the labor market" than the household survey?

The first reason is statistical reliability. The payroll or establishment survey, which the BLS calls the Employment Statistics Survey, asks employers at about 400,000 worksites how many people they employ. The payroll sample includes every firm with 1,000 employees or more and covers about one-third of the total number of workers. The household survey—its formal name is the Current Population Survey—asks people in 60,000 households about their employment status. That is a small fraction of the total number of workers; the sample size of the payroll survey is 600 times larger. As a result, the household survey is subject to a large sampling error, about three times that of the payroll survey on a monthly basis.

Second, the payroll survey is better anchored in a comprehensive count of employment than the household survey. The household survey checks its result against a direct count of employment only once a decade when the decennial census is completed. On the other hand, every year the BLS adjusts the payroll survey's estimate of employment to correspond to the unemployment insurance tax records that nearly all employers are required to file. The preliminary revision based on the March 2004 benchmark added 236,000 workers, or a two-tenths of one percent increase in employment. The Journal suggests the revision shows the payroll numbers to be faulty; on the contrary, it should be taken as sign of their reliability, especially since the household survey is "benchmarked" but once a decade.

Beyond statistical reliability, the two surveys differ conceptually as well. Some of those differences narrow the gap between the job count of the two surveys, while others widen that gap. For instance, the two surveys treat multiple jobholders differently. The payroll survey counts each job reported by employers, even if the same worker holds two jobs. The household survey, on the other hand, counts multiple jobholders as employed only once. Also, while the household survey sample is quite limited, it does equally well counting jobs at new firms and long-established firms. The more thorough payroll survey only slowly integrates new firms into its sample, which can present problems in periods of rapid job growth. Finally, the household survey counts the self-employed, while the payroll survey of business establishments does not.

It is this third point that the Journal editors have seized on to explain why the payroll survey has undercounted the growth of jobs in the current recovery. They put it this way: "[W]hen a higher ratio of people make their livelihood as independent consultants to their old company, or as power sellers on eBay, they don't show up in the establishment survey."

Perhaps—if it were true that a higher ratio of people are self-employed. But even Harvard economist Robert Barro, a senior fellow at the conservative Hoover Institute, isn't buying it. In his March *Wall Street Journal* op-ed piece, Barro called "the large expansion of self-employment" explanation "a non-starter." Self-employment in the household survey just hasn't risen that much. As a ratio of household employment, self-employment rose somewhat after 2002, but even now that ratio is barely above its level at the onset of the recession in 2001, and it remains well below its level throughout most of the 1990s. What's more, an increase in self-employment is common in a weak labor market and typically disappears as labor market conditions improve and many of the self-employed find wage and salary employment. Finally, Barro estimates that "self-employment and other measurable differences between the two surveys explain only 200,000 to 400,000 of the extra three million jobs in the household survey."

The Same Sad Story

Even the household survey indicates this recovery has done far less to create jobs than other postwar recoveries. According to the household survey, the current recovery had added just 1.5% to total employment by January 2004, some 26 months after the recession officially ended in November 2001. Other postwar recoveries added an average of 5.5% to the number of jobs over the same period. The payroll survey paints an even more dismal picture: it shows the U.S. economy losing 0.5% off its job base during 26 months of recovery, while prior recoveries since 1949 added an average of 6.9% to employment in that amount of time.

Economists Schweitzer and Venkatu agree that it is more sensible to compare each employment survey to its own results during other postwar business cycles rather than to the other survey. They compare the ratio of employment (measured by the household survey) to total population in this recovery with the average pattern over postwar business cycles. In a recession, the employment-population ratio typically declines for about a year and a half and then returns to its previous level within about three years. But in this recovery, the employment-population ratio has declined nearly continuously. As a result, after three years of economic recovery, that ratio now stands at 62.3% (in September 2004), a full two percentage points below its 2001 pre-recession level of 64.3%.

By that standard, the U.S. economy is still missing 4,252,000 jobs—the number required to simply return to the employment-population ratio in 2001, and to equal the performance of the average postwar recovery. Schweitzer and Venkatu conclude that "both measures [the payroll survey and the household survey] show a surprisingly similar picture of the weak labor market performance that has prevailed during this recovery relative to previous business cycle periods."

The continuous decline in the ratio of employment to population makes clear why the unemployment rate is not higher, given the weak labor market. It is not because new jobs have gone uncounted; after all, unemployment rates are derived from the household survey. Rather, it is because many people have stopped looking for jobs and thus have dropped out of the unemployment statistics. The labor force participation rate—the fraction of the population either working or looking for work—has fallen sharply since George Bush took office; if it had stayed at its January 2001 level, the official unemployment rate would be 7.4%.

Still Missing

By any measure—the payroll survey, the household survey, or even the unemployment rate—the *Wall Street Journal* has not managed to locate the missing jobs in the U.S. economy. An honest inspection of the data reveals what most working people already know: when it comes to creating jobs, this recovery is the weakest since the Great Depression. That truth will continue to go missing on the editorial pages of the *Wall Street Journal*.

Sources: "Missing Jobs Found," *Wall Street Journal* 10/11/04; Mark Schweitzer and Guhan Venkatu, "Employment Surveys Are Telling the Same (Sad) Story," Economic Commentary (Federal Reserve Bank of Cleveland, 5/15/04); Robert Barro, "Go Figure," *Wall Street Journal*, 3/9/04; Bureau of Labor Statistics, "Employment from the BLS household and payroll surveys: summary of recent trends," 10/8/04; Elise Gould, "Measuring Employment Since the Recovery: A comparison of the household and payroll surveys," (Economic Policy Institute, December 2003); Steven Hipple, "Self-employment in the United States: an update," *Monthly Labor Review*, July 2004.

SLOW WAGE GROWTH BUT SOARING PROFITS IN THE CURRENT RECOVERY
John Miller
September/October 2004

The current economic recovery has done less to raise wages and more to pump up profits than any of the eight other recoveries since World War II. No wonder inequality continues to worsen, and most people still doubt that the economic turnaround will ever benefit them.

A recent study conducted the Economic Policy Institute, a labor-funded think tank, reports the alarming details. Over the three-year period beginning in early 2001, when the last economic expansion peaked and the recession began, corporate profits rose 62.2%, compared to an average growth of 13.9% by the same point in the other postwar recoveries that lasted that long. Total labor compensation (the sum of all paychecks and employee benefits), on the other hand, grew only 2.8%, well under the historical average of 9.9%. (See Figure 1.) What's more, most of labor's gains came in the form of higher benefits payments to cover the increasing cost of health care and pensions, not higher wages. In fact, in 2003 median weekly wages corrected for inflation declined, for the first time since 1996.

The extreme imbalance between wage and profit growth in this recovery is hardly surprising. Corporate cost-cutting has been the hallmark of this recovery; instead of hiring new workers, bosses have squeezed more out of the old ones. Corporate restructuring, layoffs, and the global outsourcing of both white-collar and manufacturing jobs have all made new jobs scarce. This recovery is still a long way from even replacing the jobs lost since the recession began in March 2001. As of June 2004, some

FIGURE 1: GROWTH IN CORPORATE PROFITS AND LABOR COMPENSATION

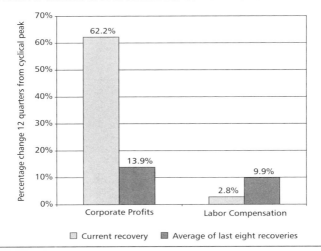

Source: Economic Policy Institute, "When do workers get their share?" Economic Snapshot, May 27, 2004. Data from the National Income and Product Accounts, Bureau of Economic Analysis, U.S. Dept. of Commerce.

39 months after the recession began—and 31 months after it officially ended—total employment was still down 1.2 million jobs. Every other economic recovery, even the jobless recovery of the early 1990s, had restored job losses and added a large number of new jobs to the economy by the 39-month mark.

Poor jobs growth has left workers in no position to push for higher wages. Only the jobless recovery of the early 1990s did as poorly as the current job-loss recovery at improving workers' wages and salaries. After adjusting for inflation, wages and salaries increased just 1.1% during the first two years of each of these two recoveries, reports economist Christian Weller of the Center for American Progress. Wages and salaries in all other postwar recoveries, on the other hand, rose an average of 12.1% in the same period, or about 11 times more quickly. (See Figure 2.)

At the same time, corporate cost-cutting measures have made for rapid increases in productivity—how much a worker can produce per hour. For instance, in 2002 and 2003, the hourly output of U.S. workers went up at a 5.3% pace, exceeding the "new economy" productivity growth rate of 2.6% from 1996 to 2001. For the first time in a postwar recovery, productivity is growing far faster than the economy.

With little wage growth, the gains from improved productivity have gone nearly exclusively to corporate profits. But few of those profits are getting reinvested. Relative to the size of the economy, real investment at the end of 2003, some 10.3% of GDP, remained well below its pre-recession level of 12.6% of GDP at the end of 2000. Weller estimates that nonfinancial corporations are investing fewer of their resources than at any time since the 1950s. And with little investment, soaring profits

FIGURE 2: REAL WAGE GROWTH IN POSTWAR RECOVERIES
(Percent Increase over the Eight Quarters after the Start of the Recovery)

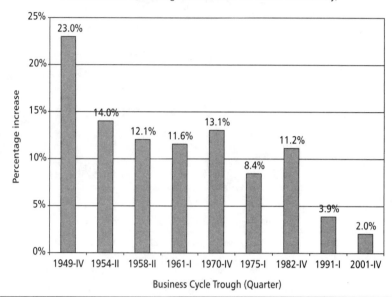

Source: Christian Weller, "Reversing the 'Upside-Down' Economy, "Center for American Progress, May 24, 2004. Data from the National Income and Product Accounts, Bureau of Economic Analysis, U.S. Dept. of Commerce.

have not translated into a hiring boom.

Only when labor markets genuinely tighten will workers be able to press for wage gains that match those of workers in earlier economic expansions. Until then, the benefits of this economic expansion, for as long as it can continue without the self-sustaining fuel of wage growth, will continue to go overwhelmingly to profits, exacerbating an economic inequality that is already unprecedented by postwar standards.

Sources: Economic Policy Institute, Job Watch Bulletin, July 2, 2004; Economic Policy Institute, "When do workers get their share?" *Economic Snapshot,* May 27, 2004; Christian Weller, "Reversing the 'Upside-Down' Economy: Faster Income Growth Necessary for Strong and Durable Growth," Center for American Progress, May 24, 2004.

Chapter 2

SHREDDING THE SAFETY NET

GOOD TIMES, BAD TIMES
Recession and the Welfare Debate
Heather Boushey
September/October 2002

When President Clinton signed the welfare reform bill in August 1996, he could not have predicted that the next five years would bring such a rapid fall in welfare caseloads and such strong growth in employment among single mothers. The economic expansion of the late 1990s brought wage gains to workers across the wage spectrum—including those at the bottom end of the pay scale—and boosted employment among groups of traditionally disadvantaged workers (single mothers, workers of color, immigrant workers). The strongest labor market in decades meant that many women who came off the welfare rolls in search of a job were able to find one. In this sense, welfare reform—at least according to its proponents—was impeccably well timed.

However, the late 1990s boom was unusual compared with earlier expansions, and there is no guarantee that future upturns will benefit those at the bottom of the earnings scale. Although studies from around the country show that nearly two out of every three women who have left welfare have found a job (for at least a while), their wages are too low to support a family—even during a period of economic growth. Most jobs that former welfare recipients have found don't pay living wages and don't offer employer-provided health insurance. Part of the problem is that women continue to earn far less than men, both because of wage discrimination and because women tend to be concentrated in lower-paying "female" jobs. This continuing gender gap becomes a larger problem as more and more women are responsible for the economic viability of their families.

Now, as the economy moves through a recession, job losses and projected slower (or negative) wage growth next year mean that it will be even tougher for low-wage workers to secure employment at wages adequate to support their families. The very sectors of the economy where former welfare recipients found jobs have been hit hard by the economic downturn. Employment rates—the proportion of Americans with a job—have fallen, and wage gains are already eroding as workers are forced to compete for jobs, instead of employers having to compete for workers. The fortuitous timing of welfare reform has now come to an end, raising urgent questions about how working single moms are going to make ends meet, not only during the slowdown but in more typical periods of economic expansion as well.

The Good Times Weren't So Good

The late 1990s economic expansion was atypical in several respects. In contrast with the economic expansion of the 1980s, low-wage workers in the late 1990s experienced low unemployment, increased job retention, and sustained (and significant) wage gains. These positive labor market trends were a result of historically low unemployment rates that lasted longer, without driving up inflation, than economists generally had thought possible.

While every demographic group saw low unemployment rates, the declines were most pronounced for minority workers, including many who had been receiving welfare. After remaining above 10% for more than 25 years, the unemployment rate for African Americans fell to 7.6% in 2000, its lowest since the Bureau of Labor Statistics began tabulating unemployment rates by race in 1972. (Even so, the 2000 unemployment rate among African Americans was still more than twice that of whites.) For Hispanic workers, the unemployment rate also reached an historic low, falling from 9.3% in 1995 to 5.7% in 2000.

Because of tight labor markets in the late 1990s, many more women, especially women of color, entered the workforce. In 2000, 60.2% of women were working—more than at any other time. While white women's labor force participation rose by less than a percentage point during the peak years of the economic expansion—1995 to 2000—African-American and Hispanic women increased their participation rates by 3.7 percentage points and 4.3 percentage points, respectively.

The tight labor market meant that workers in all wage groups earned more money. During the second half of the 1990s, workers' wages, on average, grew by 9.4%. Between 1995 and 2000, the lowest-paid women workers saw their wages rise by the same proportion as women earning high wages—about 10%. Men near the bottom of the earnings scale saw slightly higher percentage gains compared to men near the top (11.6% compared to 10.6%). In addition to favorable labor-market conditions, increases in the minimum wage in 1996 and 1997 helped to raise wages. Expansion of the Earned Income Tax Credit in 1993 further boosted incomes for the working poor. Because of these gains, women and men across the wage spectrum were able to improve their living standards.

But this picture isn't as rosy as it sounds. For example, the strong wage gains of the late 1990s were not enough to compensate for the wage declines that occurred between the late 1970s and the early 1990s. In 2001, men near the bottom of the wage scale were still earning 2.6% less than in 1979. And for women at the bottom, wages in 2001 were 2.2% below 1979 levels.

Further, although women's wages did rise during the late 1990s, this did not lead to a closing of the gender gap. In 1979, women earned only 65 cents for every dollar men earned. When male wages fell during the 1980s, men's and women's wages moved closer together, and the gender wage ratio hit a peak of 81 cents on the dollar in 1993. But the gap narrowed because men's wages were falling, not because women's wages were going up. And since wages then rose for both men and women during the remainder of the 1990s, the ratio is still hovering around 80 cents on the dollar.

Finally, in spite of low unemployment and high wages, low-income families still were not able to make ends meet. About a third of former welfare recipients did not find employment in the second half of the 1990s. Those who did find jobs—usually in low-wage sectors such as child care, home health care, and temporary help—were earning, on average, $6-8 per hour. For full-time, year-round employment, this comes out to between $12,480 and $16,640. Those earning closer to $8 per hour may have been pushed above the official poverty line of $14,269 for a family of three. However, researchers at the Economic Policy Institute have calculated that a family of three (with one school-age and one pre-school child) needs an annual income of between $21,989 (in rural Hattiesburg, Mississippi) and $48,606 (in high-priced Nassau-Suffolk County, New York) to afford the basic necessities (including food, housing, health insurance, child care, transportation, and taxes). Most former welfare recipients come nowhere near this income range.

The Bad Times Hurt Women

The economic recession, which began with job losses in manufacturing in 2000, spread across the economy last year. During the first three quarters of 2001, the economy contracted and unemployment rose.

There are a few features that make the current recession atypical. In some ways, this recession has not been as hard on low-wage workers as earlier recessions. For example, during the early 1980s recession, unemployment for workers without a high-school diploma rose by nearly four times as much as for workers with a college degree or more. During the 2000-02 recession, however, the ratio was less than two to one.

The terrorist attacks of September 11 have made this recession unusual as well. Although the recession had already begun prior to the September 11 attacks, these events wreaked havoc on certain segments of the economy, particularly hotels, air travel, and retail. As a result, the recession's impact on services, transportation, and wholesale and retail trade—sectors of the economy that usually provide more employment growth during recessions (or at least smaller employment losses, in the case of transportation)—has been especially harsh.

For example, typically in recessions, employment in the service industry (which employs about one out of every three workers) keeps growing. During the second part of the early 1990s recession, the service sector grew respectably, and transportation and wholesale trade fell at about the same rate as in the first eleven months. Retail trade actually grew in the latter part of the early 1990s recession. (See Figure 1.)

But that hasn't been the case during the current recession. From October 2000 (when unemployment began to rise) through September 2001, services continued to grow while transportation fell slightly. Since September 2001, however, services have barely grown, and transportation and retail trade (which employ about one out of every 20 and one out of every five workers, respectively) have seen sharp drops in employment. (See Figure 2.)

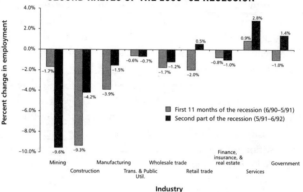

FIGURE 1: EMPLOYMENT CHANGE OVER THE FIRST AND SECOND HALVES OF THE 1990–92 RECESSION

Source: Lawrence Mishel, Jared Bernstein, and Heather Boushey, *The State of Working America 2002-3* (Ithaca, N.Y.: Cornell University Press, 2003).

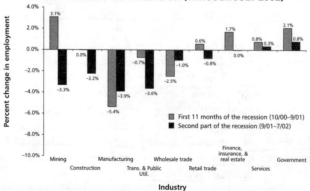

FIGURE 2: EMPLOYMENT CHANGE PRE- AND POST- SEPTEMBER 2001 DURING THE 2000–02 RECESSION (THROUGH JULY 2002)

Source: Lawrence Mishel, Jared Bernstein, and Heather Boushey, *The State of Working America 2002-3* (Ithaca, N.Y.: Cornell University Press, 2003).

These job losses have made the 2000–02 recession harder on women, compared to prior recessions, since they are more likely to work in services and retail trade than men. Typically in recessions, men experience higher unemployment rates than women. That was true during the early 1980s and early 1990s recessions, and in the current downturn as well. During the current recession, however, women have nearly "caught up" with men. Because of slower growth and greater job losses in the service sector, women's unemployment increases look more like men's than in earlier recessions. (See Figure 3.)

For former welfare recipients, the consequences have been especially severe. About a third of former welfare recipients who found employment work in the retail industry, which has seen no job growth over the course of this recession. Other sectors where women formerly on welfare found employment, such as the temporary help sector (about 5% of welfare recipients) and hotels and lodging (about 4%), have also seen employment drop substantially over the course of this recession.

Along with fewer job prospects, former welfare recipients now face slower wage growth as well. For women at the bottom of the earnings scale, wages grew by 4.3% from the first half of 2000 to the first half of 2001, but rose by only 2.7% from the first half of 2001 to the first half of 2002. For men at the bottom, wage growth fell even further, from 4.2% to 2.1%, over the same periods. If high unemployment continues, it is likely that wage growth will continue to be slow, or even negative, next year.

Reauthorization of What?

The fortunes of working families rise and fall with conditions in the labor market. During the strong economy of the late 1990s, jobs were plentiful and wages went up. Even during the economic expansion, however, low-wage families still struggled to make ends meet.

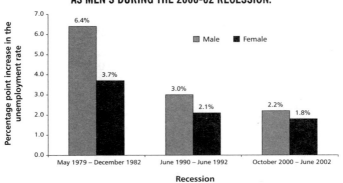

FIGURE 3: WOMEN'S UNEMPLOYMENT HAS RISEN NEARLY AS MUCH AS MEN'S DURING THE 2000-02 RECESSION.

Source: Lawrence Mishel, Jared Bernstein, and Heather Boushey, *The State of Working America 2002-3* (Ithaca, N.Y.: Cornell University Press, 2003).

That was especially true for families that once relied on welfare because the mid-1990s "reform" limited poor women's access to welfare. During the boom times, many were able to find employment, so that leaving welfare for a job was a viable option. Now that economic circumstances have changed, former welfare recipients will find it much more difficult to find and keep jobs.

Congress must reauthorize the 1996 welfare reform legislation by October 2002. In May, the House passed a reauthorization bill calling for stricter work requirements—in the form of more welfare recipients required to work, and at more hours—and only a marginal increase in child care spending, adding $1 billion over the next five years to the currently allocated $4.8 billion per year. In June, the Senate Finance Committee issued a different bill, which does not require welfare recipients to work more and also increases spending on child care by $5.5 billion over the next five years. Even this higher figure, however, is at most one tenth of what advocates believe is necessary to provide sufficient child care.

What neither bill does is recast welfare as a program that puts cash in the hands of people who need it—and will spend it—during economic contractions. When unemployment rises, families need a safety net they can rely on. But it's not just families that need the safety net; the economy needs fiscal policies that sustain demand when unemployment rises so employers will have an incentive to maintain production. Welfare—and other programs that provide assistance to families during economic slowdowns, such as unemployment compensation and Food Stamps—helps to smooth out the economy's ups and downs. With that in mind, the impact of the recession on low-wage workers should be an important part of the current welfare debate.

Sources: Heather Boushey et al., *Hardships in America: The Real Story of Working Families* (Washington, D.C.: Economic Policy Institute, 2001); Lawrence Mishel, Jared Bernstein, and Heather Boushey, *The State of Working America 2002-3* (Ithaca, N.Y.: Cornell University Press, 2003).

MARRIAGE PROMOTION, REPRODUCTIVE INJUSTICE, AND THE WAR AGAINST POOR WOMEN OF COLOR

Sarah Olson

January/February 2005

On December 22, at the stroke of midnight, Renita Pitts became a single woman. Renita is 44 years old, a mother of five with 14 grandchildren. She has been on and off of welfare for most of her life. After she had her fifth child, her husband brought crack cocaine into their house, telling her that it would help her lose weight. She became addicted and struggled for 13 years with that addiction. Throughout her marriage, Renita says, she was afraid to leave her house. "I couldn't trust my husband with our children long enough to go to school. If I left for even an hour, he would have a full-fledged party going on when I came back," she says. In addition to being a drug addict, Renita's husband was verbally, emotionally, and physically abusive. She says they fought frequently, and she had to call the police again and again.

Renita and her husband separated shortly after she stopped using drugs and returned to college. She had also begun attending church. According to Renita, her husband "was insecure because of my security." He gave her an ultimatum, saying she must leave school and stop going to church. When she refused, he left.

Despite the abuse and the drugs, Renita says, she felt many social pressures to stay married. Regardless, she says, "it was important not to have him in my life, constantly pumping me full of drugs." She says the relationship had become so abusive that if she had stayed in it any longer, "someone would have ended up dead."

With the help of California's welfare program, Renita is currently enrolled in the African American Studies and Social Welfare departments at the University of California at Berkeley and works on social justice issues at the Women of Color Resource Center. She was happy to see her divorce finalized in December.

The life stories of Renita and many other women like her are not on the radar screen in Washington, however. Legislation that would promote marriage among low-income people is currently wending its way through Congress. The so-called "Healthy Marriage Initiative" includes a range of provisions designed to encourage women on welfare to get and stay married: providing extra cash bonuses to recipients who get married, deducting money from welfare checks when mothers are living with men who are not the fathers of their children, increasing monthly welfare checks for married couples, offering marriage and relationship education classes, and putting up billboards in low-income communities promoting the value of marriage. Several provisions specifically target Latino and African-American communities. So-called marriage promotion policies, such as those in the Healthy Marriage Initiative, have been touted by the Bush administration and enjoy wide bipartisan support in Washington. Many advocates, however, are concerned that, if the bill passes, it would become more difficult for Renita and domestic violence survivors like her to get a divorce and to survive without a husband.

Married Good, Single Bad

The administration's point man for marriage promotion is Dr. Wade Horn, assistant secretary of Health and Human Services, whose Administration for Children and Families would run the initiative. In July 2002 Horn wrote, "On average, children raised by their own parents in healthy and stable married families enjoy better physical and mental health and are less likely to be poor. They're more successful in school, have lower dropout rates, and fewer teenage pregnancies. Adults, too, benefit from healthy and stable marriages." Critics say Horn sees the wedded state as a cure-all for society's ills, while ignoring the difficulties of promoting something as intensely personal as marriage. Horn and others in the ACF refused repeated requests for comment.

Marriage promotion legislation has its roots in the 1996 welfare reform act. This legislation ended welfare as an entitlement—it allowed states to deny assistance to fully qualified applicants, and resulted in the abrogation of some applicants' constitutional rights. It also created a five-year lifetime limit for welfare recipients, denied aid to many immigrant communities, created cumbersome financial reporting requirements for welfare recipients, and set up work rules that, according to many recipients, emphasize work hours over meaningful employment opportunities and skill development. The legislation explicitly claimed promoting marriage as one of its aims.

When welfare reform was passed, Congress required that it be revisited in five years. The Healthy Marriage Initiative that Congress is considering today was introduced in 2002 as part of the welfare reform reauthorization package. Welfare—now known as Temporary Aid to Needy Families (TANF)—was set to be reauthorized that year, but that reauthorization is now two years overdue.

In September, Senators Rick Santorum (R-Pa.) and Evan Bayh (D-Ind.) introduced a bill to reauthorize welfare for six months without overall changes, but with $800 million for marriage promotion and fatherhood programs over a two-year period. Sen. Santorum has been a strong proponent of marriage promotion. In an October 2003 speech to the Heritage Foundation, he promised to aggressively press for legislation that supported marriage between one man and one woman. "The government must promote marriage as a fundamental societal benefit. ... Both for its intrinsic good and for its benefits for society, we need marriage. And just as important, we need public leaders to communicate to the American public why it is necessary." The reauthorization bill has died in the Senate, but because of its strong bipartisan support, it is likely to be re-introduced. Sen. Santorum refused repeated requests for comment for this story.

Diverting Dollars

Although the debate about marriage promotion has focused on the Healthy Marriage Initiative, this is just one piece of the Bush administration's pro-marriage agenda. The Department of Health and Human Services has already diverted over $100 million within existing programs into marriage promotion. These are programs that have no specific legislative authority to promote marriage. Some examples: $6.1 million has been diverted from the Child Support Enforcement Program, $9 million from the Refugee Resettlement Program, $14 million from the Child Welfare Program, and $40 million from the Social and Economic Development Strategies Program focusing on Native Americans, among others. Plus, another nearly $80 million has been awarded to research groups studying marriage.

One beneficiary is in Grand Rapids, Michigan. Healthy Marriages Grand Rapids received $990,000 from the federal government in 2003 to "facilitate the understanding that healthy marriages between parents is [sic] critical to the financial well-being of children, increase effective co-parenting skills of married and non-married parents to improve relationships between low-income adults who parent children, increase active, healthy participation of non-custodial fathers in the lives of their children, increase the number of prepared marriages among low-income adults, and decrease the divorce rate among low-income adults." The program coordinates local public media campaigns plugging marriage as well as relationship counseling classes, many offered by faith-based providers.

It is precisely this emphasis on marriage as a cure for economic woes that worries many welfare recipients and advocates. According to Liz Accles at the Welfare Made a Difference National Campaign, "Marriage promotion is problematic for many reasons. It is discriminatory. It values certain families over others. It intrudes on privacy rights. The coercive nature of this is lost on a lot of people because they don't realize how deeply in poverty people are living." Accles says that adequate educational opportunities, subsidized child care, and real job skills and opportunities are the answer to the financial concerns of women on welfare. She joins many domestic violence counselors in saying that marriage education funded by government coffers and administered via faith-based providers and welfare case workers is at best a waste of taxpayer money, and at worst pushes women deeper into abusive relationships that may end in injury or death.

In Allentown, Pa., a program called the Family Formation and Development Project offers a 12-week marriage education course for low-income, unmarried couples with children. Employment services are offered as part of the program, but only to fathers. In its application for federal funding, the program set a goal of 90% of the participating fathers finding employment. No such goal was set for the mothers. According to Jennifer Brown, legal director at the women's legal rights organization Legal Momentum, which filed a complaint with the Department of Health and Human Services, "What we fear is that this kind of sex stereotyped programming—jobs for fathers, not for mothers—will be part of marriage promotion programs funded by the government."

Experts at Legal Momentum are concerned that the administration is diverting scarce funds from proven and effective anti-poverty programs and funneling the money into untested marriage-promotion programs. They say there is little information about what is happening on the ground, making it difficult to determine what activities have been implemented.

Feminist economists point out that the mid-1990s welfare reform law served larger economic interests by moving women out of the home and into the work force at a time when the economy was booming and there was a need for low-paid service workers. Now that the economy is in a recession, the government has adopted a more aggressive policy of marriage promotion, to pull women out of the work force and back into the home. According to Avis Jones-DeWeever, Poverty and Welfare Study director at the Institute for Women's Policy Research, "We are talking about putting

$1.5 billion into telling women to find their knight in shining armor and then everything will be okay."

Jones-DeWeever says the view that marriage creates more economically stable individuals is not grounded in reality. She notes that individuals are likely to marry within their own socioeconomic group, so low-income women are likely to marry low-income men. According to author Barbara Ehrenreich's estimates, low-income women would need to have roughly 2.3 husbands apiece in order to lift them out of poverty. Jones-DeWeever points out that in African-American communities, there are simply not enough men to marry: there are approximately two and a half women for every African-American man who is employed and not in jail. In addition, many social policy analysts are quick to point out that in general, poor people are not poor because they're unmarried. Rather, they may be unmarried because they're poor: the socioeconomic conditions in low-income communities contribute to a climate in which healthy marriages are difficult to sustain.

Another criticism of marriage promotion comes from survivors of domestic violence and their advocates. Studies consistently show that between 50% and 60%—in some studies up to 80%—of women on welfare have suffered some form of domestic violence, compared to 22% of the general population. In addition, between 3.3 and 10 million children witness domestic violence each year. Domestic violence survivors say their abuse was often a barrier to work, and many have reported being harassed or abused while at work. Most survivors needed welfare to escape the relationship and the violence. Any policy that provides incentives for women to become and stay married is in effect coercing poor women into marriage. Many women on welfare, like Renita Pitts, say that their marriages, rather than helping them out of poverty, set up overwhelming barriers to building their own autonomous and productive lives.

According to Kaaryn Gustafson, associate professor of law at the University of Connecticut, policies that attempt to look out for women's safety by restricting or coercing their activities are paternalistic and misguided. "The patriarchal model is really troubling. The gist is that if there isn't a man in the house there isn't a family. The studies of family well-being are all very problematic because you cannot parse out the issues of education, socioeconomic status, and other emotional and psychological issues that are tied up in who gets married and who doesn't."

Reproductive Straitjacket

While marriage promotion as a federal policy began in 1996, many say it is only one part of a much larger system of control over, and sanction of, the sexual and reproductive freedoms of poor women and women of color. Another part of this system is child exclusion legislation, which has been adopted by 21 states. Child exclusion laws permit states to pay benefits for only one child born to a woman on welfare. Social policy experts say it is a response to the myth that African-American welfare recipients were having more children in order to get larger benefit checks. Such laws push women either deeper into poverty, or into abortions. In some states, a woman who chooses to have another child instead of an abortion may end up trying to raise two or more children on less than $300 a month.

Christie, who would like to use only her first name, is a single mother of two. She has been working, supporting her children and herself, and going to college. Since her first child was born, she has also been receiving welfare. While on welfare, she fought to get a college degree in general education; now she hopes to get a job as a Spanish language translator. During her time in college, her welfare caseworker told Christie to quit going to school and instead report to a welfare-to-work program. She says, "I felt that it was a punishment. Just because I was on welfare, they could make me quit school and come and sit in a room and listen to people talking about the jobs I should get. Most of the jobs that they wanted you to have were geared towards the lower poverty level where you stay in poverty and you can never climb the socioeconomic ladder. It's like that's your position and that's where you have to stay."

When Christie became pregnant with her second child, her caseworker told her she could not receive an increase in her benefit. This forced Christie into some tough choices. "My religion kept me from having an abortion. I worked after I had my daughter, because I felt like it was a mistake that I made, and so I tried to do what I could for my daughter." Christie says this legislation penalizes women for having children, and creates an overwhelming sense of guilt that permeates low-income families. Rather than celebrating the birth of her daughter, Christie felt that she needed to work twice as hard to make up for her "mistake."

When states began adopting child exclusion policies in the early 1990s, they were implemented under federal scrutiny. States were required to keep data about the financial status of affected families. These data showed that child exclusion policies resulted in women and children being thrust further into poverty. One of the more sinister effects of the 1996 welfare reform law is that it did away with the requirement that states monitor the outcome of child exclusion policies. Since 1996, states have been able to impose sanctions on families without paying any attention to the results.

According to a July 2002 report by the Children's Sentinel Nutrition Assessment Program (C-SNAP), a research and advocacy collaborative, child exclusion policies are directly correlated to a number of risks to the health and well-being of children. Infants and toddlers in families that have been sanctioned under the child exclusion provisions are 30% more likely to have been hospitalized than children from families who have not been sanctioned, and these children are 90% more likely to require hospitalization at the time of an emergency room visit. In addition, child exclusion sanctions lead to food insecurity rates that are at least 50% higher than those of families who have not faced sanction. The negative health and welfare impacts reported in the C-SNAP study increase dramatically with each year that a family experiences sanctions.

Proponents of child exclusion legislation, including many members of the Bush administration and a bipartisan array of senators and representatives, claim that women on welfare have no business bringing a new child into the world whom they cannot support financially.

The United Sates has a long history of regulation of poor women's reproductive activities. From the forced sterilizations performed in low-income communities of color in the 1940s, 1950s, and even later, to state child services departments appropriating poor Native American children and giving them to upper-class white foster parents, many U.S. historians say that sexuality among lower-income communities of color has traditionally been viewed as something that should be controlled. The University of Connecticut's Gustafson responds, "There is this idea that if you pay taxes you have the right to control those who don't, and it smacks of slavery. There should be some scope of liberty that should be unconditional, and that especially includes sexuality and family formation."

There's no such respect for freedom and privacy under TANF. The program requires women to submit to a barrage of invasive questions and policies; TANF applicants must provide private details about every aspect of their lives. In California, for example, the application asks for the names of up to 12 men with whom a woman has had sexual relations on or around the time of her pregnancy. In San Diego county, before a woman can receive a welfare check, she must submit to a "surprise" visit by welfare case workers to verify that there isn't an unreported man in the household, among other things.

One of the problems with all of these sexual and reproductive-based policy initiatives is that, according to Gustafson, they distract people from the actual issues of poverty. While TANF accounts for less than 2% of the federal budget, the hysteria surrounding whether and how to assist poor families with children has created an uproar about whether low-income women should even be allowed to have children.

Because the 1996 welfare reform law eliminated the concept of welfare as an entitlement, welfare recipients lack certain protections other U.S. citizens have under the Constitution. In effect, when you apply for welfare you are signing away many of your constitutional rights. For this reason, many advocates today are critiquing welfare through the lens of human rights rather than constitutional rights. International human-rights agreements, including the United Nations Convention on the Elimination of All Forms of Discrimination against Women, afford women many universal human rights. "Those include access to education, access to reproductive choice, rights when it comes to marrying or not marrying," says Gustafson. "When you look at the international statements of human rights, it provides this context, this lens that magnifies how unjust the welfare laws are in the United States. The welfare system is undermining women's political, economic, and social participation in society at large."

On September 30, Congress passed another extension of the 1996 welfare legislation. This extension contained no policy changes—for now. When Congress does finally reauthorize welfare, child exclusion policies and marriage promotion are likely to be hot-button issues that galvanize the debate. According to Liz Accles at the National Welfare Made a Difference Campaign, there are three steps to a successful welfare strategy. "Access. Adequacy. Opportunity. All three of these hold equal weight. You cannot have benefits so low that people live deeply in poverty. You can't have good benefits that only a few people get access to. You also need to have opportunity for economic mobility built in."

Although the marriage promotion bill was defeated this time, it continues to enjoy strong bipartisan support—including support from the White House now that George W. Bush has a second term. Welfare recipients and social policy experts are worried that whenever welfare reform is debated, politicians will deem regulating the reproductive activities of poor women to be more important than funding proven anti-poverty measures like education and meaningful job opportunities.

Sources: Joan Meisel, Daniel Chandler, and Beth Menees Rienzi, "Domestic Violence Prevalence and Effects on Employment in Two California TANF Populations," (California Institute of Mental Health, 2003); Richard Tolman and Jody Raphael, "A Review of the Research on Welfare and Domestic Violence," *Journal of Social Issues*, 2000; Sharmila Lawrence, "Domestic Violence and Welfare Policy: Research Findings That Can Inform Policies on Marriage and Child Well-Being: Issue Brief," (Research Forum on Children, Families, and the New Federalism, National Center for Children in Poverty, 2002); E. Lyon, "Welfare, Poverty and Abused Women: New Research and Its Implications," Policy and Practice Paper #10, *Building Comprehensive Solutions to Domestic Violence*, (National Resource Center on Domestic Violence, 2000).

BUSH STRIKES OUT ON HEALTH CARE
Elise Gould
May/June 2004

In his State of the Union address in January, President Bush claimed to be addressing the twin crises of rising health care costs and declining access. He touted the Medicare bill Congress passed late last year for adding a prescription drug benefit for seniors, creating tax-free health savings accounts, and generally "strengthening Medicare." He then made some new proposals, including a tax credit to help uninsured people buy health insurance and a tax deduction to encourage people to buy catastrophic (or high-deductible) health insurance policies.

Dollars & Sense asked Economic Policy Institute economist Elise Gould to explain what these programs are—or are not—likely to accomplish.

Private Insurers and Prescription Drugs: Strike One
The 2003 Medicare Modernization Act is an inadequate, poorly-devised excuse for Medicare expansion. Its key provisions include new money for private insurers involved with Medicare, a prescription drug benefit, and tax-advantaged Health Sav-

ings Accounts. Originally scored at $395 billion, now estimated to cost $534 billion, the bill makes big payments to private insurance and pharmaceutical companies, but provides little bang for the buck for Medicare beneficiaries.

One aspect of the new law has received almost no attention: it raises payments to private insurers to entice them into the business of providing insurance for the Medicare population. Actually, Medicare is already partially privatized. For a number of years, the government has contracted with private insurance companies to offer their own Medicare plans to seniors. As it turned out, many of these companies, unable to turn a profit, ended up dropping their Medicare plans. (Meantime, traditional Medicare has rolled right along, with an excellent track record of beneficiary satisfaction and a super-low overhead cost under 4%.) The new, higher payments included in the 2003 law are designed to attract private companies back into the Medicare business. Proponents argue that private industry is more efficient than government and that privatization will lower Medicare's costs. But if private insurance companies are so efficient, why do they need higher reimbursement rates?

In one respect, private insurers may prove to be cheaper—but not because they're more efficient. Private insurers can tailor their plans—what's covered, what's not, whether patients have a choice of specialists, and so forth—to attract the healthiest of the Medicare population and discourage sicker elders from signing on. Of course, the healthiest are also the least expensive to insure. Splitting the Medicare pool in this way decreases the viability of the system in the long run.

What about the prescription drug benefit? It's full of holes—literally. There's the so-called donut hole in the coverage: for seniors who spend between $2,250 and $5,100 annually on prescription drugs, the amount they spend above $2,250 is entirely out-of-pocket.

Then there are the rate increases. The premiums and deductibles for the new drug coverage are expected to rise at average annual rates of 7.5% and 8.6%, respectively, from 2006 to 2013. This far exceeds the annual cost-of-living adjustments Social Security recipients get, which have averaged just 2.4% over the past 10 years. Medicare Part B (the section that provides coverage for doctor visits) has built-in protections that keep out-of-pocket expenses from rising faster than seniors' Social Security checks; the prescription drug benefit, however, includes no such protection. Even with the new benefit, then, drug costs will eat up a growing share of Medicare beneficiaries' incomes over time.

The new law also fails to treat "dual eligibles"—that is, low-income seniors eligible for both Medicare and Medicaid—fairly. The law prohibits the use of federal Medicaid dollars to pay for prescription drugs not covered by the new Medicare drug plan. This means that individuals currently on Medicaid can actually lose some of their existing coverage.

If the prescription drug benefit is offering less-than-meets-the-eye to seniors, then who does benefit from the massive new expenditure? Primarily, the pharmaceutical companies. The new law specifically prohibits the government from negotiating lower prices with drug companies. The Medicare population accounts for about half the pre-scription drug market. If the government were allowed to negotiate over prices—the same type of negotiation that goes on between private insurers and providers already—costs of the program would go down substantially.

Private insurers also stand to gain. The new prescription drug benefit will not be administered as part of traditional Medicare. Instead, seniors who want the benefit will have to choose a private drug plan; the plans will in turn be paid by Medicare. It's no surprise that the drug benefit is structured so as to accelerate the privatization of Medicare.

Instead of an inadequate program that wastes billions of dollars subsidizing private insurers and pharmaceutical companies, the government should offer a drug benefit that helps people who most need the care and cannot afford it.

Health Savings Accounts: Strike Two

The new law also provides for health savings accounts (HSAs). HSAs provide tax benefits for individuals and families who buy eligible high-deductible health insurance plans—those with an annual deductible of at least $1,000 (for individuals, or $2,000 for a family). If you purchase such a plan, which typically has relatively low premiums, you can contribute to an HSA up to a set maximum. HSA contributions are fully tax deductible. Nor do you pay any tax—even on accrued interest—when you withdraw funds from the account to pay medical expenses.

HSAs were billed as a health cost-containment vehicle and a savings mechanism designed to help people prepare for future medical expenses. Their most likely primary use, however, will be as a generous tax shelter for the upper-income set. Consider two people with HSAs, a higher-income person in the 35% tax bracket and a lower-income person in the 10% bracket. The lower-income person pays 90 cents for every dollar she puts in her HSA then withdraws for medical bills, while the higher-income person pays only 65 cents. (Assuming that the lower-income person has any extra money to contribute to the HSA in the first place!) Clearly, higher-income families have much more to gain from these accounts than middle- or low-income families. And unlike many tax deductions, there is no phase-out range or maximum income limit. Further, wealthy people who have exhausted their other tax-advantaged savings vehicles or who have income too high to qualify for traditional IRAs will be most likely to participate. Since people over 65 can withdraw money from their accounts tax-free for any reason—not only for medical expenses—with no penalty, HSAs subsidize the retirement savings of wealthy people at the expense of lost tax revenue.

Because the benefits of an HSA come through a tax deduction, they are of no use to the many Americans who do not file taxes or who have little tax liability. A married couple with two children would receive no tax benefit whatsoever from contributing to an HSA unless their income was at least $40,200—more than twice the poverty level.

HSAs are not an effective means of cost containment as they create conflicting incentives. It's true that moving people to high-deductible plans ought to induce lower spending on health care. But by giving people a tax break when they spend money on health care, this plan reduces the cost-containment advantage of high-deductible insurance.

Nor is encouraging people to move to high-deductible plans good for the health insurance system as a whole. High-deductible plans have lower premiums and are a good deal for healthy people who don't need much care. When the healthy are siphoned off into these plans, risk pools become unbalanced and costs rise for everyone else. The result: it gets harder and harder for the less healthy to afford adequate coverage.

Tax Proposals: Strike Three

New Bush administration proposals for improving health care access suffer from the same problems. The president proposes an income tax deduction for high-deductible health insurance premiums. Only families with income tax liability gain from the proposal; it will do little to reduce the number of uninsured, about half of whom are from households with income too low to benefit from the deduction at all.

The Health Insurance Tax Credit (HITC), another administration proposal introduced in the Senate this March, is intended to help the uninsured obtain coverage. The HITC would provide low-income Americans with a tax credit of up to $1,000 for individuals and $500 per child to assist them in buying private health insurance. Individuals with incomes up to $30,000 and families with incomes up to $60,000 who have no job-based or government health insurance are eligible for the credit, which is refundable—in other words, those with little or no income tax liability will receive the amount of the credit as a direct payment from the government.

The HITC has three major problems as a vehicle for widening health insurance access: it doesn't help the sick, it isn't age adjusted, and it simply isn't generous enough. The HITC applies only to the purchase of individual or non-group health coverage. People who are already sick have an extremely difficult time getting insurance in the individual market. When they are not turned down outright, the premiums are prohibitively high, and insurers often add riders that disallow coverage on pre-existing conditions and reserve the right not to renew. The benefit isn't age adjusted, but premiums are. So the HITC disproportionately benefits younger people, the least in need of health insurance.

Non-group insurance is expensive: premiums and deductibles are higher and overall plan benefits are less generous than for group plans. In one market, premiums for non-group family plans average $13,214 a year. Even with the maximum $3,000 per family credit, eligible families would still have to pay over $10,000 a year for coverage—far beyond the means of most low- and moderate-income families. And while non-group health plans are a poor substitute for employer-provided health insurance, tax preferences for these plans may give companies an excuse to stop offering insurance to their employees.

A Whole New Ballgame

If the administration really wants to lower the number of uninsured, there are better ways than through the tax system. For the estimated cost of $95 billion in the first five years, researchers estimate the HITC and the new tax deduction for high-deductible plan premiums combined will insure an additional 1.3 million people—barely a dent in the estimated 43 million uninsured Americans. Why not expand Medicaid to cover more people, encourage the creation of risk pools to cover the sick, provide an afford-able safety net for the unemployed—or dare to think about a single-payer system?

Sources: U.S. Congressional Budget Office, "Estimating the Cost of the Medicare Modernization Act," testimony before the House Ways and Means Committee, 3/24/04; U.S. Treasury Dept., "General Explanations of the Administration's Fiscal Year 2005 Revenue Proposals," February 2004; Kaiser Family Foundation, Employer Health Benefits 2003 Annual Survey; Kaiser Family Foundation, "Coverage and Cost Impacts of the President's Health Insurance Tax Credit and Tax Deduction Proposals," March 2004; Massachusetts Blue Cross and Blue Shield; U.S. Census Bureau, "Health Insurance Coverage in the United States: 2002," September 2003.

Chapter 3

LABOR REVIVES— AND FACES NEW ATTACKS

SEPTEMBER 11 AND THE RESTRUCTURING OF THE AIRLINE INDUSTRY
Rodney Ward
May/June 2002, updated May 2003

On September 11, 2001, stunned flight attendants and pilots learned that workplaces just like theirs had been transformed into lethal missiles. Flight workers lucky enough not to be on one of the hijacked planes prepared frantically for orders to land at the nearest airport. Crews then worked to calm passengers and arrange for transportation and lodging. In some cases, school gymnasiums accommodated passengers and crew, while church buses provided rides to the nearest sizeable city.

Through the four-day grounding of the U.S. civilian airlines, airline unions' Employee Assistance Programs worked overtime to provide support for traumatized workers. Crews themselves huddled together in front of TVs, watching as the nightmare unfolded before them, worrying about their friends and future.

As the first flights began again on September 15, some crews refused to fly, not confident of airport security. Those who steeled themselves to work entered a strange new workplace. With no guidance from the airlines or the Federal Aviation Administration (FAA) on how to handle potential future Hijackings, flight attendants inventoried galleys for objects they could use as defensive weapons. Shell-shocked passengers sometimes hugged flight attendants as they boarded. Many crew members barely contained tears, often hiding in galleys to avoid alarming passengers.

But as airline workers returned to the skies, a new danger loomed: layoffs. On September 15, Continental announced that it would cut 12,000 jobs. One by one, the other airlines followed suit: United and American announced 20,000 layoffs each; Northwest, 10,000; US Airways, 11,000. Delta forecast eliminating 13,000. As the toll topped 140,000, *Washington Post* writer David Montgomery quipped: "What thanks are flight attendants getting? How does this sound: You're fired."

The September 11 catastrophe hit the airline industry hard, but it also opened the door for airlines to accelerate the restructuring they already had underway. Many airlines, including giants like US Airways, were in bad shape before September 11. And the industry's agenda already included layoffs, mergers, greater restrictions on airline workers' rights, and a global deregulation of air travel. If post-9/11 politics allow the airlines to impose these changes, this will hurt not only airline workers, but also working people beyond the aviation industry.

The Executive Response

Within hours of the September 11 hijackings, an army of airline lobbyists descended on Congress (whose members have received $12 million in airline-industry contributions since 1998). The mission: Demand a massive taxpayer bailout for the industry (as much as $24 billion). If Congress failed to pony up the cash, the airlines would become "a major casualty of war," argued Delta CEO Leo Mullin.

While pleading their case, the airlines neglected to request any aid for the airline workers they were preparing to dump. Both houses of Congress defeated amendments, proposed by House Minority Leader Richard Gephardt (D-MO) and Sen. Jean Carnahan (D-MO), to provide relief to laid-off workers. Greg Crist, the spokesperson for House Majority Leader Dick Armey (R-TX), rationalized his boss's opposition as "focused on getting the airline industry back on its feet and [thus] getting these people back on the job. An expanded unemployment insurance benefit won't do anything to get you back on the job." It took six more months for Congress to provide even meager aid supplements for airline workers. (Even then, the March 9, 2002 unemployment extension legislation tacked on $8 in corporate tax breaks for every $1 spent on aid to laid-off workers.)

Rather than simply neglecting workers, however, the bailout does worse—it encourages attacks on union contracts and working conditions. Office of Management and Budget regulations state that airlines getting bailout money should provide a "demonstration of concessions by the air carrier's security holders, other creditors, or employees...." Not surprisingly, it's the employees who are bearing the brunt.

With the war on Iraq, the airlines received yet another bailout of $3.2 billion, as well as commercial airlift contracts worth nearly half a billion dollars. Once again, the wartime bailout requires airlines to cut operating costs, which will certainly mean more pressure for concessions from workers.

Leaving aside tax cuts and new military contracts, Congress has handed the airlines $18.2 billion in taxpayer money since 2001: $8.2 billion in direct grants and $10 billion in loan guarantees. At the depressed prices of airline stocks, the government could have easily bought a controlling interest in the entire industry for $18.2 billion. In another place or another time, the airlines might have been nationalized under management by airline workers. But this is far from the reality in Washington, D.C., today.

Downsizing Stock Prices, Downsizing Airlines

September 11, of course, delivered a serious hit to the airlines' bottom line. Troubled Midway Airlines closed up shop on September 12, 2001. (The company has since resumed limited operations, aided by bailout money.) In the following weeks, airplanes flew mostly empty. As the airlines shed workers, they also mothballed planes. Today there are approximately 2,400 planes, about 11% of the world's civilian air fleet, parked in the Mojave Desert.

Airline shares plummeted when the stock markets reopened on September 17. US Airways and America West shares each lost over half their value in just one day. The rest of the airlines suffered declines as well. Recently, some airline stocks have recovered to pre-September 11 levels, but several, like US Airways, are still in the dumps.

Competitive pressure, already at a high pitch, intensified. While big carriers like United, American, and Northwest downsized, Southwest and startup carrier JetBlue refused to lay employees off and began to move into markets the industry giants had evacuated. The economic shockwaves rolled through the aviation industry globally. Sabena and Swissair collapsed. British Airways carried out massive layoffs. British and Japanese carriers sought mergers. Other carriers (including Iberia and Air India) announced capacity cuts and restructurings. So did aircraft manufacturers.

Not All Bad News, If You're An Airline Executive

Not all economic impacts on the airlines have been negative, however. The industry is extremely capital intensive, its two largest costs being airplanes and fuel. Deferrals on airplane orders, the retirement of older and less fuel-efficient planes, and a tremendous drop in global fuel prices have dramatically cut costs. Though labor costs represent a small portion of overall airline costs (flight attendants represent less than 4.5% of operating expenses at United, for example), slashing the workforce also cut airline expenses.

So far, over 300 airlines have collected over $8 billion in bailout money. The lion's share has gone to industry giants United, American, and Delta. Also, on March 9, Congress passed a new tax break for the airlines. Airlines are now allowed to claim losses from 2001 and 2002 on their taxes over the last five years, a change that could mean $2 billion in cash for the companies.

In addition, the airlines routinely carry "business-interruption" insurance to cover losses due to weather, strikes, or other unforeseen circumstances. It's not clear how much airlines are collecting on claims stemming from the four-day shutdown of U.S. airports in September. The *Baltimore Sun* reported that, when asked about business-interruption insurance, US Airways spokesperson David Castelveter replied guiltily, "That's something I don't think we would publicly discuss with anyone." The insurance firm Swiss Re, however, estimated in March that September 11-related business-interruption claims (to all industries) will amount to $3.5–$7 billion. Undoubtedly, a big chunk will go to the airlines.

The Aviation World Before September 11

Deregulation Degradation

The airline industry's chaotic state is not just a result of the September 11 attacks, but also the culmination of a quarter century of deregulation. Advocates had touted the 1978 Airline Deregulation Act as a way to increase competition and bring down ticket prices. Indeed, deregulation initially enabled upstart carriers to get in the air and made flying affordable for many people who had never flown before.

But that was not the whole story. Since deregulation, service to smaller, less profitable cities has suffered and pricing has become a crazy quilt of discriminatory arrangements. Travel to and from many airports has become monopolized by one or a few airlines. Nonetheless, airlines operate on very tight profit margins compared to other industries. As airline bottom lines have been squeezed, argues author Paul Stephen Dempsey, so has the margin of safety.

Deregulation resulted in a host of problems for airline workers, too. New competitive pressures caused the airline industry to lose more money in a few years than it had made in all the years prior to 1978 combined. These losses led to mergers and bankruptcies, and set the stage for leveraged buyouts. Financier Frank Lorenzo took over both Continental and Eastern, and then used Chapter 11 bankruptcy to break union contracts at both airlines.

Consolidation or death became the choices for many carriers. The competitive carnage destroyed once-great airlines such as Braniff and PanAm, and saw many others gobbled up. USAir bought PSA and Piedmont (ultimately dismantling PSA's entire West Coast operation). Delta swallowed up Western and the remains of PanAm, while Northwest took over Republic. More recently, American Airlines absorbed the venerable TWA. Not only did these mergers lead to route disruptions, but they also destroyed thousands of jobs, as overlapping sections of newly merged companies created "redundancies." The mergers also created challenges for union workforces—how to integrate seniority lists, for example. Conflicts over seniority in the American-TWA merger will likely sow internal union conflicts for years to come.

Management Mishaps

Spectacularly inspired mismanagement by airline executives actually deserves much of the blame for the state of the industry. Airline workers frequently complain that they could run the airlines better than the executives. Meanwhile, management jealously guards its decision-making prerogatives against labor input. Who's right? You be the judge.

Over a year ago, the Airline Pilots Association (ALPA), proposed to US Airways management "hedging" on fuel (purchasing options to buy fuel in the future at current prices) while prices were low. This would protect the airline against expected increases in fuel costs. Company management rejected the suggestion. After that, fuel prices skyrocketed and so did a major portion of the airline's costs. Several pilots have bitterly joked to me that the entire pilot group could work for free for a year and a half and still not make up for management's mistake.

In another case, in 2000, United Airlines stonewalled its pilots in contract negotiations to the point that pilots refused to volunteer for overtime. This led to 9,000 flight cancellations that summer. A key demand of the pilots was that the company hire more pilots (who wants exhausted pilots working overtime anyway?). Eventually the company gave in to the pilots' demands, but only after alienating huge numbers of passengers.

Frank Reeves of Avitas, a Virginia airline consulting firm, told the *Pittsburgh Post-Gazette* that the post-September 11 crisis has given management "a golden opportunity … to write off all the bad decisions they made over the last 10 years."

September 11 and the Airline Labor Movement

Airline management, of course, still has workers—and their unions—to contend with. Despite working under the restrictive Railway Labor Act (RLA), 80–85% of airline workers are unionized. This makes the airline industry one of the most heavily unionized sectors in the U.S. economy. The airline unions operate along craft lines, with separate unions for pilots, flight attendants, baggage handlers, mechanics, customer service agents, and flight instructors. The Airline Pilots Association (ALPA) is the largest pilots' union, while the Association of Flight Attendants (AFA) represents most flight attendants. Most mechanics and baggage handlers belong to the International Association of Machinists (IAM).

Force Majeure

The most immediate impact of September 11 on workers throughout the airline industry, of course, was massive job loss. Most airline unions have job security or "no furlough" clauses in their collective bargaining agreements. Airline management, however, claimed that since the hijackings were an "act of war," the airlines could activate "force majeure" clauses in the agreements to escape their contractual obligations. Force majeure (literally, "greater power") is a commercial contract law doctrine that releases parties to a contract from their obligations due to circumstances outside their control (an "act of God," act of war, that sort of thing). There is little or no precedent for the use of force majeure in labor contract law. Nonetheless, several airlines invoked the phrase as an excuse to disregard seniority rights, severance packages, and advance notice as they laid off thousands.

The business press dutifully reported airline claims that the union contracts contained "little-known" force majeure clauses. In reality, the alleged "clauses" in union contracts were little known because they did not exist. The airlines are simply trying to use this doctrine in the same way Frank Lorenzo used bankruptcy in the 1980s: to smash union contracts and attack airline workers. Though subsequent uproar has forced airline management to reverse itself on seniority and severance pay, the violation of no-layoff clauses is still working its way through the arduous process of arbitration under the RLA (even "expedited arbitration" can take nine months or more).

Delta Union Election

Airline union elections are different from those in most of the private sector. Under the RLA, ballots only have a "yes" box. If a ballot is not mailed in, for whatever reason, the National Mediation Board (NMB), the body that oversees airline labor relations under the RLA, counts it as a "no" vote. To win, a union must get a majority of the eligible votes. (Under the National Labor Relations Act [NLRA], which governs most workers in the private sector, the union only needs a majority of the votes cast.)

On August 29, 2001, the Association of Flight Attendants (AFA) filed for an RLA election at Delta. Delta management had already been planning a sophisticated campaign of anti-union propaganda and interference in the election. The September 11 attacks, however, gave management the opportunity to claim that now was not the time to talk about a union. Now was the time to save Delta!

Delta was afraid to provoke workers by inflicting massive layoffs in the middle of a union campaign. So the airline offered "voluntary" leaves of absence to flight attendants. An estimated 4,000 to 5,000 accepted. In reality, many of the "voluntary" leaves resulted from management threats and harassment, so they might as well have been involuntary. Soon after, a management newsletter incorrectly stated that flight attendants on leave would be ineligible to vote in the union election. Management later corrected itself, but only in an email message to which on-leave flight attendants had no access. The airline also subjected workers to frequent captive meetings devoted to anti-union harangues. Many supervisors implied that union supporters were disloyal, in a time of crisis, to the company and the country.

During the election campaign, union activists spoke to many flight attendants who either said they wanted a union but that now was not the time, or that they just couldn't make up their minds. In the end, 5,609 flight attendants voted for AFA, about 60% of the 9,517 the union needed to win.

The story, however, does not end there. The AFA has filed a case with the NMB alleging illegal interference by Delta. If the board rules in favor of the union, it may order a new election. The board has no power to make Delta management follow the law, so the airline could certainly interfere again. A fairer election solution would be a "Laker Ballot" (named in honor of former British carrier Laker Air, which was once punished for interference with a new, simple-majority election). This would mean an election held along the lines of an NLRA election, with ballots that read "yes/no" and only ballots actually cast counted in the total.

A Blank Check for Concessions

In December, all the airlines turned their attention to United's negotiations with its International Association of Machinists (IAM)-represented mechanics, waiting to see how talks unfolded before demanding concessions themselves. The United-IAM contract, the first big one to be negotiated since September 11, would be the first test of the airlines' ability to extract concessions in the wake of the attacks.

The 15,000 mechanics (and related classifications), represented by IAM Lodge 141M, first voted on a Presidential Emergency Board Recommendation. The proposed agreement included a "linkage" clause, which would require mechanics to participate in any "recovery plan" (meaning concessions) to which other United employee groups agreed, or to make concessions if United declared there was a threat of bankruptcy. The mechanics soundly rejected it—over two thirds voted "no." When the IAM's international leadership endorsed an almost-identical agreement, however, it passed. The contract includes major wage increases for better-paid IAM members. By ratifying the agreement with "linkage" included, however, the IAM basically handed United a blank check for future concessions.

Some 23,000 other United Airlines ground workers (baggage handlers, customer service workers, and others) represented by IAM Lodge 141 still remain without a contract. In March, they requested the NMB formally declare an impasse so they could move towards a strike. The airline said it would conclude negotiations with the ground workers before demanding across-the-board wage cuts. (Union activists believe Lodge 141 and United will come to an agreement before the United board meeting in May.) Meanwhile, the independent Airline Mechanics Fraternal Association (AMFA) has challenged the IAM for representation of United machinists, and some workers at the airline have begun rank-and-file organizing in response to the mechanics' contract. (An excellent analysis can be found in the April 2002 edition of *Labor Notes* <www.labornotes.org>.)

Nonetheless, the IAM has set an important precedent for concessions. Other airlines already smell blood in the water. The current US Airways-ALPA contract includes a pay provision (a system demanded by management in the last contract talks) called "parity + 1." This means pilots' wages are adjusted every year to equal the average at other major carriers, plus 1%. Since US Airways adopted the system, pilots at Delta and United have made major wage gains, pushing up pay for US Airways pilots as well. In response, new US Airways CEO David Siegel declared that parity + 1 made no sense for the airline (despite the fact that it was management's idea to begin with). It is the opening volley in US Airways' attack on the unions.

The Challenges for Airline Labor

The long-term trend of airline consolidation continues to the present. American Airlines absorbed TWA in 2000, and United and US Airways proposed to merge. Though the United-US Airways merger was blocked by the Justice Department on anti-trust grounds, the question of consolidation lingered on before September 11. There was serious talk of a merger between Delta and either Northwest or Continental.

Delta CEO Leo Mullin spent last fall and winter parading around the country declaring that the government must shed its aversion to big airline mergers. Rumors now abound about new mergers in the works. According to Holly Hegeman of the business-news website TheStreet.com, Delta and America West may be in serious negotiations. Even if large-scale mergers fall through, it is likely that larger airlines will gobble up small to medium-sized carriers. Further consolidation would certainly result in layoffs for large numbers of airline workers.

Merger discussions have even contemplated treaties to allow international consolidation. Presently, U.S. regulations limit foreign ownership of airlines, as well as landing rights for foreign carriers. Some proposals to change this are bilateral, like the Transatlantic Common Aviation Area, which would allow mergers between airlines in the United States and the European Union. More ambitiously, the International Chamber of Commerce argues that the world airline industry should be deregulated all at once by including commercial aviation in the proposed General Agreement on Trade in Services (GATS). In addition to allowing global airline mergers, this would likely introduce the "flag of convenience" status for airlines. Carriers could formally register themselves in any country, potentially choosing those with lax labor laws and low wages (as cruise ships do).

Airline workers also face more direct attacks as part of the current industry restructuring. A chorus of industry voices has gone up advocating reforms to the Railway Labor Act. Though the RLA, through a maze of waiting periods, makes it extremely difficult for airline employees to strike, even this is too much for some in management and in Congress. Legislation sponsored by Sen. John McCain (R-AZ), proposes a binding arbitration system that would virtually eliminate airline workers' right to strike. Delta, United, and Federal Express are among the companies championing the legislative attack. Not surprisingly, all three are major contributors to both parties. Fedex made a $5,000 contribution to McCain in the 1999–2000 election cycle.

Airline unions are not quite ready for the challenges coming their way. Though the industry is highly unionized, the unions are extremely balkanized. For example, five different unions represent flight attendants (including the Teamsters at Northwest, the IAM at Continental, Transport Workers Union at Southwest, and the Independent Association of Professional Flight Attendants at American).

Moreover, while unions representing different work groups have formed coalitions, the craft structure of the unions and the dramatic pay disparities between different work groups represent barriers to building solidarity. Pilots represent the elite of the airline workforce, with jumbo-jet pilots at mainline carriers making up to $200,000 a year. Yet junior pilots at "regional jet" carriers (RJs) can make as little as $15,000 a year, hardly an elite salary. The mainline-RJ disparity also exists, to a lesser magnitude, for flight attendants. Even within the same bargaining units, mechanics get higher pay than other ground workers. Customer service agents, meanwhile, are among the lowest paid of all airline workers. Just go to any airline-worker electronic bulletin board to witness the sniping about pay differentials. This only gets worse among workers at different airlines.

The good news is that a coalition of flight-attendant unions has fought, in the wake of September 11, for safer workplaces, federal whistleblower protection for airline workers, and relief for laid-off airline workers. Within some airlines, coalitions of airline unions from different work groups are forming united fronts against management concession demands.

But much of the coalition building, even among union locals, takes place only within the leadership. Membership meetings at airline unions are rare—the constant travel inherent for pilots and flight attendants certainly contributes to this problem—and rank-and-file participation is generally reserved for contract- negotiation times. Rank-and-file members, meanwhile, generally regard their unions as service providers for negotiations and grievances. Many members assume that this is what they pay dues for and expect the union to function, in the words of one veteran activist, as "a giant grievance machine."

This "service" model, however, is completely inadequate in the current crisis. To build the necessary capacity for struggle, the unions need to become social movements again. We need greater rank-and-file participation, more member education, and greater mobilization (not just at contract negotiation time). We need more solidarity among different work groups, between workers at different airlines, among airline workers from different countries, and between the airline unions and the rest of the labor movement. And we need to fight for labor-law reform that makes it easier, not harder, to organize and strike.

Unless we rise to these challenges, we will see far worse than just the decline of the airline unions. The airline industry has been a bellwether for the labor movement as a whole since Reagan fired striking air traffic controllers in 1981. If management succeeds in weakening the unions and eroding working conditions in such a densely unionized industry, it will encourage further attacks on unions and workers far beyond the airlines. What happens next will depend upon how well airline workers and their unions understand these threats, and on the potential power of their solidarity.

IMMIGRANT WORKERS IN THE CROSSHAIRS
David Bacon
January/February 2003

Erlinda Valencia came from the Philippines almost two decades ago. Like many Filipina immigrants living in the San Francisco Bay area, she found a job at the airport, screening passengers' baggage.

For 14 years she worked for Argenbright Security, the baggage-screening contractor used by airlines across the country. For most of that time, it was a minimum-wage job, and she could barely support her family working 40 hours a week. Then, two years ago, organizers from the Service Employees International Union (SEIU) began talking to the screeners. Erlinda Valencia decided to get involved, and eventually became a leader in the campaign that brought in the union. "We were very happy," she remembers. "It seemed to us all that for the first time, we had a real future." The new contract the union negotiated raised wages to over $10 an hour, and workers say harassment by managers began to decrease.

Erlinda Valencia's experience reflected a major national shift in immigrant workers' organizing. In recent years, immigrant workers made hard-fought gains in their rights at work, and in using these rights to organize unions and fight for better wages and conditions. Despite the hostile reaction embodied in measures like California's Propositions 187 and 227, which sought to penalize undocumented immigrants and ban bilingual education, the political and economic clout of immigrants has increased, in large part because of successful labor organizing efforts. Some, like the janitors' strike in Los Angeles, have become well-known.

As a result, the AFL-CIO changed its position on immigration, and began calling for the repeal of employer sanctions, the federal law making it illegal for an undocumented worker to hold a job. The national movement for amnesty for undocumented workers began to grow, and the U.S. and Mexican governments started to negotiate over variants of the proposal. Under pressure from unions and immigrant rights organizations, the Immigration and Naturalization Service (INS) reduced the number of raids it carried out from 17,000 in 1997 to 953 in 2000.

Then the airplanes hit the twin towers in New York and the Pentagon in Washington. The mainstream media universally portrayed the September 11 attacks as the actions of immigrants. Political figures across the board proposed restrictions on immigration (by students, for instance) and crackdowns against undocumented workers, despite the fact that none of this would have prevented the attacks. The movement towards amnesty, and away from immigration raids and heavy-handed enforcement tactics, halted abruptly. Many public agencies, from local police departments to the Social Security Administration, which previously faced pressure to stop aiding the INS, took up immigration enforcement as a new responsibility. The Bush administration took advantage of the anti-immigrant fever to undermine the rights of workers, especially the foreign-born. The nativist scapegoating also provided a rationale for attacks on civil liberties, including the open use of racial profiling, indefinite detention, and other repressive measures.

Everything Changes—for Transportation Workers

Screeners like Erlinda Valencia were among the first, and hardest, hit. Media and politicians blamed the screeners for allowing terrorists to board airplanes in Boston and New York with box cutters and plastic knives, despite the fact that these items were permitted at the time. But the whispered undercurrent beneath the criticism, that the screeners were undependable, and possibly even disloyal, was part of the rising anti-immigrant fever which swept the country.

Screeners in California airports, like those in many states where immigrants are a big part of the population, are mostly from other countries. In fact, the low pay for screeners was one of the factors that led to the concentration of immigrants and people of color in those jobs. In the search for scapegoats, they were easy targets.

In short order, Congress passed legislation setting up a new Transportation Security Authority (TSA) to oversee baggage and passenger screening at airports, and requiring that screeners be federal government employees. That could have been a good thing for Valencia and her coworkers, since federal employees have decent salaries, and often, because of civil service, lots of job security. Federal regulations protect their right to belong to unions, as well—at least they used to.

The TSA, however, was made part of the recently established Homeland Security Department. Legislation passed after the November elections—and after some Democrats did an about face and voted for it—allows Homeland Security Czar Tom Ridge to suspend civil-service regulations in any part of the new department. By doing so, he can eliminate workers' union rights, allow discrimination and favoritism, and even abolish protection for whistleblowers.

In the anti-immigrant fever of the times, moreover, Congress required that screeners be citizens. Valencia had never become one, because of a Catch-22 in U.S. immigration law. She is petitioning for visas for family members in the Philippines. As a citizen, however, she would actually have to wait longer to petition for them than she has to as a legal resident.

At the San Francisco airport, over 800 screeners were non-citizens. The INS, however, refused to establish any fast-track to citizenship, to help them qualify for the new federalized jobs. So just as she and her coworkers finally made the job bearable and capable of supporting a family, she lost it in November, when the citizenship requirement went into effect nationwide. "It's so unfair," she said. "I've done this job for 14 years, and we're all really good at it. Instead of wanting us to continue, they're going to hire people with no experience at all, and we'll probably have to train them too. You can fly the airplane, even if you're not a citizen, and you can carry a rifle in the airport as a member of the National Guard doing security, without being a citizen either. But you can't check the bags of the passengers."

In recent years, screeners working for private contractors like Argenbright have organized unions at airports in a number of cities, including San Francisco and Los Angeles. By federalizing the workforce, the government was also, in effect, busting those unions and tearing up their newly won contracts. The act creating the Homeland Security Department—which, with 170,000 employees, will be the largest in the federal government—may be invoked to prevent the new screener workforce from forming new unions and bargaining with the TSA. The American Federation of Government Employees, which represents federal workers, has protested against the exemption of the TSA from federal regulations recognizing employees' collective bargaining rights, and announced its intention of organizing the new workforce. But it does not challenge the citizenship requirement for screeners.

Taking the "War" to the Workplace

Valencia was caught up in a wave of anti-immigrant legislation and repression that has profoundly affected immigrants and workers across the country in the wake of the September 11 terrorist attacks. The INS has launched a series of large-scale raids—Operation Tarmac. In airports around the country, the agency has told employers to provide the I-9 form for their employees. Using this information, agents have organized raids to pick up workers, and demanded that employers terminate those it says lack legal status. Close to 1,000 workers have been affected.

Initially, the INS stated publicly that it would only concentrate on workers who had access to the planes themselves, using aviation security as a pretext (hence the name Operation Tarmac). But once the raids got going, the crackdown expanded to workers in food preparation, and even in food service within passenger areas of the airports. A late-August raid at the Seattle-Tacoma International Airport led to the arrest of workers at the Sky Chef facility, which prepares on-board meals for airlines. The Hotel Employees and Restaurant Employees International Union (HERE), which is negotiating a contract with the company, claims that workers were called to an employee meeting, where they were met by INS agents in company uniforms. Some arrested workers had worked as long as 10 years at the facility, which ironically is owned by a foreign airline, Lufthansa.

Another 81 airport workers were arrested in raids on the Los Angeles, Orange County, Ontario (Calif.), Palm Springs, and Long Beach airports on August 22. The detained immigrants were working in janitorial, food service, maintenance, and baggage-handling jobs. They were picked up because they apparently were using Social Security numbers which didn't match the INS database. While federal authorities admit that none of them—in fact none of the people arrested in any Operation Tarmac raid—are accused of terrorist activity, U.S. Attorney Debra Yang claimed that "we now realize that we must strengthen security at our local airports in order to ensure the safety of the traveling public." Eliseo Medina, executive vice-president of the SEIU, which has mounted organizing drives among many of the workers in Southern California airports, called the arrests unwarranted. "These people aren't terrorists," he fumed. "They only want to work." Unions like the Communications Workers of America (CWA) have protested Operation Tarmac raids in Washington, D.C., and elsewhere.

While the anti-immigrant campaign may have started at U.S. airports, it has now expanded far beyond their gates. The agency taking the new anti-immigrant attitude most to heart has been the Social Security Administration (SSA). Following the September 11 attacks, the SSA has flooded U.S. workplaces with "no-match letters," which the agency sends to employers informing them of employees whose Social Security numbers don't correspond to the SSA database.

In the last few years, employers have used no-match letters to fire immigrant workers during union organizing drives, or to intimidate those attempting to enforce worker protection laws. Until September 11, unions were making some headway in preventing these abuses. Two years ago, San Francisco's hotel union, HERE Local 2, won an important arbitrator's decision, which held that finding the name of a worker in a no-match letter was not, by itself, sufficient reason for terminating her. In addition, pressure on the SSA resulted in the inclusion, in the text of the letter, of a similar caveat, saying that inclusion in a no-match list was not to be taken as evidence of lack of immigration status.

In the wake of September 11, however, SSA has consciously embraced the no-match letter as an immigration-enforcement device. In 2001, the agency sent out 110,000 letters, and only when there were more than ten no-matches at a company or if the no-matches represented at least 10% of a company's total workforce. This year it plans to increase the number of letters to 750,000, and all it takes is one no-match to generate a letter. The pretext is September 11: "Concerns about national security, along with the growing problem of identity theft, have caused us to accelerate our efforts," according to SSA Commissioner Jo Anne Barnhart. The Internal Revenue Service has also sharply increased the number of letters sent to employers questioning incorrect numbers, and has threatened to begin fining employers who provide them. As in the case of Valencia and the screeners, however, there is no logic that connects a worker's immigration status with national security. And proponents of these changes don't even bother trying to produce an explanation that does.

The new attitude at Social Security marks an important change. In Nebraska in 1998, Operation Vanguard, a large-scale INS program to enforce employer sanctions, relied on the SSA's database to sift out the names of possible undocumented immigrants from the rolls of all the state's meatpacking employees. Over 3,000 people lost their jobs as a result. The INS had plans to extend the operation to other states, but was unable to do so when the SSA expressed misgivings about the INS's use of its database, and denied further access. The SSA had faced pressure from immigrants' rights groups and labor unions, who questioned why information intended to ensure that workers receive retirement and disability benefits was suddenly being used to take their jobs. After September 11, 2001, such objections were brushed aside.

The net effect of the new enforcement efforts has been to turn the Social Security card into a de facto national ID card, especially for employment, without any act of Congress creating one. Immigrant rights and civil liberties advocates have fought for years against the creation of a national ID, saying that it would inevitably lead to abuse by government and employers, and that it would eventually become a kind of internal passport. And Congress has been unwilling to establish such a national identification system, at least until September 11.

An Injury to All

The wave of repression against immigrant workers hasn't just affected immigrants themselves. Limitations on workers' rights affect all workers. But because immigrants have been in the forefront of organizing unions and fighting sweatshop conditions, the threat against them has increased the danger that such conditions will spread, and affect workers throughout the labor force.

INS enforcement has increased the pressure on undocumented workers to avoid anything that could antagonize their employers, whether organizing a union, asking for a raise, or filing a complaint about unpaid overtime. There are almost 8 million undocumented people in the United States—4% of the urban workforce, and over half of all farm workers—according to a recent study by the Pew Hispanic Trust. When it becomes more risky and difficult for these workers to organize and join unions, or even to hold a job at all, they settle for lower wages. And when the price of immigrant labor goes down as a result, so do wages for other workers.

Attacks on immigrant workers have an especially big effect on unions trying to organize industries where immigrants are a large part of the workforce. The Operation Tarmac raids, for instance, hurt hotel unions' efforts to organize food service workers. The unions organizing immigrants are some of the most progressive in the labor movement. Unions like the Hotel Employees and Restaurant Employees have been disproportionately hit by the anti-immigrant offensive. Other unions, like the Teamsters and Laborers, have also led immigrant rights activity in many local areas, and suffered the impact of no-match letters and raids. Although the Bush administration has courted these unions' national leaders, the relationship doesn't seem to have provided any political leverage for stopping anti-immigrant abuses.

Organizing a Fightback

Today, employers illegally fire workers for union activity in 31% of all union organizing campaigns, affecting immigrant and native-born workers alike. Companies treat the cost of legal battles, reinstatement, and back pay as a cost of doing business, and many consider it cheaper than signing a union contract. Labor rights for all workers need to be strengthened, not weakened. But, as former National Labor Relations Board chair William Gould IV points out, "There's a basic conflict between U.S. labor law and U.S. immigration law." In its recent Hoffman decision, the Supreme Court has held that the enforcement of employer sanctions, which makes it illegal for an undocumented immigrant to hold a job, is more important than the right of that worker to join a union and resist exploitation on the job.

Despite the decision, however, and the growing anti-immigrant climate, immigrants workers are still organizing. In May, four hundred workers won a hard-fought union election at the ConAgra beef plant in Omaha, a city where INS raids destroyed immigrant-based union committees only a few years ago. New Jersey recycling workers at KTI also finally won a union vote, on their fourth attempt to join the Laborers Union, which is also organizing successful campaigns among asbestos workers on Long Island. HERE won a 22-year battle for a contract at San Francisco's Flagship Marriott Hotel, the hotel chain's first corporate-managed property to sign a union agreement.

The union-based efforts for amnesty and the repeal of employer sanctions were dealt a serious blow by the post-September 11 climate, but there are signs of renewed forward movement. SEIU Local 790, in cooperation with Filipinos for Affirmative Action and the Phillip Veracruz Justice Project, led efforts to fight for screeners' jobs at the San Francisco airport. The SEIU also initiated a national postcard campaign, called A Million Voices for Justice, to restart the national campaign for amnesty. In August, the SEIU and the ACLU sued the Department of Transportation over the citizenship requirement, and in mid-November Federal District Court Judge Robert Takasugi ruled the requirement illegal. The decision, however, only applies to the nine workers in whose names the suit was filed. Lawyers for the plaintiffs hope to broaden it to a class-action, while federal authorities predictably announced they would appeal.

Last summer, HERE announced plans for a Freedom Ride on Washington, D.C., for immigrant rights. The union deliberately chose the name and used the language of the civil-rights movement in an effort to establish a greater level of unity between African Americans, Latinos, and Asian-Americans. HERE officials also said they intended to challenge the color line—employers have kept African-Americans out of hotel employment, while hiring immigrants at lower wages—in hotels across the country. Massive layoffs and the economic downturn in tourism made plans to challenge hiring discrimination a moot point, but in the spring, HERE announced that it would again begin organizing its Freedom Ride, and set it for fall 2003.

And while Erlinda Valencia was one of the nine named plaintiffs in the suit against the citizenship requirement, the favorable court decision only means, at best, that she can take a test to qualify for her old job. If she takes it and passes, she will be put on a list of eligible potential employees. Her old job at the airport and those of her coworkers have already been filled. Preliminary studies indicate that many new hires are ex-members of the military and law enforcement agencies, and that the new workforce does not include nearly as many immigrants or people of color as the old one.

Valencia, like may other former screeners, has found herself looking for another job. The labor councils, unions, and immigrant rights activists who supported the screeners mounted food drives, tried to help former screeners get retraining, and tried to help them find stable new employment. But the larger challenge, they believe, is building a political movement to roll back the anti-immigrant atmosphere in which Valencia, and many like her, have become ensnared.

U.S. LABOR LAW

How the United States' stacked labor laws make it nearly impossible for workers to gain union representation.

Andrew Strom
September/October 2003

Ever wish you had a union at work? Surveys show that half of all non-union workers do. Still, less than 10% of private sector workers in this country enjoy the benefits of union representation. How is this possible? U.S. labor laws that are stacked against workers can take much of the blame.

Under the National Labor Relations Act (NLRA)—the law that governs labor relations for most of the private sector—to obtain bargaining rights a union must represent a majority of the employees in an appropriate "bargaining unit." So, first you and your co-workers have to figure out who counts as an "employee." According to the NLRA, supervisors—anyone who uses "independent judgment" to "responsibly direct" the work of others—are not "employees." This excludes millions of workers who would qualify as workers under any common sense definition and leaves millions more unsure if they have a legal right to unionize.

Let's say there are 60 people at your workplace; five are clearly supervisors, five more are borderline supervisors, and 35 of the remaining 50 workers want a union. You should be home free, right?

Not so fast. Your employer is not required to bargain with your chosen union just because all or a majority of workers sign a petition. Instead, your employer can demand a secret ballot election held by the National Labor Relations Board (NLRB, the federal agency that administers the NLRA). The law gives employers any number of ploys they can use to drag out the election process and to craft a bargaining unit where they'll win the vote. Before the election, your employer can insist on a hearing about whether the bargaining unit the workers have selected is "appropriate." For instance, if workers at a retail chain store want a union, the company will argue that the bargaining unit must include every store in the metropolitan area. The employer may also demand a hearing about the borderline supervisors, trying to exclude them from the union if they are pro-union and insisting on their right to vote if they are anti-union.

If you clear these hurdles, your employer will almost certainly wage an anti-union campaign in the months before the election. When the NLRA was first passed in 1935, the NLRB held that employers were prohibited from interfering in union elections, but the 1947 Taft-Hartley Act allowed employers to express anti-union views as long as they do not make threats or promises.

Now, employers may require workers to attend anti-union meetings without providing equal time to pro-union workers. (By contrast, under federal election law, if an employer invites one candidate to address employees, it must give the same opportunity to all other candidates.) Supervisors can meet individually with workers and ask them to vote against the union. (Compare this with sexual harassment law, which recognizes that it can be inherently coercive for a supervisor to ask a subordinate for a date.) The company may also post and distribute anti-union propaganda while simultaneously prohibiting workers from distributing union literature in work areas. (Imagine a political election where only the incumbent is allowed to advertise.) And thanks to a 1992 Supreme Court decision, nonemployee union organizers have no right to campaign on the employer's private property, even if the property includes a large parking lot open to the public.

If you work in the airline industry you are covered by the Railway Labor Act (RLA), and a different set of rules applies. The National Mediation Board, which regulates elections under the RLA, has found that it is inherently coercive for employers to hold small group or one-on-one meetings to campaign against the union. But in other ways, the RLA makes obtaining union representation especially difficult for those it covers. Under the RLA, for example, you must organize as part of a nationwide bargaining unit, making it highly impractical for workers to organize at large, geographically-dispersed companies. This is why Federal Express got Congress to amend the RLA in 1996 so that it would be covered.

Some anti-union tactics are illegal. But even where the law does place limits on employers' actions during an organizing drive, it fails to provide meaningful remedies or deterrents. You may think that if you were fired for trying to organize a union, a clear violation of the NLRA, you could sue and win a multi-million dollar verdict. But unlike laws that protect workers from other forms of discrimination, there is no private right to sue under the NLRA. Your only recourse is to file a charge with the NLRB. The Regional Director will conduct an investigation, but won't give you access to the information it gets from your employer. Your chances aren't good; Regional Directors dismiss almost two-thirds of all cases without a hearing. Even if the Regional Director decides to take your case, the only remedy is an order of reinstatement and back wages, less any wages you earned in the interim. There are no fines, no penalties, and no punitive damages. And reinstatement only comes at the end of a lengthy legal process—a hearing before an Administrative Law Judge, an appeal to the five-member NLRB in Washington, followed by an appeal to the U.S. Court of Appeals. The process routinely takes five years. No wonder companies regularly fire workers for trying to organize.

What if, despite your employer's anti-union campaign, you and your co-workers stick together and vote for union representation? Your employer has one more chance to contest the result, by claiming (again) that the bargaining unit was inappropriate, or that workers were threatened by union organizers, or any of a dozen other reasons to invalidate the election. Whether or not the arguments succeed, the employer can usually buy two more years of delay until the U.S. Court of Appeals orders it to bargain.

Once bargaining finally begins, your employer's only obligation is to bargain in

Labor Law in Action at Overnite

In 1994, the employees of Overnite Transportation Company, one of the largest nonunion trucking companies in the country with approximately 14,000 employees at 175 service centers, began organizing with the Teamsters. By February 1995, workers had voted to unionize at four locations, elections were scheduled at 22 others, and petitions for elections had been filed at five additional service centers.

The next month, Overnite's president, Jim Douglas, sent a letter to service center managers describing the organizing drive as "the biggest war of our lives," and urging them to "muster troops to all out attack" and to "unleash the fury of the Overnite machine." Douglas personally traveled to more than fifty service centers to threaten workers against voting for the union. Managers held compulsory meetings with workers where they threatened alternately that workers would never get a contract, or that if they did get a contract it would drive the company out of business. Supervisors threatened harsher working conditions if workers unionized. Workers were also illegally prohibited from talking about the union or distributing union literature in break rooms. The company used both carrots and sticks in its anti-union campaign, granting wage increases, but informing all employees that the wage increases were being withheld at the service centers that had already voted to unionize.

Not surprisingly, the illegal anti-union campaign succeeded at many locations. At eleven of the service centers where majorities of workers had signed union cards, the workers ultimately voted against unionizing. The Teamsters filed charges challenging the election results. Due to the extensive nature of the violations and the large number of locations involved, the hearings dragged on for months. Eventually the union won; the Administrative Law Judge (ALJ) set aside the election results and further found that Overnite's illegal conduct was so pervasive that fair elections would not be possible. As a result, the ALJ recommended the strongest possible remedy—an order requiring Overnite to bargain with the Teamsters despite the outcome of the elections. The full NLRB agreed with the ALJ, and so did a three-judge panel of the Fourth Circuit Court of Appeals,

"good faith." One-third of the time, workers who vote to unionize never even get a first contract. Why? If your employer fails to bargain in good faith, the only remedy is ... an order requiring it to bargain in good faith. Workers cannot recover damages for the deprivation of their right to bargain.

Suppose your employer does negotiate in good faith. Getting a good contract is still hardly a given. Traditionally, workers would strike if their employer refused to give in to their demands. But strikes rarely succeed these days. Your employer can't fire you for striking, but it can hire "permanent replacements." When strikers try to return to work, the employer does not have to take them back, it merely has to place them on a preferential hiring list in case any of the permanent replacements quit.

Of course, any strike would be more effective if you could expand it beyond your own employer. But the Taft-Hartley Act made it illegal for workers to strike or picket one employer in order to put pressure on another. This prohibition against "secondary" strikes applies even to strikes against another subsidiary owned by the

the most conservative court in the country. But Overnite appealed the ruling to eleven judges on the Fourth Circuit. By the time the full court finally ruled on the c it was 2002. The judges unanimously agreed that Overnite had committed serious and widespread violations of the law. Unfortunately, a majority of the judges decided that since most of the illegal conduct took place in 1995, and there had been substantial employee turnover since then, a fair election would now be possible—so it lifted the bargaining order. Even if the court had affirmed the NLRB order, Overnite would have successfully delayed bargaining for seven years. But the court essentially penalized the workers for the delays inherent in the NLRB enforcement process, requiring them to restart their organizing drive from zero.

At more than two dozen other locations, workers withstood the anti-union assault and voted to unionize. At four of these, Overnite simply refused to bargain. Overnite contested the election results at these sites on grounds that the NLRB and the Court of Appeals both found without merit. But the Court of Appeals did not issue its decision until seven years after the elections, so no bargaining took place at these sites during all that time. In those locations where bargaining did take place, negotiations dragged on for years with little progress.

In 1999 the Teamsters decided to call a strike in order to put pressure on the company to stop its illegal anti-union campaign and to bargain in good faith. By this point, the Teamsters had filed over 1,000 charges against Overnite with the NLRB. Despite initial support for the strike among the workers, Overnite was able to outlast them. While the strike undoubtedly hurt the company's bottom line, workers became discouraged as it dragged on, and many eventually returned to work. After three years, less than 600 workers were still supporting the strike, and the Teamsters finally called an end to it. At the peak of the organizing drive, the NLRB certified the Teamsters as the bargaining representative for 3,600 Overnite workers at 37 service centers. But today, not a single Overnite worker is covered by a union contract.

same company. It also prohibits actions that go one step up the corporate food chain; for example, janitors who work for a cleaning contractor cannot picket the building owner. And workers at Ford or GM are prohibited from striking to support workers at a parts supplier.

Nevertheless, there are still some workers who have enough power to wage an effective strike by themselves. But once again Taft-Hartley is there to keep the workers in check. The law allows the President to enjoin any strike that poses a threat to "health and safety"—a provision courts have interpreted broadly to include threats to the nation's economic well-being.

Unions grew rapidly after the NLRA was passed in 1935, but the percentage of unionized workers has declined steadily since the passage of Taft-Hartley in 1947, when over 40% of private sector workers belonged to unions. A comprehensive labor law reform bill was introduced during the Carter administration that would have given unions equal time when employers hold anti-union meetings, strengthened the remedies for violations of the law, and speeded up the enforcement process. The bill was filibustered to death by Republicans. During the Clinton administration, there was a proposal to limit the ability of employers to hire permanent replacements for strikers, but again it didn't get the backing of the 60 Senators necessary to prevent a filibuster. Since that defeat, unions have virtually given up on achieving labor law reform.

In a few instances workers have, with union backing, waged successful campaigns that get around one-sided labor laws by using shareholder activism, marches and rallies, reaching out to elected officials, handbilling, and the Internet. But with labor law so stacked against workers, it's a miracle that any workers manage to gain union representation at all.

JUST IN TIME?
Emerging alliances between unions and day laborers
Ricky Baldwin
March/April 2004

The unionized hotel and restaurant workers on strike at Chicago's Congress Hotel are facing an increasingly common threat: temporary or day laborers hired as replacement workers to bust the union. Exploding numbers of vulnerable workers, often homeless or undocumented, are being recruited by opportunistic temp agencies that target desperate communities and exploit the struggles of unionized workers.

With the pool of needy workers steadily growing, unions are painfully aware that walkouts could spell suicide. Not only this: the presence of temps at (otherwise) union worksites, performing the same work for far less pay, erodes union workers' efforts at improvements. Day labor, says Tim Costello of the North American Alliance for Fair Employment (NAAFE), "is essentially a gun at the head of organized labor."

Today, in stark contrast to the long-time hostility between strikers and "scabs," unions and day laborer groups in Chicago and across the country are forming alliances against the common threats of unscrupulous employers and predatory temp agencies.

Some unions are still wary of this radical shift in strategy, and in union tradition. But as union density (the percentage of workers who are union members) shrinks, and the day labor workforce swells, the practical benefits of alliance are bringing more and more of the skeptics around.

Day Labor Explosion
Formal temp work originated in Chicago in the 1920s, then all but disappeared following the reforms of the New Deal and the economic boom after World War II. But economic shifts in the 1970s spurred a comeback for the temp industry, which

quadrupled in size between 1982 and 1997. (See box "The Contingent Economy," for a taxonomy of temp work.) Now an estimated one in eight new jobs is a temp job. Moreover, 57% of employers report that they seldom or never promote temps into permanent jobs.

The rejuvenated temp industry has also branched out from its earlier concentration in clerical work; now over 60% of temp jobs are non-clerical, including industrial, technical, professional, and even health care jobs. Of particular signifi-

The Contingent Economy

Temporary work is divided into at least three types: agency temps hired through professional personnel suppliers like Manpower or Labor Ready; internal temps employed by companies directly; and corner day laborers who gather on street corners each morning hoping for work. Agency temps who perform industrial, warehouse, construction, or other unskilled manual labor are also called day laborers.

Temp jobs are one part of the expanding sphere of contingent work, which also includes independent contracting, involuntary part-time work, and other insecure, low- or no-benefit job arrangements.

Nobody really knows how many temps there are, but recent government estimates of agency temps alone range as high as 5.3 million, compared to 250,000 temps in 1973. With turnover as high as 600% in many temp jobs, however, these figures are misleading. According to industry reports, more than 15 million workers, or 12% of the U.S. workforce, held temporary or contingent jobs at one time or another during 1998, again not including either corner day laborers or temps hired directly by firms. Corner day laborers are essentially impossible to count, because many are undocumented immigrants and most work unofficially or "off the books."

In addition to this growth, the composition of the contingent workforce has shifted in recent years from an overwhelmingly clerical phenomenon (now only 40% of agency temps) to largely industrial (35%), technical (11%), and professional (6%), according to a 1999 Ford Foundation review by Nik Theodore and Chirag Mehta. Another survey by Theodore examining homeless day laborers for the University of Illinois-Chicago in 2000 found the most common jobs in the recent past were loading, unloading or warehouse work (47.5%); light industrial or factory work (33.9%); janitorial (6.1%); and construction (4.2%). According to Labor Research Associates, day laborers now fill over one-third of construction jobs.

Among agency temps, around half are women, over 80% are white, and less than half are under 35, according to federal data. Day laborers in particular are, however, by all reports mostly black or Latino (depending on the location) and younger.

In 1997, the median weekly wage for agency temps was 64.5% of that for full-time non-contingent workers, but much lower for women and Latino workers at 59.8% and 55.0% respectively. In 1999, 29.8% of agency temps had an annual family income of less than $15,000, compared to 7.7% of non-contingent full-time workers. Also, 70% of agency temps had no health insurance, compared to 44% of non-contingent full-time workers. It is also not uncommon for day laborers to receive less than minimum wage.

cance is unskilled manual temporary work, or "day labor," which has exploded in the last decade.

Day laborers regularly earn less than $9,000 a year, according to a study by Nik Theodore, director of the Center for Urban Economic Development at the University of Illinois-Chicago. Many are homeless. The study, conducted in homeless shelters in Chicago, found that 75% of the homeless had worked in day-labor in the past year. Over a quarter had worked day labor assignments for the City of Chicago itself. Fully 82% had earned less than the federal minimum wage of $5.15 on their most recent job—often as a result of check-cashing fees or paycheck deductions for transportation or safety equipment.

Many day laborers work in the informal economy—panhandling, selling newspapers or blood plasma, or gathering on certain street corners to jockey for favor from contractors who drive up, known as "corner day labor." Corner day laborers frequently work "off the books" and are often overcharged, underpaid, or not paid at all. Some are even abandoned at distant worksites with no way to get home.

"Some guys get part of their pay this week, and the boss promises more next week," says Pablo Alvarez, director of the National Day Laborers Organizing Network. "But when next week comes, the same thing happens. We've had guys that were owed $6,000 or $15,000 or more in some cases."

The growth of contingent work is reshaping the economy. It was a significant reason for stagnant or falling wages during the economic boom of the 1990s, according to a March 2000 study by the Campaign on Contingent Work. And companies are increasingly turning to temp agencies to help them break strikes.

In the strike and lockout at Kaiser Aluminum from 1998 to 2000, the largest and longest strike in United Steelworkers history, temps were a central issue. Temp giant Labor Ready supplied Kaiser with hundreds of strikebreakers. The use of strikebreakers prolonged the strike, keeping the $3 billion operation in production during the walkout and enabling management to resist all settlement offers—months after the strikers had offered to return to work. Labor Ready also recruited out-of-state strikebreakers, according to the union, a violation of Washington state law. Eventually the National Labor Relations Board ruled the lockout illegal, and the conflict ended in binding arbitration. But by then, over 540 jobs out of 3,000 had been lost.

The temp agencies are "essentially professional strikebreakers," in business to keep a supply of desperate workers at the ready, says Jennie Busch of the Day Labor Organizing Project (DLOP). The project, a joint effort by Chicago Jobs with Justice and the Chicago Coalition for the Homeless, was founded in 1998 to advocate for individual workers and for systematic reform of the day labor industry. Temp agencies not only prolong strikes and weaken unions' position, Busch says, they also put day laborers in a particularly vulnerable position. During a strike, employers often cut corners on training and other health and safety measures. Also, in an operation run almost entirely by temps who may have never done similar work, the risk of injury on the job is much higher.

Crossing the Line

Exposing these health and safety concerns, says Busch, is one important way that day laborers can improve working conditions at temp agencies and help strikers build a case against the boss. But in order to accomplish this, unions and day laborers have to cooperate across the picket line.

In the ongoing Congress Hotel strike in Chicago, for example, the union had a history of advocating for day laborers' rights. The hotel's 130 housekeepers, phone operators, bellmen, and others belong to Hotel Employees and Restaurant Employees (HERE) Local 1, a member-run union that in 2002 stood up to and prevailed against a hotel management association representing 27 Chicago hotels, although not the Congress. Central to HERE's winning strategy was to coordinate with the DLOP in a campaign against local temp agencies, which had been advertising job openings beginning on the strike deadline.

Together, HERE and DLOP organized marches and rallies that exposed temp agency abuses, mainly wage and hour violations and failing to inform temps when they were being sent into a strike situation as required by Illinois law. As a result, two temp agencies publicly agreed not to supply strikebreakers in the event of a walkout, and in the end the hotels signed a citywide agreement raising the wages of 7,000 hotel workers to $10.00 an hour.

When its own contract negotiations began in late 2002, Congress Hotel's management balked. The hotel not only refused to follow the citywide agreement, as it typically had in the past—it actually cut wages by 7%, to $8.21 for housekeeping staff. Last May, the workers voted to strike, and took their case to the DLOP. As the strike progressed, temp workers at the hotel began to report open paint cans and other containers of hazardous materials in open closets, as well as open electrical boxes with exposed wires and water leaking nearby. Workers reported rodent droppings and rat poisons in the employee cafeteria and by vending machines, says Local 1's Claire Fauke.

The testimony of temps inside the hotel, along with photographs of safety violations, provided the union with critical ammunition. The picture they painted of conditions at the hotel convinced Travelocity.com, Hotels.com, and Expedia.com to post travel advisories for the Congress, contributing to a drastic drop in the hotel's business during the peak summer months. Community and labor organizations also held protests at temp agencies used by the Congress, highlighting the mistreatment of temps and causing a number of agencies to revoke their relationships with the hotel.

Then in December, temps and customers testified at a city council meeting, yielding a sweep by local building inspectors. A court ordered the hotel to correct 68 safety violations within 30 days or close its doors, prompting the hotel's attorney to denounce the strategy as "a dirty trick."

Temp workers' complaints about health and safety conditions played a similar role in the recent tortilla workers strike at Azteca Foods in Chicago, organized by the United Electrical Workers (UE). Workers at Azteca complained of health and safety problems even before the strike. The low paid, mostly Latina workers routinely suffered from chemical rashes and burns from sulphuric acids and bleaches used in the flour. But the temps Azteca managers called in to replace the strikers faced all that and more. One day laborer lost the use of his arm after it was caught between two rotating belts and none of the other temps knew how to shut down the machine.

The incident prompted a federal safety inspection and two citations against Azteca. News of the accident and subsequent violations also helped promote the union's call for a consumer boycott. Eventually, the company settled the unfair labor practice charges that had sparked the strike, and the workers returned to work. Their contract fight and boycott, however, continue.

Likewise, striking Teamsters at cheese producer V&V Supremo and striking UE workers at seat manufacturer Coach and Car both found cooperation with temporary workers invaluable. At V&V, where workers struck in 2001 (and were later locked out) over the company's failure to recognize their union vote, some day laborers refused to cross the picket line, and others reported on conditions in the plant. A community-labor coalition organized a boycott, and finally V&V signed a contract including 12% to 24% wage increases. Similarly, during a 2001 walkout at Coach and Car, some temps refused to scab and others reported from inside. The temp agencies' violations of licensing regulations as well as wage and hour laws led state senator Miguel del Valle to denounce the agencies in public and helped shoehorn state legislative reforms that passed the next year. Strikers voted to end the walkout when the National Labor Relations Board upheld most of the union's unfair labor practice charges.

But this kind of cooperation between traditional antagonists does not happen overnight. In the last four years, Chicago's DLOP has developed a strong core of leaders among day laborers and simultaneously built a network of relationships among community and labor organizations. Working together to win back pay for hundreds of underpaid temps, then to pass legislative reforms, these groups have developed mutual trust.

Safe Havens

Now the DLOP is trying to establish a community hiring hall like the one that opened last summer in Cleveland. Over 50 of these nonprofit hiring halls are now operating around the country. Like for-profit temp agencies, they match workers with jobs; however, they are run by and for workers and provide a safe haven where day laborers know they won't be victimized.

The benefits to day laborers from these hiring halls are obvious. In Takoma Park, Maryland, for example, the Center for Employment and Leadership has been offering training, legal advocacy, and a nonprofit hiring hall for day laborers since 1991. The center is a project of CASA de Maryland, a community organization established in 1985 by Central American refugees and North American activists. CASA works closely with building trades unions and has placed day laborers in over 9,000 jobs.

But unions benefit too, says Dan Kerr of Cleveland's Day Laborers Organizing Committee. Kerr's group began as a grassroots effort at a homeless shelter, providing free meals and trying to sever the relationship between temp agencies and the shelters. The group made its first contacts with organized labor through the local living-wage campaign. Kerr says many unions were initially skeptical of working with day laborers—normally thought of as low-wage competitors at best or "scabs" at worst. HERE and the Service Employees International Union (SEIU) were enthusiastic from the start, though, perhaps because both unions represent workers from many of the same communities as day laborers: poor, and mostly black or Latino. Both unions also represent workers who often work side by side with temp workers being paid significantly less and often doing the dirtiest, most dangerous jobs with little or no training. This two-tier workforce exerts downward pressure on union wages and other improvements by sheer competition.

When Kerr's group suggested a nonprofit community hiring hall, HERE was looking for a "higher end" temp agency to write into their contract at the Sheraton Hotel to serve as the employer's first choice whenever it needed temp workers. SEIU had a similar need for a nonexploitive agency at Jacobs Field, the Cleveland Indians' home base, where SEIU represents concession stand workers but the cleaning crews are nonunion temps. The community hiring hall fit the bill perfectly, and now virtually all the new hiring hall's work has been obtained through ties with unions.

Still, as Ed Shurma of Chicago's Coalition for the Homeless points out, these hiring halls, though a vast improvement, fall far short of the goal of helping homeless and other day laborers gain a stable livelihood. "So now our focus is on full-time jobs that pay a living wage."

Unionizing Day Laborers

One tried and true means of raising wages and improving conditions at work is of course through unionization, which many consider impossible for workers as vulnerable and transient as day laborers. Before trying it, Chicago organizers began making regular visits to day labor agencies to distribute information on day laborers' rights. They established a worker center at a church where day laborers could come with complaints, and held "accountability sessions" with day labor agencies, churches, and community groups to discuss unpaid wages and overtime, discrimination in assignments, unsafe working conditions, and illegal paycheck deductions.

Now the DLOP is actively helping workers achieve full-fledged union representation, by providing education, union contacts, and rank-and-file leadership development.

Larry W. Hamilton is one of those new leaders. Hamilton works at McCormick Place, an exhibition hall run by Chicago's Metropolitan Pier and Exposition Authority, where he and 39 coworkers set up trade shows. As the only nonunion workers in a huge building, they earn minimum wage with no benefits. Most of them have been setting up shows at McCormick Place for several years—as temps.

"If I told Mr. Webster I had been working here for 11 years as a temporary worker," Hamilton jokes, "he'd say, you haven't looked at my dictionary lately, have you?"

Rather than bouncing from job to job, Hamilton and his coworkers stay put while their employer of record, the temp agency, changes at the whim of a contractor called Wieland Services. "[Wieland] tells us where to go to pick up our checks," says Hamilton. "He tells them when to give us a raise. Some of the men here have worked for this contractor for five to fifteen years. We worked for his father."

At times, Hamilton and his coworkers pull ten or twelve hour shifts, but only get paid for eight. "He says he'll pay us the rest next week or ten days later," says Hamilton. "But we're not getting paid very much, so when he holds $10 or $20, that's a lot to a person on minimum wage." He says this explains why workers find it hard to leave. "We need to stay and pick up the rest of our money. It's almost like sharecropping."

Despite the hurdles, Hamilton is enthusiastic about the set-up crew's prospects for unionization, perhaps thanks to previous experience with the DLOP and its member organizations. Homeless until about a year ago, Hamilton says the Homeless Coalition helped him get a voucher and raise the deposit money to get his own apartment. "I feel indebted to them," he says, "both for the work they have done with homeless children and parents and for myself." Hamilton volunteered first for the Homeless Coalition and now sits on the steering committee for the DLOP.

So-called "perma-temps" like Hamilton are increasingly common in today's workforce, as employers seek to cut costs and shift risks onto their workers. This arrangement provides the employer with all the benefits of a stable workforce but allows the worker none of the benefits of permanent work.

Organized Corners

But day labor is still far more commonly characterized by rapid turnover, which makes traditional union organizing next to impossible. In some cities, corner day laborers have formed their own brand of unions, organized corner by corner, to fight abuses by employers, police, and others. Among them are the Coalition for Humane Immigrant Rights of Los Angeles (CHIRLA) and the Latino Union in Chicago, a spin-off of the Day Laborers Organizing Project. These are unions without collective bargaining rights, but they can still have a tangible impact by, for example, convincing all the day laborers at a specific corner not to accept wages below an agreed-upon minimum. Some also negotiate with local officials and neighborhood associations to establish official corners or indoor waiting areas for day laborers to congregate.

Day laborer organizations like CHIRLA typically have less contact with organized labor since they're almost exclusively called out for nonunion jobs with small firms or individual homeowners. Nevertheless, they can make common cause with unions, says Alvarez, even when this is not easy.

When Los Angeles janitors went on strike in 2000, for example, employers approached day laborers at several organized corners looking for strikebreakers. In a heroic show of solidarity, the workers refused the jobs, even though it meant they might go without income that day—a situation most of them could scarcely afford.

Again recently, says Alvarez, in the ongoing national supermarket strike and lockout affecting almost 90,000 employees, day laborers at organized corners in Los Angeles refused similar offers. After all, many of the strikers, especially the janitors, belong to the same communities as the day laborers. More than this, says Alvarez, "They declined because they didn't want to be scabs."

Day laborer organizations "have an affinity with unions," he explains, "because they do what unions do. Their goal is improving the lives of all workers." Alvarez also says his network cooperates with several building trades unions, especially Ironworkers, Laborers, Carpenters and Painters.

Unfinished Business

In 2001, the building trades unions carried out what was by most accounts a highly successful campaign to stop the spread of temporary labor in the construction industry, reportedly forcing the largest temp agency in construction to close upwards of 10% of its hiring offices. Organizers joined forces with over 100 local community coalitions already providing services to day laborers both to expose the conditions in temporary work and to organize the temps wherever they could.

The primary target was Washington-based Labor Ready, which claims to employ 140,000 construction workers, making it the largest employer in U.S. construction and "a cancer growing in our industry," according to the AFL-CIO Building and Construction Trades department's organizing director Jeff Grabelsky.

The campaign succeeded in exposing Labor Ready's abuses, resulting in numerous citations, fines, and in one case $100,000 in back pay for underpaid temps at California state college construction projects. The state of Washington found that Labor Ready had cheated the state out of another $730,000 in workers comp premiums. The National Labor Relations Board cited Labor Ready for blacklisting pro-union employees, and the Occupational Safety and Health Administration handed the company more inspections, violations, and fines than its top ten competitors combined, according to the Labor Research Association.

In all, the campaign may have cost the company as much as $3 million. "It alerted government regulators to the extent of the problems," says NAAFE's Tim Costello. "But it's over. It was a specific campaign that came to an end, and the unions were not ready to take the next step"—yet.

That step, Costello says, would feature coalition efforts such as opening hiring halls as well as advocating for public policy changes.

Will Collette agrees. Collette was a strategic researcher for the building trades department of the AFL-CIO at the time of the campaign against Labor Ready and outlined a detailed proposal for a nationally coordinated campaign to address day labor in a much more extensive way. The plan calls for an all-out organizing drive with apprenticeship and membership programs for day laborers, many more community-labor partnerships such as those in Chicago and Cleveland—about ten times the present number—and worker centers, hiring halls, and grant-funded education and legal services.

Collette's plan draws on successful models from all around the country to design a much-needed comprehensive strategy, one that national labor organizations would seemingly do well to adopt. But in the process it also illustrates the scope, creativity, and successes of the emerging alliances between unions and day laborer groups. "There's a lot of exciting work going on around day labor," notes Jennie Busch, "and more and more unions are recognizing the urgency of it."

MISREPORTING THE NEW OVERTIME RULES

The way the mainstream media reported on the recent changes to overtime rules is a perfect illustration of the bias of supposedly "balanced" news coverage.

David Swanson
September/October 2004

On August 23, the Bush administration's Department of Labor eliminated the right to time-and-a-half pay for overtime work for millions of Americans. That's the biggest pay cut in American history. The facts that should have made that statement a headline in every paper in the country were easily obtainable. Reporters had had months in which to review the changes. Experts had written helpful analyses. The specific ways in which various categories of workers were being stripped of their rights would have been no secret to any sixth grader with Internet access.

And if our national media couldn't take the time to read the rule changes themselves, the Department of Labor and others pressing for the changes had made their goals abundantly clear. The DOL had published advice to employers on how to avoid paying overtime. Both houses of Congress had passed an amendment to prevent the new changes from stripping workers of overtime pay, but a conference committee under Republican leadership had surreptitiously removed that measure. Business groups supported the changes. Labor unions opposed them. And the Bush administration had spent four years attacking worker rights and lying about it.

For the media to take seriously the administration's claims that these changes would benefit workers would require not only a strict avoidance of research, but also the assumption that the administration was as likely as workers' organizations be honest about what would help workers. Of course, the media made this assumption, illustrating a fundamental problem with contemporary journalism. Reporters believe they cannot arbitrate between competing views. They tend to give extra deference to the government as well. As a result, whether or not they do their own research, they do not report on what they learn.

This was the lead of the Associated Press story by Leigh Strope on August 23: "Paychecks could surge or shrink for a few or for millions of workers across the country starting Monday, when sweeping changes to the nation's overtime pay rules take effect." The rest of the article was no more enlightening, unless you've learned to read between the lines. Strope betrayed no evidence of having read the changes or of having drawn any conclusions. To have done so would have violated the "balanced reporting" ethic that calls for the reporter to be simply a stenographer for two sides—regardless of their credibility or the actual evidence.

It's not as if Strope didn't know who the players were in this drama: one day earlier, she had published an article that in its first two sentences did more than almost any other to make clear what interests were at stake—before moving on in the third sentence to the traditional "balanced" approach:

"In an unprecedented overhaul of the nation's overtime pay rules, the Bush administration is delivering to its business allies an election-year plum they've sought for decades. The new rules take effect Monday after surviving many efforts by Democrats, labor unions and worker advocates to block them in Congress and kill them through public and political pressure. The administration and business groups say the old regulations were out of date and confusing, and were sparking multimillion dollar lawsuits. The Labor Department says no more than 107,000 workers will lose overtime eligibility from the changes, but about 1.3 million will gain it. The Economic Policy Institute, a liberal Washington think tank, says 6 million will lose, and only a few will get new rights to premium pay for working more than 40 hours a week. But no one really knows."

What could be more even-handed and professional? It just depends what side you take. And if the media can't figure out which side is right, how should I presume? That has to be the reaction many readers had to articles bearing these and similar headlines:

Overtime Law Clarification Is Hard to Figure
—*San Diego Union-Tribune*

Labor Experts Disagree on What Overtime Overhaul Will Mean
—*Orlando Sentinel*

Rules for Overtime Pay to Take Effect: Employers, Workers Confused by Regulations on Eligibility, Classification
—*Washington Post*

Overdue Overtime Overhaul Is Overly Confusing
—*Lewiston Morning Tribune*

Reading the articles that follow these headlines is like reading the sports section.

There are always two competing sides, and they just can't seem to agree. This is what the *Tallahassee Democrat* told us, in a typical article: "Labor department officials say the new rules will expand overtime coverage to 1.3 million low-income workers. But labor groups and other opponents charge the new rules could result in at least 6 million people who now get overtime being moved into classes of workers not eligible for time-and-a-half pay." (The Labor Department always simply "says" things, while "opponents" usually "charge" or "argue" or "claim.")

Yet the Economic Policy Institute had explained in a July report exactly how the rule changes would eliminate the right to overtime for millions of white- and blue-collar workers. And three former DOL officials who had served under Reagan, Bush Sr., and Clinton had released a report in July with a very similar analysis. (See www.epinet.org/content.cfm/briefingpapers_bp152 and www.aflcio.org/yourjobeconomy/overtimepay/upload/OvertimeStudyTextfinal.pdf.) These weren't just claims, but detailed explanations. Most of the media neither presented nor refuted those explanations, but simply cited their conclusions as "claims."

Editors at the *New York Times* were able to recognize the importance of these analyses and published an admirable editorial on August 25, including this sentence (emphasis added): "The administration goes so far as to say that its changes will expand the pool of people eligible for overtime, but research by liberal and labor advocates persuasively argues that the changes would cut the number, by as many as 6 million."

The *Hartford Courant* published an excellent column called "Selling Workers Snake Oil." The author of the EPI report had a good column printed in the *Contra Costa Times* and the *St. Louis Post-Dispatch*. AFL-CIO President John Sweeney published a column in the *Charleston Gazette* and the *Seattle Post-Intelligencer*. The president of the New Hampshire AFL-CIO published a column in the *Manchester Union Leader*. And Cox News Service ran a column called "Chutzpah and George Bush" that merits quoting:

"It will probably be years until the changes settle and the outcomes are clear. But if you think this is an administration that would set out to do workers a great big favor and pester employers' bottom lines, you ought to check your zip code. It may be time for you to move back to Earth."

But columns and editorials are framed as opinion, not fact. They're the one place the media occasionally admit that their government sources are telling whoppers.

The *Times*' August 23 article by Steven Greenhouse made no such admission. Greenhouse simply gave both sides. Greenhouse lacks neither intelligence nor familiarity with the topic. It's impossible to believe he hasn't formed some conclusion in his own mind. Yet, against the enormous weight of evidence, he presented two camps as equally worth listening to.

Is "balanced reporting" a policy that benefits the public or merely one that allows the Bush administration to use the media to deceive under the guise of "objectivity"? If our elected leaders can obtain a respectful one-half share of the media coverage by telling obvious lies, what motivation do they have to tell the truth?

On August 23, the AFL-CIO organized a rally outside the DOL attended by two U.S. senators. Strope from the AP wrote an article that described the rally in detail without substantively presenting the union's position on the issue, but giving the administration's view. The rally had become another opportunity for the administration to present its point of view.

Television coverage followed that same outline. ABC's "World News Tonight" showed union members yelling and then included a sound bite from a Commerce Department official who said "Most of their opposition is simply political. Substantively there really is not that much to complain about in this regulation." CBS's "MarketWatch" gave seven sentences to what the DOL "says" followed by one on what labor "claims." NPR allowed some time to a speaker from the National Employment Law Project, but primarily pounded home again and again the notion that the rule changes are too complicated to be understood.

Fox News claimed: "[T]he people who will be affected the most are those earning between $12,000 and $25,000 a year. They'll now be guaranteed mandatory overtime." Fox, to my knowledge, stood alone in claiming that so many more workers were going to be paid more that businesses were worried they would have to raise prices.

Many labor and other alternative media outlets did an excellent job of telling this story. On the ILCAonline.org website are articles by *Press Associates Inc.*, the *Union Advocate*, the Newspaper Guild of New York, and the AFL-CIO. TomPaine.com published Sweeney's column, and countless other labor papers and other alternative outlets published excellent articles. Given the corporate media's deference to government sources, the alternative media is often the only place to turn for news, including the story of the biggest pay cut in U.S. history.

Reprinted from <www.ilcaonline.org>.

Chapter 4

WHAT SOCIAL SECURITY CRISIS?

THE GREAT STOCK ILLUSION
Ellen Frank
November/December 2002

During the 1980s and 1990s, the Dow Jones and Standard & Poor's indices of stock prices soared ten-fold. The NASDAQ index had, by the year 2000, skyrocketed to 25 times its 1980 level. Before the bubble burst, bullish expectations reached a feverish crescendo. Three separate books—Dow 36,000, Dow 40,000 and Dow 100,000—appeared in 1999 forecasting further boundless growth in stock prices. Bullish Wall Street gurus like Goldman's Abby Cohen and Salomon's Jack Grubman were quoted everywhere, insisting that prices could go nowhere but up.

But as early as 1996, skeptics were warning that it couldn't last. Fed chair Alan Greenspan fretted aloud about "irrational exuberance." Yale finance professor Robert Shiller, in his 2001 book titled Irrational Exuberance, insisted that U.S. equities prices were being driven up by wishful thinking and self-fulfilling market sentiment, nourished by a culture that championed wealth and lionized the wealthy. Dean Baker and Marc Weisbrot of the Washington-based Center for Economic and Policy Research contended in 1999 that the U.S. stock market looked like a classic speculative bubble—as evidence they cited the rapidly diverging relationship between stock prices and corporate earnings and reckoned that, to justify the prices at which stocks were selling, profits would have to grow at rates that were frankly impossible.

In 1999 alone, the market value of U.S. equities swelled by an astounding $4 trillion. During that same year, U.S. output, on which stocks represent a claim, rose by a mere $500 billion. What would have happened if stockholders in 1999 had all tried to sell their stock and convert their $4 trillion into actual goods and services? The answer is that most would have failed. In a scramble to turn $4 trillion of paper gains into $500 billion worth of real goods and services, the paper wealth was bound to dissolve, because it never existed, save as a kind of mass delusion.

The Illusion of Wealth Creation

Throughout the 1990s, each new record set by the Dow or NASDAQ elicited grateful cheers for CEOs who were hailed for "creating wealth." American workers, whose retirement savings were largely invested in stocks, were encouraged to buy more stock—even to bet their Social Security funds in the market—and assured that stocks always paid off "in the long run," that a "buy-and-hold" strategy couldn't lose. Neither the financial media nor America's politicians bothered to warn the public about the gaping disparity between the inflated claims on economic output that stocks represented and the actual production of the economy. But by the end of the decade, insiders saw the writing on the wall. They rushed to the exits, trying to realize stock gains before the contradictions inherent in the market overwhelmed them. Prices tumbled, wiping out trillions in illusory money.

The case of Enron Corp. is the most notorious, but it is unfortunately not unique. When Enron filed for bankruptcy protection in November of 2001 its stock, which had traded as high as $90 per share a year before, plummeted to less than $1. *New York Times* reporter Jeffrey Seglin writes that the elevators in Enron's Houston headquarters sported TV sets tuned to CNBC, constantly tracking the firm's stock price and acclaiming the bull market generally. As Enron stock climbed in the late 1990s, these daily market updates made employees— whose retirement accounts were largely invested in company shares—feel quite wealthy, though most Enron workers were not in fact free to sell these shares. Enron's contributions of company stock to employee retirement accounts didn't vest until workers reached age 50. For years, Enron had hawked its stock to employees, to pension fund managers, and to the world as a surefire investment. Many employees used their own 401(k) funds, over and above the firm's matching contributions, to purchase additional shares. But as the firm disintegrated amid accusations of accounting fraud, plan managers froze employee accounts, so that workers were unable to unload even the stock they owned outright. With employee accounts frozen, Enron executives and board members are estimated to have dumped their own stock and options, netting $1.2 billion cash— almost exactly the amount employees lost from retirement accounts.

Soon after Enron's collapse, telecommunications giant Global Crossing imploded amid accusations of accounting irregularities. Global Crossing's stock, which had traded at nearly $100 per share, became virtually worthless, but not before CEO Gary Winnick exercised his own options and walked away with $734 million. Qwest Communications director Phil Anschutz cashed in $1.6 billion in the two years before the firm stumbled under a crushing debt load; the stock subsequently lost 96% of its value. The three top officers of telecom equipment maker JDS Uniphase collectively raked in $1.1 billion between 1999 and 2001. The stock is now trading at $2 per share. An investigation by the *Wall Street Journal* and Thompson Financial analysts estimates that top telecommunications executives captured a staggering $14.2 billion in stock gains between 1997 and 2001. The industry is now reeling, with 60 firms bankrupt and 500,000 jobs lost. The Journal reports that, as of August 2002, insiders at 38 telecom companies had walked away with gains greater than the current market value of their firms. "All told, it is one of the greatest transfers of wealth from investors—big and small—in American history," reporter Dennis Berman writes. "Telecom executives ... made hundreds of millions of dollars, while many investors took huge, unprecedented losses."

Executives in the energy and telecom sectors were not the only ones to rake in impressive gains. Michael Eisner of Disney Corp. set an early record for CEO pay in 1998, netting $575 million, most in option sales. Disney stock has since fallen by two-thirds. Lawrence Ellison, CEO of Oracle Corp., made $706 million when he sold 29 million shares of Oracle stock in January 2001. Ellison's sales flooded the market for Oracle shares and contributed, along with reports of declining profits, to the stock's losing two-thirds of its value over the next few months. Between 1999 and 2001, Dennis Kozlowski of Tyco International sold $258 million of Tyco stock back to the company, on top of a salary and other compensation valued near $30 million. Kozlowski defended this windfall with the claim that his leadership had "created $37 billion in shareholder wealth." By the time Kozlowski quit Tyco under indictment for sales tax fraud in 2002, $80 billion of Tyco's shareholder wealth had evaporated.

Analyzing companies whose stock had fallen by at least 75%, Fortune magazine discovered that "executives and directors of the 1035 companies that met our criteria took out, by our estimate, roughly $66 billion."

The Illusion of Retirement Security

During the bull market, hundreds of U.S. corporations were also stuffing employee savings accounts with corporate equity, creating a class of captive and friendly shareholders who were in many cases enjoined from selling the stock. Studies by the Employee Benefit Research Council found that, while federal law restricts holdings of company stock to 10% of assets in regulated, defined-benefit pension plans, 401(k)-type plans hold an average 19% of assets in company stock. This fraction rises to 32% when companies match employee contributions with stock and to 53% where companies have influence over plan investments. Pfizer Corporation, by all accounts the worst offender, ties up 81% of employee 401(k)s in company stock, but Coca-Cola runs a close second with 76% of plan assets in stock. Before the firm went bankrupt, WorldCom employees had 40% of their 401(k)s in the firm's shares. Such stock contributions cost firms virtually nothing in the short run and, since employees usually aren't permitted to sell the stock for years, companies needn't worry about diluting the value of equity held by important shareholders—or by their executive option-holders. Commenting on recent business lobbying efforts to gut legislation that would restrict stock contributions to retirement plans, Marc Machiz, formerly of the Labor Department's retirement division, told the *Wall Street Journal*, "business loves having people in employer stock and lobbied very hard to kill this stuff."

Until recently, most employees were untroubled by these trends. The market after all was setting new records daily. Quarterly 401(k) statements recorded fantastic returns year after year. Financial advisers assured the public that stocks were and always would be good investments. But corporate insiders proved far less willing to bank on illusory stock wealth when securing their own retirements.

Pearl Meyer and Partners, an executive compensation research firm, estimates that corporate executives eschew 401(k) plans for themselves and instead negotiate sizable cash pensions—the average senior executive is covered by a defined-benefit plan promising 60% of salary after 30 years of service. Under pressure from the board, CEO Richard McGinn quit Lucent at age 52 with $12 million in severance and a cash pension paying $870,000 annually. Lucent's employees, on the other hand, receive a 401(k) plan with 17% of its assets invested in Lucent stock. The stock plunged from $77 to $10 after McGinn's departure. Today it trades at around $1.00. Forty-two thousand Lucent workers lost their jobs as the firm sank.

When Louis Gerstner left IBM in 2002, after receiving $14 million in pay and an estimated $400 million in stock options, he negotiated a retirement package that promises "to cover car, office and club membership expenses for 10 years." IBM's employees, in contrast, have been agitating since 1999 over the firm's decision to replace its defined benefit pension with a 401(k)-type pension plan that, employee representatives estimate, will reduce pensions by one-third to one-half and save the firm $200 million annually. Economist Paul Krugman reports in the *New York Times* that Halliburton Corp. eliminated its employee pensions; first, though, the company "took an $8.5 million charge against earnings to reflect the cost of its parting gift" to CEO Dick Cheney. *Business Week*, surveying the impact of 401(k)s on employee retirement security, concludes that "CEOs deftly phased out rich defined-benefit plans and moved workers into you're-on-your-own 401(k)s, shredding a major safety net even as they locked in lifetime benefits for themselves."

Since 401(k)s were introduced in the early 1980s their use has grown explosively, and they have largely supplanted traditional defined-benefit pensions. In 2002, three of every four dollars contributed to retirement accounts went into 401(k)s. It is thanks to 401(k)s and other retirement savings plans that middle-income Americans became stock-owners in the 1980s and 1990s. It is probably also thanks to 401(k)s, and the huge demand for stocks they generated, that stock prices rose continuously in the 1990s. And it will almost certainly be thanks to 401(k)s that the problems inherent in using the stock market as a vehicle to distribute income will become glaringly apparent once the baby-boom generation begins to retire and liquidate its stock.

If stocks begin again to rise at historical averages—something financial advisors routinely project and prospective retirees are counting on—the discrepancy between what the stock market promises and what the economy delivers will widen dramatically. Something will have to give. Stocks cannot rise faster than the economy grows, not if people are actually to live off the proceeds.

Or rather, stock prices can't rise that fast unless corporate profits—on which stocks represent a legal claim—also surpass GDP gains. But if corporate earnings outpace economic growth, wages will have to stagnate or decline.

Pension economist Douglas Orr believes it is no accident that 401(k)s proliferated in a period of declining earnings and intense economic insecurity for most U.S. wage-earners. From 1980 until the latter half of the 1990s, the position of the typical American employee deteriorated noticeably. Wages fell, unemployment rose, benefits were slashed, stress levels and work hours climbed as U.S. firms "downsized" and "restructured" to cut costs and satiate investor hunger for higher profits. Firms like General Electric cut tens of thousands of jobs and made remaining jobs far less secure in order to generate earnings growth averaging 15% each year. Welch's ruthless union-busting and cost-cutting earned him the nickname "Neutron Jack" among rank-and-file employees. GE's attitude towards its employees was summed up by union negotiator Steve Tormey: "No matter how many records are broken in productivity or profits, it's always 'what have you done for me lately?' The workers are considered lemons and they are squeezed dry." Welch was championed as a hero on Wall Street, his management techniques widely emulated by firms across the nation. During his tenure, GE's stock price soared as the firm slashed employment by nearly 50%.

The Institute for Policy Studies, in a recent study, found that rising stock prices and soaring CEO pay packages are commonly associated with layoffs. CEOs of firms that "announced layoffs of 1000 or more workers in 2000 earned about 80 percent more, on average, than the executives of the 365 firms surveyed by Business Week."

Throughout the 1980s and 1990s, workers whose jobs were disappearing and wages collapsing consoled themselves by watching the paper value of their 401(k)s swell. With labor weak and labor incomes falling, wage and salary earners chose to cast their lot with capital. In betting on the stock market, though, workers are in reality betting that wage incomes will stagnate and trying to offset this by grabbing a slice from the profit pie. This has already proved a losing strategy for most.

Even at the peak of the 1990s bull market, the net wealth—assets minus debts—of the typical household fell from $55,000 to $50,000, as families borrowed heavily to protect their living standards in the face of stagnant wages. Until or unless the nation's capital stock is equitably distributed, there will always be a clash of interests between owners of capital and their employees. If stocks and profits are routinely besting the economy, then either wage-earners are lagging behind or somebody is cooking the books.

Yet surveys show that Americans like 401(k)s. In part, this is because savings accounts are portable, an important consideration in a world where workers can expect to change jobs several times over their working lives. But partly it is because savings plans provide the illusion of self-sufficiency and independence. When retirees spend down their savings, it feels as if they are "paying their own way." They do not feel like dependents, consuming the fruits of other people's labor. Yet they are. It is the nature of retirement that retirees opt out of production and rely on the young to keep the economy rolling. Pensions are always a claim on the real economy—they represent a transfer of goods and services from working adults to non-working retirees, who no longer contribute to economic output. The shift from defined-benefit pensions to 401(k)s and other savings plans in no way changes the fact that pensions transfer resources, but it does change the rules that will govern how those transfers take place—who pays and who benefits.

Private defined-benefit pensions impose a direct claim on corporate profits. In promising a fixed payment over a number of years, corporations commit to transfer a portion of future earnings to retirees. Under these plans, employers promise an annual lifetime benefit at retirement, the amount determined by an employee's prior earnings and years of service in the company. How the benefit will be paid, where the funds will come from, whether there are enough funds to last through a worker's life—this is the company's concern. Longevity risk—the risk that a worker will outlive the money put aside for her retirement—falls on the employer. Retirees benefit, but at a cost to shareholders. Similarly, public pension programs, whether through Social Security or through the civil service, entail a promise to retirees at the expense of the taxpaying public.

Today, the vast majority of workers, if they have pension coverage at all, participate in "defined contribution" plans, in which they and their employer contribute a fixed monthly sum and invest the proceeds with a money management firm. At retirement, the employee owns whatever funds have accrued in the account and must make the money last until she dies. Defined-contribution plans are a claim on nothing. Workers are given a shot at capturing some of the cash floating around Wall Street, but no promise that they will succeed. 401(k)s will add a huge element of chance to the American retirement experience. Some will sell high, some will not. Some will realize gains. Some will not.

Pearl Meyer and Partners estimate that outstanding, unexercised executive stock options and employee stock incentives today amount to some $2 trillion. Any effort to cash in this amount, in addition to the stock held in retirement accounts, would have a dramatic impact on stock prices. American workers and retirees, in assessing their chances for coming out ahead in the competition to liquidate stock, might ponder this question: If, as employees in private negotiations with their corporate employers, they have been unable to protect their incomes or jobs or health or retirement benefits, how likely is it that they will instead be able to wrest gains from Wall Street where corporate insiders are firmly in control of information and access to deals?

SOCIAL SECURITY Q&A
Ellen Frank
November/December 2001

Q: Is there or is there not an actual Social Security trust fund?

A: Since the mid-1980s, the Social Security Administration (SSA) has been collecting more in payroll taxes each year than it pays out in pension, survivor, and disability benefits. The difference between receipts and payments grew significantly in the 1990s, and now amounts to some $160 billion each year. The Social Security system is expected to continue running annual surpluses at least through 2025.

Each year, SSA turns over any surplus funds to the U.S. Treasury, which spends the funds. In return, SSA receives special-issue, non-negotiable U.S. Treasury securities, which represent an implicit promise by the U.S. government to repay Social Security when and if additional money is needed to cover benefits. These bonds are what we call the "trust fund." In 2000, the trust fund contained bonds valued at $1.2 trillion; by 2025, the accumulated surpluses should top $3 trillion.

These, of course, are projections—the surpluses (and thus the trust fund) could be larger or smaller than anticipated, depending on wage growth, population changes, the overall state of the economy, and so on. Under the SSA's "low-cost" (or best-case) scenario, the Social Security trust fund will grow continuously until late in the 21st century.

So, yes, there is a trust fund, representing the excess of payroll taxes over benefit claims, and it is "invested" in promissory notes issued by the government.

Q: Is there actually money in the Social Security trust fund? And if not, where is it?

A: There is not actually "money" in the trust fund, any more than there is actually "money" in your bank account. When you open a bank account, the bank lends your money out. You exchange money for a promise from the bank to repay you, subject to whatever limitations and provisions you may have agreed to in advance. Your money is replaced with a piece of paper laying out those terms and obligations—a bank statement, passbook, quarterly notice, whatever. Your money has become a claim on a financial firm and is as good as the stability of that financial firm.

Similarly, the surplus revenues flowing into Social Security over the years have all been lent to the Treasury and spent—all, that is, except this year's $160 billion surplus. Before the attacks in September, Congress was still arguing over this money. By December, the surplus is almost certain to have disappeared in any case.

Some critics of Social Security use alarmist rhetoric in discussing the trust fund: The SSA is bankrupt, our hard-earned money is gone, the government has blown it all. They're right that there's no money in the trust fund. But there's nothing duplicitous in this. All money gets lent or spent and replaced with other kinds of paper claims. Banks and other financial firms don't keep money lying around either.

Q: Then why do I keep hearing about a "crisis" in Social Security?

A: The problems with Social Security are not really financial in nature. They stem from the fact that, over the last 30 years or so, birth rates have declined in the United States, while life expectancies have increased. If these trends continue (and there's no reason to suppose they will not), the ratio of retirees to workers will rise. Unless the economy grows faster than the SSA predicts—unless those future workers are more productive than the SSA projects, or the workforce grows faster than expected due to immigration—the cost of supporting all these retirees will exceed the revenues that would accrue from current tax rate of 12.4% on payroll.

According to SSA's none-too-optimistic projections, the Social Security system will have enough revenue from payroll taxes alone to cover benefits at their current levels (adjusted for inflation) up until 2016. For seven years after that, there will be enough revenue from payroll taxes and interest on the bonds held by the trust fund to cover benefits at current levels. Then, in 2023, SSA will need to begin redeeming the bonds. When that happens, the system will have enough revenue—from payroll taxes, interest, and bond redemption combined—to cover legislated benefits for another 15 years or so.

The problem is this. Once we reach a point where payroll tax receipts fall below projected benefit payments—once the SSA actually needs the interest and principle from the bonds to meet its obligations—the U.S. Treasury will have to find resources to pay the SSA, just like it has to find resources to pay back any other creditor. They can do this by raising taxes, cutting spending on other federal programs, or borrowing from the private financial markets.

Q: But if the government has to raise money to pay the SSA in the future anyway, then what's the point of collecting these surpluses today?

A: Good question. From a purely economic perspective, there is no point. The federal government is collecting surplus payroll taxes and then spending them, and will have to raise revenue somehow in the future to pay Social Security benefits. The bonds in the trust fund do nothing to alter this.

Realize that the bonds are non-negotiable, and SSA cannot redeem them for cash unless Congresses allocate money for this purpose. But if future Congresses choose not to repay Social Security, they can simply raise payroll taxes or cut benefits and avoid altogether the need to redeem the bonds. Understanding this, some Democrats have insisted in recent years that Social Security surpluses be used exclusively to repay debts that the government currently owes to the financial markets. This is the idea behind the so-called Social Security "lockbox."

In fact, it makes absolutely no difference to the trust fund whether the surpluses are used to repay public debt, cut taxes, or pay for expanded federal programs, any more than you, as a depositor, need concern yourself with where a bank lends your deposits. But the defenders of the trust fund apparently feel that using the surpluses to repay debt will harden the federal government's commitment to the security of future retirees. If the money has purportedly been "saved" in a rhetorical "lockbox," the reasoning goes, it will be pretty hard for opponents of Social Security to turn around 10 or 20 years from now and argue that benefits need to be cut.

Now look at this from the perspective of anti-government Republicans. They oppose higher taxes, have little faith in the ability of government to cut spending (and plenty of ideas on how to raise spending for defense and corporate subsidies), and object to the government borrowing cash from the financial markets. They are also none too keen on the idea of workers retiring into extended periods of idleness. Back in the 1930s, when Social Security was established, conservative business groups vehemently opposed it. They gave their support grudgingly, and only when then-President Roosevelt assured them that the system would be funded entirely by payroll taxes on working stiffs. General tax revenues, which are paid largely by upper-income groups, were never to be tapped for Social Security.

But if governments of the future are to honor the commitment implicit in the trust fund, then general revenues will have to be tapped. Real resources will need to be transferred to retirees, above and beyond the 12.4% payroll tax, so that retirees can survive without a paycheck. The amount needed is not that large, but it's large enough to worry those corporate and wealthy taxpayers who neither need nor want Social Security and who are likely to be asked to foot the bill.

This is why proponents of privatization are claiming that the Social Security trust fund is on the verge of collapse. The trust fund was designed to solve a potential economic problem—transferring resources to seniors in the future so that American workers can continue to enjoy retirement—with a political accounting device. Privatization boosters are today exploiting the contradictions inherent in that accounting device to attack Social Security and to justify regressive policies such as raising current payroll taxes or cutting current benefits.

Q: But there will be a shortfall in Social Security at some point in the future. What can we do about that?

A: It's difficult to say for sure whether the projected shortfalls will materialize. But they may. And if they do, privatization is definitely not the answer. The economic problem of caring for a large number of retirees in the future cannot be solved with private accounts. Even if they worked as their boosters claim (and they won't—see Ellen Frank, "The Hidden Costs of Private Accounts," page 80), private stock accounts are just another sort of accounting device. Eventually, all those private account holders are going to retire and try to sell their stock for the cash needed to buy real resources—food, shelter, health care. If the economy has not grown sufficiently to provide the resources, the stocks will rapidly become worthless.

The only real investment we can make today to strengthen Social Security is in economic growth and enhanced economic well-being. Next time your Congressional representative talks about Social Security, ask her what she's doing today to ensure that America's future workers will be healthy enough, happy enough, secure enough, and skilled enough to care for their aging parents. That's the only security we can count on.

THE HIDDEN COSTS OF PRIVATE ACCOUNTS
Ellen Frank
November/December 2001

As Bush's handpicked commission on Social Security grapples with the details of diverting Social Security revenue into private accounts, it will almost certainly confront a knotty little logistical problem—an issue that so stumped privatization boosters in the past that most either finessed the problem or threw up their hands entirely. The problem is how to actually manage the 150 million plus personal accounts even a partially privatized system would require.

When privatization was initially floated several years back, advocates had in mind something along the lines of the current employer-sponsored 401(k) programs. In a 401(k) plan, employers contract with a fund manager to invest employee contributions. To minimize paperwork and oversight costs, they limit the number of available investment options, generally to around 10 funds, though sometimes to as few as three or four, so that workers are not wholly free to actively manage their own portfolios.

Even so, tracking this money is neither easy or cost-free. Employers need to set up accounting and compliance systems, select investment options, and monitor fund performance. The U.S. Department of Labor estimates that administrative costs run somewhere between $100 and $200 per year for each person enrolled in a plan. On top of that, fund managers rake off fees—usually 1 to 2% of the balance—to cover costs and leave some profit. And the system doesn't work seamlessly. Contributions get lost, delayed, misdirected; sometimes willfully, sometimes by accident.

Consider, then, how a national 401(k)-type program, funded out of payroll taxes and covering every single worker in the United States, would operate. Each and every employer in the country would need to set up a monitoring system and contract with financial firms to manage the accounts of even part-time, transient workers. The plan Bush put forth during his presidential campaign would divert two percentage points of the 12.4% payroll tax to personal investment accounts. Presumably, the law would require employers to offer some minimum array of investing options. Let's say they would have to offer five options, and let's imagine further that the typical employee would choose to allocate her savings equally among the five funds.

Consider, as an example, the local donut franchise with several part-time employees, typically working 20 hours each week at $7.50 an hour. Currently, the business owner sends $18.60 per worker to the Social Security Administration (SSA)—the combined employee and employer share of payroll taxes. Now, though, the donut shop will need to send out two checks—$15.60 to the government, and $3 to the financial contractor managing the employee's investment accounts. That's 60 cents in each of the five funds. The cost to the donut shop owner of setting up and monitoring these accounts could add up to thousands of dollars each year.

Now, imagine that our representative fast food worker quits after 10 weeks and takes a job with the pizza shop down the road. Does she shift her $30 in accumulated savings to the pizza maker's plan? Must the pizza shop owner offer the same five investment options as the donut franchiser? If not, who will arrange for the transfer of her funds from one financial contractor to another?

Or can the worker simply leave her miniscule balances—$6 in each of five funds—where they are, opening new funds with new financial firms as she shifts from part-time job to part-time job in the low-wage sector of the economy? If so, who will pay the administrative costs of maintaining all these accounts? The donut shop? The pizza store? The worker herself? Will the typical U.S. teenager complete high school with perhaps 20 different accounts, each containing a few dollars apiece, and those few dollars destined to be eaten away by annual management fees and administrative costs? And what happens if funds are lost, or deliberately withheld, or sent to the wrong fund manager? Would the federal government oversee this? Would the grocer, the baker, and the pizza maker pay for independent oversight? Would the mutual fund industry want this headache? Would anyone?

Chewing over this logistical nightmare, earlier advocates of privatization proposed to streamline the process. To ease the burden on small businesses, employers would instead send all payroll tax money to the SSA, as they do now, and the SSA would place two percentage points in privately managed accounts, nominally owned by the covered workers. Acting like a centralized human resources office for the entire U.S. labor force, the SSA could offer a wider array of investment choices and set up a system, similar to those offered today by a number of large employers, that would allow workers to actively manage their savings.

This is undoubtedly much simpler. But it is not cheap. The SSA would now be responsible for two major administrative functions—managing the flow of funds to current pensioners, and handling the mutual fund monitoring and record-keeping for 150 million private accounts. Economists estimate that this would at least double the administrative costs of running Social Security, raising the annual cost of administration from nearly 1% to just under 2% of payroll taxes. Will these costs be paid by workers? If so, nearly half of the projected returns from private accounts will be lost to administrative costs—and this is before we even talk about fees charged by the finance industry.

Or will Social Security's extra costs be paid by the Treasury out of general tax revenues? In this case, the government could save itself the trouble. If general revenues amounting to an additional 1% of payroll taxes were shifted to the SSA, that would go a long way towards solving Social Security's long-range financing problems, adding a number of years to the life of the trust fund.

Then there's another question. If all the money targeted for private accounts must, in any case, flow through the SSA, why bother with private accounts in the first place? Why not let the SSA invest the same share of its own revenues in private assets, manage its own portfolio, and use the presumably higher returns to fund higher benefits, or close future operating deficits?

"Absolutely not!" say privatization boosters. Allowing a federal agency to manage billions in private assets in its own name on behalf of 150 million taxpayers is socialism. Allowing the same agency to contract with financial firms to manage those same stocks in the name of said taxpayers is free-market capitalism. So does ideology trump common sense in the Social Security debate.

Last year, the conservative Federalist Society invited me to debate Charles Rounds, Suffolk University law professor and supporter of private accounts. The audience questioned Rounds closely on how the accounts would operate. Would workers actually own their own savings? If so, could they withdraw funds and spend them as they chose? Or invest them in anything at all—say, Florida real estate or an Internet start-up? And what would happen if their investments went sour or they spent down their savings before retiring?

These are the sorts of questions privatization boosters prefer not to address. A libertarian and Cato Institute researcher, Rounds criticized Social Security as a big-government welfare scheme which, disguised as a pension plan, coerces American workers to support retirees. Yet he conceded that a privatized system would itself necessitate quite a lot of federal coercion—workers would be required to save, to place their savings in a few pre-selected stock funds, and to keep them there until retirement. He also acknowledged that Congress might need to saddle the SSA with yet another task—administering a supplementary welfare program for those who outlived their savings.

That is the dirty little secret of privatization. A system of private accounts would be so expensive to set up and monitor, and would expose workers to so much risk and so many fees, that the federal government would almost certainly have to manage the whole mess, from choosing investment options and monitoring accounts, to establishing a parallel welfare system for those whose investments prove unprofitable.

So the push for privatization is not about freedom and individual choice after all. It's about diverting the money now going to SSA into the coffers of Wall Street.

SOCIAL SECURITY ISN'T BROKEN
So Why the rush to "fix" It?
Doug Orr
November/December 2004

Federal Reserve Chairman Alan Greenspan told Congress earlier this year that everyone knows there's a Social Security crisis. That's like saying "everyone knows the earth is flat."

Starting with a faulty premise guarantees reaching the wrong conclusion. The truth is there is no Social Security crisis, but there is a potential crisis in retirement income security and there may be a crisis in the future in U.S. financial markets. It's this latter crisis that Greenspan actually is worried about.

Social Security is the most successful insurance program ever created. It insures millions of workers against what economists call "longevity risk," the possibility they will live "too long" and not be able to work long enough, or save enough, to provide their own income. Today, about 10% of those over age 65 live in poverty. Without Social Security, that rate would be almost 50%.

Social Security was originally designed to supplement, and was structured to resemble, private-sector pensions. In the 1930s, all private pensions were defined-benefit plans. The retirement benefit was based on a worker's former wage and years of service. In most plans, after 35 years of service the monthly benefit, received for life, would be at least half of the income received in the final working year.

Congress expected that private-sector pensions eventually would cover most workers. But pension coverage peaked at 40% in the 1960s. Since then, corporations have systematically dismantled pension systems. Today, only 16% of private-sector workers are covered by defined-benefit pensions. Rather than supplementing private pensions, Social Security has become the primary source of retirement income for almost two-thirds of retirees. Thus, Congress was forced to raise benefit levels in 1972.

What has happened to private-sector defined benefit pensions? They've been replaced with defined-contribution (DC) savings plans such as 401(k)s and 403(b)s. These plans provide some retirement income but offer no real protection from longevity risk. Once a retiree depletes the amount saved in the plan, their retirement income is gone.

In a generous DC plan, a firm might match the worker's contribution up to 3% of his or her pay. With total contributions of 6%, average wage growth of 2% a year, and an average return on the investment portfolio of 5%, after 35 years of work, a retiree would exhaust the plan's savings in just 8.5 years even if her annual spending is only half of her final salary. If she restricts spending to just one-third of the final salary, the savings can stretch to 14 years.

At age 65, life expectancy for women today is about 20 years, and for men about

15 years, so DC savings plans will not protect the elderly from longevity risk. The conversion of defined-benefit pensions to defined-contribution plans is the source of the real potential crisis in retirement income. Yet Greenspan did not mention this in his testimony to Congress.

No Crisis

Opponents of Social Security have hated it since its creation in 1935. The first prediction of a Social Security crisis was published in 1936! The Heritage Foundation and Cato Institute are home to many of the program's opponents today, and they fixate on the concept of a "demographic imperative." In 1960, the United States had 5.1 workers per retiree, in 1998 we had 3.4, and by 2030 we will have only 2.1. Opponents claim that with these demographic changes, revenues will eventually be insufficient to pay Social Security retirement benefits.

The logic is appealingly simple, but wrong for two reasons. First, this "old-age dependency" ratio in itself is irrelevant. No amount of financial manipulation can change this fact: all current consumption must come from current physical output. The consumption of all dependents (non-workers) must come from the output produced by current workers. It's the overall dependency ratio——the number of workers relative to all non-workers, including the aged, the young, the disabled, and those choosing not to work—that determines whether society can "afford" the baby boomers' retirement years. In the 1960s we had only 0.62 workers for each dependent, and we were building new schools and the interstate highway system and getting ready to put a man on the moon. No one bemoaned a demographic crisis or looked for ways to cut the resources allocated to children; in fact, the living standards of most families rose rapidly. In 2030, we will have 0.98 workers per dependent. We'll have more workers per dependent in the future than we did in the past. While it is true a larger share of total output will be allocated to the aged, just as a larger share was allocated to children in the 1960s, society will easily produce adequate output to support all workers and dependents, and at a higher standard of living.

Second, the "demographic imperative" ignores productivity growth. Average worker productivity has grown by about 2% per year, adjusted for inflation, for the past half-century. That means real output per worker doubles every 36 years. This productivity growth is projected to continue, so by 2040, each worker will produce twice as much as today. Suppose each of three workers today produces $1,000 per week and one retiree is allocated $500 (half of his final salary)—then each worker gets $833. In 2040, two such workers will produce $2,000 per week each (after adjusting for inflation). If each retiree gets $1,000, each worker still gets $1,500. The incomes of both workers and retirees go up. Thus, paying for the baby boomers' retirement need not decrease their children's standard of living. A larger share of output going to retirees does not imply that the standard of living of those still working will be lower. Those still working will have a slightly smaller share of a much larger pie.

So why the talk of a Social Security crisis? Social Security always has been a pay-as-you-go system. Current benefits are paid out of current tax revenues. But in the 1980s, a commission headed by Greenspan recommended raising payroll taxes to expand the trust fund in order to supplement tax revenues when the baby boom generation retires. Congress responded in 1984 by raising payroll taxes significantly. As a result, the Social Security trust fund, which holds government bonds as assets, has grown every year since. As the baby boom moves into retirement, these assets will be sold to help pay their retirement benefits.

Each year, Social Security's trustees must make projections of the system's status for the next 75 years. In 1996, they projected the trust fund balance would go to zero in 2030. In 2000, they projected a zero balance in 2036 and today they project a zero balance in 2042. The projection keeps changing because the trustees continue to make unrealistic assumptions about future economic conditions. The current projections are based on the assumption that annual GDP growth will average 1.8 % for the next 75 years. In no 20-year period, even including the Great Depression, has the U.S. economy grown that slowly. Each year the economy grows faster than 1.8%, the zero balance date moves further into the future. But the trustees continue to suggest that if we return to something like the Great Depression, the trust fund will go to zero.

Opponents of Social Security claim the system will then be "bankrupt." Bankruptcy implies ceasing to exist. But if the trust fund goes to zero, Social Security will not shut down and stop paying benefits. It will simply revert to the pure pay-as-you-go system that it was before 1984 and continue to pay current benefits using current tax revenues. Even if the trustees' worst-case assumptions come true, the payroll tax paid by workers would need to increase by only about 2% points, and only in 2042, not today.

If the economy grows at 2.4%—which is still slower than the stagnant growth of the 1980s—the trust fund never goes to zero. The increase in real output and real incomes will generate sufficient revenues to pay promised benefits. By 2042, we will need to lower payroll taxes or raise benefits to reduce the surplus.

The claim that benefits of future retirees must be reduced in order to not reduce the standard of living of future workers is simply wrong. It is being used to drive a wedge between generations and panic younger workers into supporting Bush's plan to destroy Social Security. Under the most likely version of his privatization proposal, according to Bush's own Social Security Commission, the guaranteed benefits from Social Security of a 20-year-old worker joining the labor force today would be reduced by 46%. That Commission also admitted that private accounts are unlikely to make up for this drop in benefits. An estimate made by the Goldman-Sacks brokerage firm suggests that even with private accounts, retirement income of younger workers would be reduced by 42% compared to what they would receive if nothing is done to change the Social Security system. Private accounts are a losing proposition for younger workers.

The Real Fear: An Oversupply of Bonds

So why did Greenspan claim cutting benefits would become necessary? To understand the answer, we need to take a side trip to look at how bonds and the financial markets affect each other. It turns out that rising interest rates reduce the selling price of existing financial assets, and falling asset prices push up interest rates (see box "How Does the Bond Market Work?").

For example, in the 1980s, President Reagan cut taxes and created the largest government deficits in history up to that point. This meant the federal government had to sell lots of bonds to finance the soaring government debt; to attract enough buyers, the Treasury had to offer very high interest rates. During the 1980s, real interest rates (rates adjusted for inflation) were almost four times higher than the historic average. High interest rates slow economic growth by making it more expensive for consumers to buy homes or for businesses to invest in new infrastructure. The GDP growth rate in the 1980s was the slowest in U.S. history apart from the Great Depression.

But high interest rates also depress financial asset prices. A five percentage point rise in interest rates reduces the selling price of a bond (loan) that matures in 10 years by 50%. It was the impact of the record-high interest rates of the 1980s on the value of the loan portfolios of the savings and loan industry that caused the S&L crisis and the industry's collapse.

Greenspan is worried because he sees history repeating itself in the form of President Bush's tax cuts. In his testimony, Greenspan expressed concern over a potentially

---

How Does the Bond Market Work?

A bond is nothing more than an IOU. A company or government borrows money and promises to pay a certain amount of interest annually until it repays the loan. When you buy a newly issued bond, you are making a loan. The amount of the loan is the "face value" of the bond. The initial interest rate at which the bond is issued, the "face rate," multiplied by this face value determines the amount of interest paid each period. Until the debt is paid back, events in the financial markets affect the bond's value.

If market interest rates fall, prices of existing bonds rise. Why? Suppose you buy a bond with a face value of $100 that pays 10%. You then collect $10 per year. If the current interest rate falls to 5%, newly issued bonds will pay that new rate. Since your bond pays 10%, people would rather buy that one than one paying 5%. They are willing to pay more than the face value to get it, so the price will be bid up until interest rates equalize. The price at which you could sell your bond will rise to $200, since $10 is 5% of $200.

But changes in bond prices also affect interest rates. If more people are selling bonds than buying them, an excess supply exists, and prices will fall. If you need to sell your bond to get money to pay your rent, you might have to lower the price of the bond you hold to $50. Because the bond still pays $10 per year to the owner, the new owner gets a 20% return on the $50 purchase. Anyone trying to issue new bonds will have to match that return, so the new market interest rate becomes 20%.

large rise in interest rates. This is his way of warning about an excess supply of bonds. Starting in 2020, Social Security will have to sell about $150 billion (in 2002 dollars) in trust fund bonds each year for 22 years. At the same time, private-sector pension funds will be selling $100 billion per year of financial assets to make their pension payments. State and local governments will be selling $75 billion per year to cover their former employees' pension expenses, and holdings in private mutual funds will fall by about $50 billion per year as individual retirees cash in their 401(k) assets. Private firms will still need to issue about $100 billion of new bonds a year to finance business expansion. Combined, these asset sales could total $475 billion per year.

This level of bond sales is more than double the record that was set in the 1980s following the Reagan tax cuts. But back then, the newly issued bonds were being purchased by "institutional investors" such as private-sector pension funds and insurance companies. After 2020, these groups will be net sellers of bonds. The financial markets will strain to absorb this level of asset sales. It's unlikely they will be able to also absorb the extra $400 billion per year of bond sales needed to cover the deficit spending that will occur if the new Bush tax cuts are made permanent. This oversupply of bonds will drive down the value of all financial assets.

In a 1994 paper, Sylvester Schieber, a current advisor to President Bush on pension and Social Security reform, predicted this potential drop in asset prices. After 2020, the value of assets held in 401(k) plans, already inadequate, will be reduced even more. More importantly, at least to Greenspan, the prices of assets held by corporations to fund their defined benefit pension promises will fall. Thus, pension payments will need to come out of current revenues, reducing corporate profits and, in turn, driving down stock prices.

It's this potential collapse in the prices of financial assets that worries Greenspan most. In order to reduce the run-up of long-term interest rates, some asset sales must be eliminated. Greenspan said, "You don't have the resources to do it all." But rather than rescinding Bush's tax cuts, Greenspan favors reducing bond sales by the Social Security trust fund. Doing that requires a reduction in benefits and raising payroll taxes even more.

Framing a question incorrectly makes it impossible to find a solution. The problem is not with Social Security, but rather with blind reliance on financial markets to solve all economic problems. If the financial markets are likely to fail us, what is the solution? The solution is simple once the question is framed correctly: where will the real output that baby boomers are going to consume in retirement come from?

The federal budget surplus President Bush inherited came entirely from Social Security surpluses resulting from the 1984 payroll tax increase. Bush gave away revenues meant to provide for workers' retirement as tax cuts for the wealthiest 10% of the population.

We should rescind Bush's tax cuts and use the Social Security surpluses to really prepare for the baby boom retirement. Public investment or targeted tax breaks could be used to encourage the building of the hospitals, nursing homes, and hospices that aging baby boomers will need. Such investment in public and private infrastructure would also stimulate the real economy and increase GDP growth. Surpluses could be used to fund the training of doctors, nurses and others to staff these facilities, and of other high skilled workers more generally. The higher wages of skilled labor will help generate the payroll tax revenues needed to fund future benefits. If baby boomers help to fund this infrastructure expansion through their payroll taxes while they are still working, less output will need to be allocated when they retire. These expenditures will increase the productivity of the real economy, which will help keep the financial sector solvent to provide for retirees.

Destroying Social Security in order to "save" it is not a solution.

Sources: Dean Baker and Mark Weisbrot, *Social Security: The Phony Crises,* University of Chicago Press, 1999; William Wolman and Anne Colamosca, *The Great 401(k) Hoax,* Perseus Publishing, 2002; Sylvester J. Schieber and John B. Shoven, "The Consequences of Population Aging on Private Pension Fund Saving and Asset Markets," National Bureau of Economic Research, Working Paper No. 4665, 1994.

AFRICAN AMERICANS AND SOCIAL SECURITY
Why the Privatization Advocates Are Wrong
William E. Spriggs
November/December 2004

Proponents of Social Security privatization are trying to claim that the current program is unfair to African Americans and that a privatized program would serve African Americans better. This argument lends support to the privatization agenda while at the same time giving its advocates a compassionate gloss. But the claims about African Americans and Social Security are wrong.

The Old Age Survivors and Disability Insurance Program (OASDI), popularly known as Social Security, was put in place by Franklin Roosevelt to establish a solid bulwark of economic rights for the public—specifically, as he put it, "the right to adequate protection from the economic fears of old age, sickness, accident, and unemployment." Most Americans associate Social Security only with the retirement—or old age—benefit. Yet it was created to do much more, and it does.

As its original name suggests, Social Security is an insurance program that protects workers and their families against the income loss that occurs when a worker retires, becomes disabled, or dies. All workers will eventually either grow too old to compete in the labor market, become disabled, or die. OASDI insures all workers and their families against these universal risks, while spreading the costs and benefits of that insurance protection among the entire workforce. Currently, 70% of Social Security funds go to retirees, 15% to disabled workers, and 15% to survivors.

Social Security is a "pay as you go" system, which means the taxes paid by today's workers are not set aside to pay their own benefits down the road, but rather go to pay the benefits of current Social Security recipients. It's financed using the Federal Insurance Contribution Act (or FICA) payroll tax, paid by all working Americans on earnings of less than about $90,000 a year. While the payroll tax is not progressive, Social Security benefits are—that is, low-wage workers receive a greater percentage of pre-retirement earnings from the program than higher-wage workers.

In the 1980s, recognizing that the baby boom generation would strain this system, Congress passed reforms to raise extra tax revenues above and beyond the current need and set up a trust fund to hold the reserve. (See "Social Security Isn't Broken," p. 83) Trustees were appointed and charged with keeping Social Security solvent. Today's trustees warn that their projections, which are based on modest assumptions about the long-term growth of the U.S. economy, show the system could face a shortfall around 2042, when either benefits would have to be cut or the FICA tax raised.

Those who oppose the social nature of the program have pounced on its projected shortfall in revenues to argue that the program cannot—or ought not—be fixed, but should instead be fundamentally changed (see "Privatization Advocates.") Privatization proponents are seeking to frame the issue as a matter of social justice, as if Social Security "reform" would primarily benefit low-income workers, blue-collar workers, people of color, and women. Prompted by disparities in life expectancy between whites and African Americans and the racial wealth gap, a growing chorus within the privatization movement is claiming that privatizing Social Security would be beneficial to African Americans.

Opponents attack the program on the basis of an analogy to private retirement accounts. Early generations of Social Security beneficiaries received much more in

Privatization Advocates

Powerful advocates for privatization include libertarian and conservative think tanks and advocacy groups such as the Cato Institute, the Heritage Foundation, Americans for Tax Reform, and Citizens for a Sound Economy, all driven by an ideological commitment to the abolition of federal social programs.

Wall Street too is thirsty for the $1.4 trillion that privatization would funnel into equities if the taxes collected to support the Social Security system were invested privately rather than reinvested in federal government bonds. That's not to mention the windfall of fees privatization would deliver for banks, brokerage houses, and investment firms.

Just after he took office, President Bush appointed a commission to examine privatizing the Social Security system. The commission could not figure out how to maintain payments to current recipients while diverting tax dollars to the savings of current workers, nor could it resolve how to cover the benefits of the disabled or resolve issues surrounding survivors' benefits. Although the president did not succeed in carrying out Social Security privatization in his first term, he has made the partial privatization of Social Security retirement accounts the top priority of his second-term domestic agenda.

benefits than they had paid into the system in taxes. Privatization proponents argue those early recipients received a "higher rate of return" on their "investment" while current and future generations are being "robbed" because they will see "lower rates of return." They argue the current system of social insurance—particularly the retirement program—should be privatized, switching from the current "pay-as-you-go" system to one in which individual workers claim their own contribution and decide where and how to invest it.

But this logic inverts the premise of social insurance. Rather than sharing risk across the entire workforce to ensure that all workers and their families are protected from the three inevitabilities of old age, disability, and death, privatizing Social Security retirement benefits would enable high-wage workers to reap gains from private retirement investment without having to help protect lower-wage workers from their (disproportionate) risks of disability and death. High-wage workers, who are more likely to live long enough to retire, could in fact do better on average if they opt out of the general risk pool and devote all their money to retirement without having to cover the risk of those who may become disabled or die, although they would of course be subjecting their retirement dollars to greater risk. But low-wage workers, who are far more likely to need disability or survivors' benefits to help their families and are less likely to live long enough to retire, would then be left with lower disability and survivors' benefits, and possibly no guaranteed benefits. This is what the Social Security privatization movement envisions. But you wouldn't know it from reading their literature.

And when the myths about Social Security's financial straits meet another American myth—race—even more confusion follows. Here is a look at three misleading claims by privatization proponents about African Americans and Social Security.

Myth #1

Several conservative research groups argue that Social Security is a bad deal for African Americans because of their lower life expectancies. "Lifetime Social Security benefits depend, in large part, on longevity," writes the Cato Institute's Michael Tanner in his briefing paper "Disparate Impact: Social Security and African Americans." "At every age, African-American men and women both have shorter life expectancies than do their white counterparts. ... As a result, a black man or woman earning exactly the same lifetime wages, and paying exactly the same lifetime Social Security taxes, as his or her white counterpart will likely receive a far lower rate of return." Or as the Americans for Tax Reform web site puts it: "A black male born today has a life expectancy of 64.8 years. But the Social Security retirement age for that worker in the future will be 67 years. That means probably the majority of black males will never even receive Social Security retirement benefits."

The longevity myth is the foundation of all the race-based arguments for Social Security privatization. There are several problems with it.

First, the shorter life expectancy of African Americans compared to whites is the result of higher morbidity in mid-life, and is most acute for African-American men. The life expectancies of African-American women and white men are virtually equal. So the life expectancy argument can really only be made about African-American men.

Second, the claim that OASDI is unfair to African Americans because their expected benefits are less than their expected payments is usually raised and then answered from the perspective of the retirement (or "old age") benefit alone. That is an inaccurate way to look at the problem. Because OASDI also serves families of workers who become disabled or die, a correct measure would take into account the probability of all three risk factors—old age, disability, and death. Both survivor benefits and disability benefits, in fact, go disproportionately to African Americans.

While African Americans make up 12% of the U.S. population, 23% of children receiving Social Security survivor benefits are African American, as are about 17% of disability beneficiaries. On average, a worker who receives disability benefits or a family that receives survivor benefits gets far more in return than the worker paid in FICA taxes, notwithstanding privatizers' attempts to argue that Social Security is a bad deal.

Survivors' benefits also provide an important boost to poor families more generally. A recent study by the National Urban League Institute for Opportunity and Equality showed that the benefit lifted 1 million children out of poverty and helped another 1 million avoid extreme poverty (living below half the poverty line).

Finally, among workers who do live long enough to get the retirement benefit, life expectancies don't differ much by racial group. For example, at age 65, the life expectancies of African-American and white men are virtually the same.

President Bush's Social Security commission proposed the partial privatization of Social Security retirement accounts, but cautioned that it could not figure out how to maintain equal benefits for the other risk pools. The commission suggested that disability and survivor's benefits would have to be reduced if the privatization plan proceeds.

This vision is of a retirement program designed for the benefit of the worker who retires—only. A program with that focus would work against, not for, African Americans because of the higher morbidity rates in middle age and the smaller share of African Americans who live to retirement.

Myth #2

African Americans have less education, and so are in the work force longer, than whites, and yet Social Security only credits 35 years of work experience in figuring benefits. Tanner says, "benefits are calculated on the basis of the highest 35 years of earnings over a worker's lifetime. Workers must still pay Social Security taxes during years outside those 35, but those taxes do not count toward or earn additional benefits. Generally, those low-earnings years occur early in an individual's life. That is particularly important to African Americans because they are likely to enter the workforce at an earlier age than whites...."

This claim misinterprets the benefit formula for Social Security. Yes, African Americans on average are slightly less educated than whites. The gap is mostly because of a higher college completion rate for white men compared to African-American men. But the education argument fails to acknowledge that white teenagers have a significantly higher labor force participation rate (at 46%) than do African-American teens (29%). The higher labor force participation of white teenagers helps to explain why young white adults do better in the labor market than young African-American adults. (The racial gaps in unemployment are considerably greater for teenagers and young adults than for those over 25.)

These differences in early labor market experiences mean that African-American men have more years of zero earnings than do whites. So while the statement about education is true, the inference from education differences to work histories is false. By taking only 35 years of work history into account in the benefit formula, the Social Security formula is progressive. It in effect ignores years of zero or very low earnings. This levels the playing field among long-time workers, putting African Americans with more years of zero earnings on par with whites. By contrast, a private system based on total years of earnings would exacerbate racial labor market disparities.

Myth #3

A third claim put forward by critics of Social Security is that African-American retirees are more dependent on Social Security than whites. Tanner writes: "Elderly African Americans are much more likely than their white counterparts to be dependent on Social Security benefits for most or all of their retirement income." Therefore, he concludes, "African Americans would be among those with the most to gain from the privatization of Social Security—transforming the program into a system of individually owned, privately invested accounts." Law professor and senior policy advisor to Americans for Tax Reform Peter Ferrara adds, "the personal accounts would produce far higher returns and benefits for lower-income workers, African Americans, Hispanics, women and other minorities."

It's true that African-American retirees are more likely than whites to rely on Social Security as their only income in old age. It's the sole source of retirement income for 40% of elderly African Americans. This is a result of discrimination in the labor market that limits the share of African Americans with jobs that offer pension benefits. Privatizing Social Security would not change labor market discrimination or its effects.

Privatizing Social Security would, however, exacerbate the earnings differences between African Americans and whites, since benefits would be based solely on individual savings. What would help African-American retirees is not privatization, but rather changing the redistributive aspects of Social Security to make it even more progressive.

The current formula for Social Security benefits is progressive in two ways: low earners get a higher share of their earnings than do higher wage earners and the lowest years of earning are ignored. Changes in the formula to raise the benefits floor enough to lift all retired Social Security recipients out of poverty would make it still more progressive. Increasing and updating the Supplemental Security Income payment, which helps low earners, could accomplish the same goal for SSI recipients. (SSI is a program administered by Social Security for very low earners and the poor who are disabled, blind, or at least 65 years old.)

The proponents of privatization argue that the heavy reliance of African-American seniors on Social Security requires higher rates of return—returns that are only possible by putting money into the stock market. Yet given the lack of access to private pensions for African-American seniors and their low savings from lifetimes of low earnings, such a notion is perverse. It would have African Americans gamble with their only leg of retirement's supposed three-legged stool—pension, savings, and Social Security. And, given the much higher risk that African Americans face of both death before retirement and of disability, it would be a risky gamble indeed to lower those benefits while jeopardizing their only retirement leg.

Privatizing the retirement program, and separating the integrated elements of Social Security, would split America. The divisions would be many: between those more likely to be disabled and those who are not; between those more likely to die before retirement and those more likely to retire; between children who get survivors' benefits and the elderly who get retirement benefits; between those who retire with high-yield investments and those who fare poorly in retirement. The "horizontal equity" of the program (treating similar people in a similar way) would be lost, as volatile stock fluctuations and the timing of retirement could greatly affect individuals' rates of return. The "vertical equity" of the program (its progressive nature, insuring a floor for benefits) would be placed in greater jeopardy with the shift from social to private benefits.

Social Security works because it is "social." It is America's only universal federal program. The proposed changes would place Social Security in the same political space as the rest of America's federal programs—and African Americans have seen time and again how those politics work.

THE SOCIAL SECURITY ADMINISTRATION'S CRACKED CRYSTAL BALL

John Miller

November/December 2004

2042. That's the year the Social Security Trust Fund will run out of money, according to the Social Security Administration (SSA). But its doomsday prophesy is based on overly pessimistic assumptions about our economic future: The SSA expects the U.S. economy to expand at an average annual rate of just 1.8% from 2015 to 2080—far slower than the 3.0% average growth rate the economy posted over the last 75 years.

What's behind the gloomy growth projections? Is there anything to them—or has the SSA's economic crystal ball malfunctioned?

Flawed Forecast

The Social Security Administration foresees a future of sluggish economic growth in which labor productivity, or output per worker, improves slowly; total employment barely grows; and workers put in no additional hours on the job. (It reasons that economic growth, or growth of national output, must equal the sum of labor productivity increases, increases in total employment, and increases in the average hours worked.)

In its widely cited "intermediate" 1.8% growth scenario, labor productivity improves by just 1.6% a year and workforce growth slows almost to a standstill at 0.2% a year—rates well below their historical averages. (See Table 1.) Under these assumptions, and if average work time holds steady, Social Security exhausts its trust fund in the year 2042, at which point it faces an initial shortfall of 27% of its obligations. After that, Social Security would be able to pay out just 70% of the benefits it owes to retirees.

The problem is not with the logic of the method the Social Security Administration uses to make its projections, but rather with its demographic and economic assumptions. Its forecast of 1.6% annual labor productivity growth is especially suspect. When the nonpartisan Congressional Budget Office (CBO) assessed the financial health of Social Security earlier this year, it assumed that productivity would improve at a rate of 1.9% per year. In the CBO forecast, faster productivity growth, along with a lower unemployment rate, boosts wages—the tax base of the system—allowing Social Security to remain solvent until 2052, 10 years longer than the SSA had projected just a few months earlier.

One doesn't have to buy into the hype about the magic of the new economy to conclude that the CBO came closer to getting the projected productivity growth rates right than the SSA did. The federal government's own Bureau of Labor Statistics esti-

TABLE 1: SOCIAL SECURITY ADMINISTRATION'S PRINCIPAL ECONOMIC ASSUMPTIONS[a]

Annual Percentage Increase

Year	Real Gross Domestic Product[b]	Productivity (Total U.S. Economy)	Total Employment[c]	Average Hours Worked
2004	4.4%	2.7%	1.7%	0.0%
2005	3.6%	1.8%	1.7%	0.0%
2006	3.2%	1.9%	1.3%	0.0%
2007	3.0%	1.9%	1.1%	0.0%
2008	1.0%	1.8%	2.8%	0.0%
2009	2.7%	1.8%	0.9%	0.0%
2010	2.6%	1.7%	0.8%	0.0%
2011	2.4%	1.7%	0.8%	0.0%
2012	2.3%	1.6%	0.6%	0.0%
2013	2.2%	1.6%	0.6%	0.0%

Average Annual Percentage Increase

2010 to 2015	2.2%	1.6%	0.6%	0.0%
2015 to 2080	1.8%	1.6%	0.2%	0.0%

[a] These are the "intermediate economic assumptions" that the Social Security Administration regards as most plausible. The SSA also reports a "low cost" forecast that projects a 2.6% real growth rate from 2015 to 2080 and a "high cost" forecast that projects a 1.1% real growth rate from 2015 to 2080.
[b] Real Gross Domestic Product is calculated in constant 1996 dollars.
[c] Total employment is the total of civilian and military employment in the U.S. economy.
Source: Social Security Administration, 2004 Annual Report of the Board of Trustees (March 23, 2004), Table V.B.1 and Table V.B.2, pp. 89 and 94.

mates that productivity rates in the nonfarm sector improved at a 2.3% average pace from 1947 through 2003. Adjusting for the gap of 0.2 percentage points between the productivity growth of the nonfarm business sector and the economy as a whole still leaves productivity across the economy growing by a healthy 2.1% over the postwar period. That historical record convinces economist Dean Baker, from the Washington-based Center for Economic and Policy Research, that a productivity growth rate of 2.0% a year is a "very reasonable" assumption.

The drastic deceleration of employment growth, from its historic (1960 to 2000) average of 1.78% to 0.2% per year, is also overstated. As the trustees see it, employment will grow far more slowly as the baby-boomers leave the labor force. That is true as far as it goes. But if their projections are correct, the country will soon face a chronic labor shortage. And in that context, the immigration rate is unlikely to slow, as they assume, to 900,000 a year. Rather, future immigration rates would likely be at least as high as they were in the 1990s, when 1.3 million people entered the United States annually, and possibly even higher if immigration laws are relaxed in response to a labor shortage. Faster immigration would boost employment growth and add workers, who would pay into Social Security, helping to relieve the financial strain on the system created by the retirement of the baby-boom generation.

In its own optimistic or "low cost" scenario, the SSA erases the shortfall in the trust fund by assuming a faster productivity growth rate (of 1.9%), a lower unemployment rate (of 4.5% per year), and higher net immigration (of 1.3 million people per year). The still rather sluggish 2.6% average growth rate that results would wipe out the rest of the imbalance in the system and leave a sizeable surplus in the trust fund—0.15% of GDP over the next 75 years.

Making Short Work of the Shortfall

Even in the unlikely event that the pessimistic predictions the SSA has conjured up actually do come to pass, the Social Security imbalance could be easily remedied.

The Social Security Trust Fund needs $3.7 trillion to meet its unfunded obligations over the next 75 years. That is a lot of money—about 1.89% of taxable payroll and about 0.7% of GDP over that period. But it's far less than the 2.0% of GDP the 2001 to 2003 tax cuts will cost over the next 75 years if they are made permanent. (Many of the tax cuts are currently scheduled to sunset in 2010.) The portion of the Bush tax cuts going to the richest 1% of taxpayers alone will cost 0.6% of GDP— more than the CBO projected shortfall of 0.4% of GDP.

Here are a few ways to make short work of any remaining shortfall without cutting retirement benefits or raising taxes for low- or middle-income workers. First, newly hired state and local government workers could be brought into the system. (About 3.5 million state and local government workers are not now covered by Social Security.) That move alone would eliminate about 30% of the projected deficit.

In addition, we could raise the cap on wages subject to payroll taxes. Under current law, Social Security is funded by a payroll tax on the first $87,900 of a person's income. As a result of this cap on covered income, the tax applies to just 84.5% of all wages today—but historically it applied to 90%. Increasing the cap for the next decade so that the payroll tax covers 87.3% of all wages, or halfway back to the 90% standard, would eliminate nearly one-third of the SSA's projected deficit.

Finally, stopping the repeal of the estate tax, a tax giveaway that benefits only the richest taxpayers, would go a long way toward closing the gap. Economists Peter Diamond and Peter Orszag, writing for The Century Fund, advocate dedicating the revenues generated by renewing the estate tax to the Social Security Trust Fund. They suggest an estate tax set at its planned 2009 level, which would exempt $3.5 million of an individual's estate. The tax would fall exclusively on the wealthiest 0.3% of taxpayers. That alone would close another one-quarter of the SSA's projected shortfall. Returning the estate tax to its 2001 (pre-tax cut) level (with a $675,000 exemption for individuals) would do yet more to relieve any financial strain on Social Security.

Any way you look at it, Social Security can remain on sound financial footing even in the dreariest of economic futures, so long as alarmist reports like those of its trustees don't become an excuse to corrupt the system.

Sources: Congressional Budget Office, The Outlook for Social Security, June 2004; Social Security Administration, 2004 Annual Report of the Board of Trustees (March 23, 2004); "What the Trustees' Report Indicates About the Financial Status of Social Security," Robert Greenstein, Center on Budget and Policy Priorities (March 31, 2004); "The Implications of the Social Security Projections Issued By the Congressional Budget Office" Robert Greenstein, Peter Orszag, and Richard Kogan, Center on Budget and Policy Priorities (June 24, 2004); "Letter to Rudolph G. Penner" from Dean Baker, co-director of the Center For Economic and Policy Research (January 26, 2004); Countdown to Reform: The Great Social Security Debate, Henry Aaron and Robert Reischauer, The Century Foundation Press, 1998.

Chapter 5

WINDFALLS FOR THE WEALTHY

"DEATH TAX" DECEPTION
Rosie Hunter and Chuck Collins
January/February 2003

The federal estate tax, or "death tax," isn't dead yet, but a powerful clique of wealthy families and interest groups will stop at nothing to kill it. Their movement makes small business owners and family farmers its poster boys. But those who stand to gain the most from repeal are a few thousand very wealthy households. The effort to turn the public against the estate tax, and ultimately abolish it, is a case study in conservative movement tactics—the campaign uses distorted facts, dirty tricks, and front groups, and it's bent on repealing the nation's only tax on inherited wealth.

The decade-long public relations and lobbying campaign seemed to pay off when President George W. Bush signed his $1.35 trillion tax cut into law in 2001. The bill included a gradual phase-out of the estate tax over ten years (see box). But because the tax bill—a bizarre assortment of delayed activation dates and gimmicks that money guru Jane Bryant Quinn called "a contemptible piece of consumer fraud"—was structured to "sunset" at the end of 2010, the estate tax will be fully repealed for only one year, after which tax rules revert back to what they were before passage of the bill.

The anti-estate tax lobby is now pushing hard to make repeal permanent. With Republicans back in control of both houses of Congress, repeal proponents on both sides of the aisle are emboldened. And they understand that they must move quickly because as the budget deficit grows, permanent repeal will become politically more difficult to justify.

Can this juggernaut be stopped? Perhaps, but only if progressives take a hard look at the anti-estate tax campaign, debunk its claims—and its "grassroots" façade—and then organize like never before.

The Case for Preserving an Estate Tax
Abolishing the estate tax would further concentrate the nation's wealth in the hands

of the super-rich at a time when the distribution of wealth is already more unequal than at any point since the 1920s. It would also drain resources from strapped states and charities. Among the pressing budgetary reasons to preserve the tax are these:

- Making the repeal of the estate tax permanent would contribute to a fiscal train wreck, draining government coffers of $850 billion between 2011 and 2021.

- Repeal would eliminate one of the few progressive taxes in our federal system, resulting in the transfer of hundreds of billions of dollars to the trust funds of the nation's wealthiest families while shifting the burden of taxation (or cuts in services) onto those less able to pay.

States—already straining to balance their budgets—stand to lose $9 billion a year in state-linked revenue by 2010 as a result of the planned estate tax phase out.

Estate tax repeal would also shrink charitable giving and bequests, particularly from estates in excess of $20 million. Without the incentives provided by the estate tax (which encourages charitable bequests during life, in anticipation of the tax, as well as at death), the Treasury Department estimates that charitable giving may decline as much as $6 billion a year.

But the estate tax was meant to do more than bolster budgets and aid charities. From its inception, it was meant to ward off the emergence of a hereditary aristocracy in the United States. Established in 1916, the tax was a populist response to the excesses of the Gilded Age. President Theodore Roosevelt justified it by arguing that society has a claim upon the fortunes of its wealthy. Roosevelt pointed out that "most great civilized countries have an income tax and an inheritance tax. In my judgment both should be part of our system of federal taxation." Such taxation, he noted, should "be aimed merely at the inheritance or transmission in their entirety of those fortunes swollen beyond all healthy limits."

A number of modern-day millionaires—who are themselves subject to the tax—understand its historical importance. As part of the opposition to repeal, over 1,200 wealthy individuals signed a petition calling for preserving—but reforming—the tax. The signers (who include William H. Gates, Sr., George Soros, and Ted Turner) argue that the tax is an essential means to moderate the excessive build-up of hereditary wealth and power. Investor Warren Buffett argued in the *New York Times* that repealing the estate tax would be comparable to "choosing the 2020 Olympic team by picking the eldest sons of the gold-medal winners in the 2000 Olympics…Without the estate tax, you in effect will have an aristocracy of wealth, which means you pass down the ability to command the resources of the nation based on heredity rather than merit." Petition-signers and other activists say they support raising the cap on exemptions to further reduce the already-miniscule number of small businesses and farms affected by the tax. For some, the call to raise exemption levels is in part tactical—a means to gain congressional support for tax preservation.

The Push for Repeal

How did legislation benefiting only a narrow slice of the wealthiest Americans advance so far? Who is behind the push to abolish the estate tax?

Repeal backers describe their movement as "grassroots," but peek behind the curtain and you find a well-funded public relations, lobbying, media, and research apparatus (led by sophisticated operatives, many with deep connections to the Republican Party).

In the early 1990s, a group including the heirs to the Mars and Gallo family fortunes embarked on a long-term effort to eliminate the tax. They enlisted the help of Patricia Soldano, an Orange County, California, advisor to wealthy families. She formed a lobbying organization (the "Policy and Taxation Group") to provide an "outlet" for wealthy families "interested in communicating their concerns to members of Congress." Soldano channeled funds to congressional backers of repeal and hired the powerful lobbying firm Patton Boggs.

By the mid-1990s, Soldano's outfit and other early pro-repeal groups had joined together with a veritable anti-tax industry of think tanks, lobbying firms, and interest groups in Washington, D.C. to form a powerful "death tax elimination" lobby. Conservative think tanks, including the Heritage Foundation and the libertarian National Center for Policy Analysis, produced "policy backgrounders" criticizing the estate tax, and made the requisite op-eds and TV appearances as well. The anti-government group Citizens for a Sound Economy encouraged its members to lobby their senators and representatives against the tax. Other groups involved in the anti-estate tax crusade include the private campaign organization Club for Growth; the political arm of the libertarian Cato Institute; the American Conservative Union; Grover Norquist's Americans for Tax Reform; and the 60 Plus Association, a self-styled conservative alternative to the American Association of Retired Persons. At the center of the lobbying effort is the National Federation of Independent Businesses (NFIB), a business trade association and one of the most influential organizations in Washington. The NFIB's lobbying web site <www.YesToGrammKyl.com> sends faxes to Congress urging estate tax repeal.

In 1993, U.S. Representative Christopher Cox (R-Calif.) introduced the first repeal legislation with just 29 co-sponsors. Soon, Sen. Jon Kyl (R-Ariz.) became a chief ally, along with Reps. Jennifer Dunn (R-Wash.) and John Tanner (D-Tenn.). Within a year, elimination of the "death tax" occupied a central plank of the G.O.P.'s 1994 "Contract with America." By 1998, repeal legislation had over 206 House sponsors including the entire Republican leadership.

At NFIB's 2002 Small Business Summit, Bush strategist Karl Rove said "the NFIB and the Bush administration work hand-in-hand because we see eye-to-eye." Referring to NFIB's failed effort in June 2002 to make the repeal of the estate tax permanent, Rove assured his audience, "Don't look at it as a defeat. This is a war, and we need to make an ongoing commitment to winning the effort to repeal the death tax."

Death Tax Lingo

In perhaps its greatest public relations feat, the pro-repeal lobby has managed to portray the estate tax as a "death tax" on most Americans. The phrase suggests a tax imposed upon death itself, although over 98% of those who die go untaxed. The "death tax" label has proven a major asset to the campaign, yet its authorship is disputed. James L. Martin, president of the 60 Plus Association and Bush family friend, credits himself. Rep. Dunn credits Seattle Times publisher Frank Blethen.

Whatever the origin of the tag, Republican pollster Frank Luntz masterminded its widespread use. Luntz urged conservative legislators and candidates to exclusively call the estate tax a "death tax," and in a 1994 memo he suggested legislators hold anti-estate tax press conferences at local funeral homes. Republicans employ the "death tax" label so effectively that the term is now used in the mainstream press.

Martin has thought up plenty of other labels for the tax as well, including "grim-reaper's tax," "grave robber's tax," "cruelest tax," "pine-box tax," and "success tax." Martin travels the country to spread the word that "taxing cadavers is gross public policy," and to ask the public, "Should Uncle Sam, rather than a blood relative, be the first in line when you die?" At one point Martin ran a contest to generate new catch phrases; the winner—"last-grasp tax"—got $100. Martin, Luntz, and other Republican spin-doctors recognize that success hinges on how the debate is framed. Martin told *The American Prospect*, "it's all a matter of marketing."

Deception Down on the Farm

Pro-repeal literature is packed with claims that the estate tax forces working farmers to sell their farms. When Congress passed legislation to repeal the tax in 2000, it delivered the bill to President Bill Clinton on a tractor to symbolize the "down on the farm" effects of the bill. On the campaign trail later that year, George W. Bush declared, "To keep farms in the family, we are going to get rid of the death tax!"

Starting in the spring of 2001, a number of investigative reports began to question the veracity of these claims. They found that stories of farmers losing the farm to the estate tax are so rare that experts and investigators have been unable to find any real examples. Neil Harl, an Iowa State University economist whose tax advice has made him a household name among Midwest farmers, said he searched far and wide but never found a case in which a farm was lost because of estate taxes. "It's a myth," said Mr. Harl, "M-Y-T-H."

The *New York Times* reported that when the pro-repeal American Farm Bureau Foundation was challenged to produce one real case of a farm that was lost because of the estate tax, it could not cite a single example. In April 2001, the Bureau's president sent an urgent memo to its affiliates stating, "it is crucial for us to be able to provide Congress with examples of farmers and ranchers who have lost farms ... due to the death tax." Still, no examples were forthcoming.

Disabled Americans Against the Death Tax?

In early 2001, Responsible Wealth (a project of the popular education organization United for a Fair Economy) initiated the petition of wealthy individuals calling for preservation of the tax. The petition prompted a swift counterattack by the pro-repeal lobby, which issued a barrage of advertising and media events to undermine the Responsible Wealth effort. One example provides an illustration of pro-repeal tactics.

In March of 2001, full-page advertisements appeared in several daily newspapers around the country including the *Wall Street Journal* and the *Washington Times*. The advertisements were produced by a new organization, dubbed "Disabled Americans for Death Tax Relief." Its leader, a young woman from Austin, Texas, named Erin O'Leary, claimed she had just formed the organization two weeks earlier and already had over 1,000 members.

O'Leary was "deeply offended by the callous and heartless comments made by 125 so-called 'millionaire' signers of the Responsible Wealth ad that appeared in the *New York Times*." She alleged that there are "2.5 million disabled people who are family members of millionaires, a number that would grow to 8 million over the next thirty years," and that with rising medical costs, these individuals needed their inheritances. The text of the advertisement continued:

> In order to live a full life, these Americans may require medical help, nursing and living assistance far beyond that which is covered by medical insurance. Warren Buffet, Bill Gates, Sr. and George Soros believe that these people should be denied full financial help from their parents.

The "Disabled Americans" stunt was the creation of conservative communications maven Craig Shirley (whose public relations firm represents the National Rifle Association, the Heritage Foundation, and the Republican National Committee). Fox News and several conservative talk shows kept O'Leary busy with interviews, but most other news media recognized O'Leary's advertisement for the charade that it was.

Disabilities experts responded, including author Marta Russell, who felt that "using disabled people to front for the interests of the wealthiest members of our society is an outrage and a disgrace." Russell disputed the claim that millions of disabled people could be adversely affected by the tax. O'Leary's figures made no sense given the economic profile of the disabled population in this country. The disabled are one of this country's poorest groups, and highly dependent on the very tax-funded social services that repeal of the estate tax could put at risk.

Shaping Public Perception

Print and radio advertisements are key weapons both in molding public perception and attacking members of Congress who vote against full repeal. The owner of the *Seattle Times*, Frank Blethen, sees estate tax repeal as his personal crusade. (Blethen believes that the estate tax is responsible for the decline of family-owned newspapers.)

He started a website <www.deathtax.com> and organizes an annual "Death Tax Summit" in Washington, D.C., to mobilize other independent newspapers and business groups to lobby Congress.

Blethen has used the *Seattle Times* as a vehicle for his anti-estate tax cause, both on the editorial page and through advertisements, stirring concerns from the paper's editors about his lack of impartiality. Further, he circulated the anti-death tax ads he developed to other newspaper owners; they were published in over one hundred independent newspapers nation-wide.

The estate tax is also a favorite issue for conservative groups seeking to exercise political influence through issue ads. In the months prior to the 2002 election, pro-repeal organizations ran estate tax issue ads in South Dakota, Missouri, Minnesota, Iowa, and Arkansas. In Missouri, the United Seniors Association and Americans for Job Security (phony grassroots organizations fronting for corporate interests) targeted former Senator Jean Carnahan's position on the estate tax. In Minnesota, Americans for Job Security ran full-page newspaper ads attacking the late Senator Paul Wellstone for voting against full repeal, and flew a banner at the Minnesota state fair: "Wellstone Quit Taxing the Dead!"

Dividing Diverse Constituencies

Another pro-repeal strategy has been to thwart progressive and diverse groups that might be inclined to preserve the estate tax. Over the past five years, pro-repeal forces worked to convince the public that the estate tax is particularly detrimental to women and people of color as well as farmers. In doing so, they spin an illusion of a rainbow coalition in opposition to the tax.

For example, the NFIB and front group called the Small Business Survival Coalition recently organized press conferences with women business owners and alleged that "women—not men—are the chief victims of the tax" because women generally outlive men. They mobilized women's business organizations including Women Impacting Public Policy and the National Association of Women Business Owners in support of repeal.

But claims that the estate tax burdens women business owners are misleading. The great majority of all businesses fall below the taxable level. Relatively few businesses of any kind face the tax, and because women-owned (and minority-owned) businesses are smaller than average, they are affected even more rarely. As for the argument that women outlive men, the only families subject to the tax are those who own assets at least 20 times greater than the net worth of the median family. Therefore few widows lose any inheritance to the estate tax. And those who do are among the wealthiest 2% of households, not hard luck cases. On the other hand, women—and people of color—benefit disproportionately from social programs (including small business loans and education spending) funded by the tax.

Anti-estate tax groups have similarly put forward minority business groups, such as the Hispanic Business Roundtable and the National Black Chamber of Commerce, as visible allies. Frank Blethen enlists minority-owned newspapers in opposing the tax. He tells readers of the <www.deathtax. com> newsletter that it is important to "educate" members of Congress that the estate tax is "a minority and female-owned business issue and an environmental issue."

In April 2001, billionaire Robert Johnson of Black Entertainment Television and a group of other African-American business people ran ads in the *New York Times* and the *Washington Post*. Johnson invoked race in his ads, claiming to speak for African Americans broadly. The ads asserted that the estate tax unfairly takes wealth away from the black community and that repeal would help African Americans gain economic power. Although there are no statistics available on the number of African Americans subject to the estate tax, African Americans are clearly far less likely than white people to inherit fortunes large enough to face taxation. The median net worth for African-American households (excluding homeownership) is $1,200, compared to $37,600 for white households. (The median Hispanic household is lower still, with zero net worth.) One in four African-American households own no positive wealth at all, compared with one in seven white households. And there are only two African Americans on the Forbes 400: Oprah Winfrey and Robert Johnson himself.

Nevertheless, President Bush moved quickly to quote Johnson in his speech to the Council of Mayors, saying "as Robert Johnson of Black Entertainment Television argues, the death tax … weighs heavily on minorities."

Soon after, Bush tried to convince the members of the National Council of La Raza, a major Latino advocacy group, to join him in supporting estate tax repeal. Bush described a Mexican-American taco-shop owner who said he wanted "to get rid of the death tax so I can pass my business from one generation to the next." It turned out, as even the *Wall Street Journal* noted, the taco shop Bush described was valued at $300,000, far below the over $1 million exemption the current law allows owners of businesses. George W. got it wrong. The taco shop would pass to heirs untaxed, just as the vast majority of small businesses do.

Like the allegations about small farms and family enterprises, pro-repeal forces repeat these allegations about women and people of color over and over through their media work and lobbying efforts.

A principal tactic of the campaign has been to get the minnows to front for the whales.

But the truth is, few or no folks are losing their taco shops—or their farms—to the estate tax. In fact, in 1998, only 776 estates where family-owned business assets represented over half the value of the estate were "taxable" under estate tax rules, out of 47,482 total taxable estates, and 2.3 million individual deaths. So the great majority of estates taxed under the estate tax are not estates built on family-owned businesses and farms, but other forms accumulated wealth—stock investments, non-productive assets, fourth homes, art collections, luxury items, etc.

All or Nothing Repeal

The architects of the repeal effort are zealots. They advocate nothing short of complete repeal and consistently oppose any reform or compromise. They understand that partial reform will not benefit the principal patrons of the repeal effort—the very wealthy interests who bankroll the campaign would not be covered by exemptions. (Their wealth is so great it would exceed even a very high cap.)

But this strategy may backfire when the groups that have bought into the misrepresentations realize that, rather than family farmers or small business owners, the vast majority of whom will never owe any estate tax, the windfall of estate tax repeal will go to the heirs and heiresses of the country's 3,000 wealthiest estates. This elite group will inherit billions in appreciated stock and real estate, enormous capital gains that have never been subject to taxation. The *Wall Street Journal* has estimated that George W. Bush's heirs alone would stand to gain from $6 to $12 million if the tax is repealed, assuming his estate remains the same size up to his death. Cheney's heirs would save between $10 and $45 million. And the heirs of the Gallos and Marses stand to make even more.

Conclusion

In the bid to eliminate the estate tax, anti-repeal forces have used slick advertising, explicit falsehoods and deception. But we should not have to endure the triple whammy of lost federal revenue, state revenue and charitable giving in order to give a handful of millionaires and billionaires a tax break, no matter how well disguised in a misinformation campaign.

With Republicans back in control of the U.S. Senate, the push is already on to permanently repeal the federal estate tax. For now, even with their new majority and Democratic party supporters, repeal proponents fall short of the 60 votes they need under budget rules that expire in April 2003. If the budget rules are not extended, however, they will be able to advance their anti-estate tax agenda with only a simple majority. This juggernaut can be stopped, but time is running out.

DOUBLE TAXATION DOUBLE SPEAK
Why Repealing Dividend Taxes Is Unfair
John Miller
March/April 2003

Concerned that the most well off in our society might be suffering a bout of the post-holiday blues, the *Wall Street Journal's* day-after-Christmas editorial urged the Bush Administration to end the "double taxation" of dividends—payments of corporate profits to stockholders. Nothing lifts the spirits of the wealthy like yet another tax giveaway.

But for the editors of the Journal, making dividends tax exempt is not just psychotherapy for stock investors. It's a matter of economic justice and sound economic policy. (See excerpts.) In their hands, however, notions of a fair and effective policy response to today's stagnant economy become "double taxation" doublespeak. Let's try to set the record straight.

The equity argument [for ending the dividend tax] is that it is unfair to tax anything twice, even at the highest levels of income. Americans will favor repealing the double tax on dividends because it offends their sense of fair play.

The "double taxation" of dividends is the heart of their argument. But there is nothing about double taxation that ought to offend Americans' sense of fair play. True enough, the government collects income taxes on dividends paid out of the profits of corporations that have already been taxed. But being taxed more than once on the same income is a fact of life for every taxpayer, not just dividends collectors. Most workers, for instance, pay Social Security payroll taxes and income taxes on their wages, and then sales taxes when they spend what remains of their paycheck.

Beyond that, the claim that dividends are "double" taxed is an exaggeration. To begin with, in the year 2000 more than half of corporate dividends went to tax-exempt pension funds, individual retirement accounts, and non-profit foundations or to individuals who owed no income tax. In addition, corporate income is hardly taxed the first time around. Relative to GDP, U.S. corporate income taxes are no more than half those of other wealthy industrial (OECD) countries. By our own historical standards, corporate income taxes have fallen from 4.1% of GDP in 1960 to just 1.7% of GDP in 2001. In addition, the average rate of taxation on corporate profits currently stands at 15%, far below the top corporate tax rate of 35%. Worse yet, in 1998, twenty-four highly profitable major corporations, including Pfizer, PepsiCo, MCI Worldcom, General Motors, and Texaco, paid no corporate income taxes—and received a tax rebate. Robert McIntyre, director of Citizens for Tax Justice, estimates that "barely more than half of corporate profits are subject to tax at any level."

More importantly when it comes to fairness, the issue is not how often we pay taxes, but how much we pay in taxes. By that standard, eliminating taxes on dividends would surely violate most people's sense of fair play. As even the *Wall Street Journal* allows, the beneficiaries would be those "at the highest levels of income." Some 42% of the benefits from repealing taxes on dividends would go to the richest 1% of taxpayers, and three-quarters of the tax benefits would go the richest 10%, reports the Tax Policy Center of the Urban Institute and the Brookings Institution. The top 1% of taxpayers, those with yearly incomes greater than $373,000, also benefited most from the economic growth of the last two decades. After adjusting for inflation, their real average before-tax income more than doubled (a 138% increase) from 1979 and 1997, according to the Congressional Budget Office, while their tax burden, much like that of large corporations, has declined. By 1997, the richest 1%

of U.S. families paid out about 1/3 of their income in all federal taxes, far less than the 2/5 they paid in 1977. These figures will only get worse due to the 2001 Bush tax cut or the elimination of dividends taxation.

[Taxing dividends] creates huge distortions in both corporate and investor behavior... [O]n the corporate side, taxation creates incentives for companies to finance themselves via debt (interest on debt is tax deductible, dividend payouts are not). Increased debt can of course result in increased financial fragility for the company and risk for investors.

The *Journal* editors argue that repealing the taxation of dividends might reduce corporations' reliance on debt financing. Interest payments are currently tax-exempt. By putting the taxation of interest payments and dividends on an equal footing, the government would take away the incentive for corporations to finance themselves through borrowing. But so too would several other changes in the tax code that would not result in a tax windfall for the super wealthy. For instance, to eliminate the tax bias in favor of "growth stocks" (which benefit investors by increasing in price), we could just remove the 20% cap on income taxes on capital gains (the sale of stocks and other assets). But the editors of the *Wall Street Journal* are loathe to consider any proposal that would boost government revenues and arrest the decline in the tax burden of the rich or large corporations.

The tax penalty also prompts companies to retain earnings ... rather than paying profits to investors. This can freeze capital—rather than allowing investors to reinvest cash in other businesses where rates of return might be higher, thus permitting capital to flow to more productive uses.

Cutting taxes on dividends is surprisingly less than popular with corporate managers. Both Carter and Reagan administration proposals to reduce or eliminate the double taxation found little support among business elites. Joel Slemrod, a former Reagan administration White House aide and tax economist, told the *Wall Street Journal* that business executives dismissed the Reagan proposal to cut dividend taxes as "just for shareholders," saying that they preferred tax relief that comes directly to corporations. While the *Wall Street Journal* editorial touts dividend paying corporations as a good investment in today's bear market, some economists are not convinced. Economist Alan Auerbach argues, for instance, that with lower dividend taxes, investors would expect corporations to pay out more of their earnings in the form of dividends, reducing the cash available for new corporate investments.

Finally, repealing the tax on dividends is unlikely to provide the stimulus necessary to counteract today's economic stagnation. As Slemrod's comments suggest, business investment is unlikely to pick up in response to cutting dividend taxes, especially in face of the overcapacity in today's economy. Even if shareholders do pour new money into stocks paying dividends, that will do little to spark new corporate investment. The vast majority of stock sales are not new issues, but resales of existing stock from one stock investor to another, which do not provide corporations with new funds for investment. During the 1990s stock boom, economists Robert Pollin, Dean Baker, and Marc Schaberg put the ratio of stock resales to new stock sales at 113.8 to 1.

If fairness and effectiveness are the issues, then a cut in the Social Security payroll taxes will do more to spread widely the benefit of cutting taxes and do far more to get the economy going again than eliminating dividend taxes. Today, three quarters of taxpayers pay more in payroll taxes than income taxes. In addition, we can count on those middle- and low-income households, many of them strapped for cash with the economic slowdown, to spend more of their income than the super-rich who would make out with the repeal of taxes on dividends.

A one-year payroll-tax holiday on the first $10,000 of wages would give workers a tax cut of up to $765, with much of the benefit going to middle- and low-income taxpayers. The AFL-CIO, the Business Roundtable, and the Economic Policy Institute all support proposals similar to this one. The Tax Policy Center estimates that 45.4% of the benefits of a Social Security payroll-tax holiday would go to the bottom 60%, as opposed to 4.7% of the benefits from repealing dividend taxation.

A payroll tax holiday would do as much to lift the spirits of most people as repealing dividends taxation would do to buck up the super-rich. It's the right thing to do. Don't let all the double taxation doublespeak make you doubt that for one minute.

RED INK, BLUE BLOODS, AND BAD POLICY
Bush Squanders the Budget Surplus
John Miller
May/June 2003

It's worse than we thought.

In January 2001, when George W. Bush took office, the bipartisan Congressional Budget Office (CBO) projected federal budget surpluses as far as the eye could see. Some $5.6 trillion in budget surpluses would accumulate over the next decade. This was Dubya's post-Cold War "peace dividend," a sum with the potential to reverse decades of neglect of the nation's pressing social needs.

By the spring of 2002, two-thirds of that projected surplus was gone. The largest single share went to the first round of Bush tax cuts. Now, one year later, the rest of the projected surplus is gone, and then some. Current federal tax and spending policies will saddle the federal government with budget deficits through fiscal year 2007, according to the latest CBO study, and leave a net deficit of $378 billion in place of the $5.6 trillion surplus for the ten years from 2002 to 2011. (See Table 1.)

TABLE 1: FEDERAL BUDGET SURPLUS (OR DEFICIT) IN TRILLIONS OF DOLLARS*

	FY 2002–2011
January 2001 CBO Projection	5.644
January 2003 CBO Projection	0.020
March 2003 CBO Projection	–0.378
March 2003 CBO Projection with FY2004 Presidents Budget	–2.122

* The federal budget surpluses and deficits in the table are for the unified budget which combines on-budget and off-budget (principally Social Security) federal government surpluses and deficits. *Sources:* Congressional Budget Office, Jan. 2001, Jan. 2003, March 2003.

A $6 trillion reversal of fiscal fortune is a stunning accomplishment, even for a president with a proven knack for losing money in the private sector. Did the Bush administration—full of remorse over the tax giveaways to the rich of its first year in office—spend this past year bolstering the budget for social programs? Did the president decide that government borrowing is reasonable if the money is invested in meeting important human and infrastructure needs?

Not a chance.

The CBO report is clear about where the rest of that projected surplus did go. First off, the recession and worsening economic prospects made mincemeat of the CBO projections. A deeper than anticipated economic slump in 2001, slow growth since then, and a collapsing stock market made the CBO revenue estimates far too optimistic. When combined with unanticipated cost increases, especially escalating health care costs, these "technical changes" ate about 45% of the projected ten-year surplus.

These factors—arguably beyond the control of the Bush administration—aside, there was still $3 trillion in projected surpluses that the Bush budgets have entirely depleted. The major culprit in pushing the Bush budget into the red? That's easy: tax cuts, targeted to the wealthy. Tax cuts in the past two years accounted for nearly three-fifths of the lost surplus due to legislative changes (in other words, the remaining 55% of the lost surplus). That $1.757 trillion went to finance the Bush tax cuts enacted in 2001, including the phase-out of the estate tax and an across-the-board cut in income tax rates, and a far smaller rebate for income taxpayers in 2002. Over one-third of the benefits of those tax cuts, according to Citizens for Tax Justice, will go to the richest 1% of taxpayers, all with incomes greater than $384,000.

Increased government spending, the great bulk of which went to military appropriations, explains the remaining deterioration in the Bush budget picture. Additional military appropriations are more than double the new spending for discretionary nonmilitary domestic spending—programs such as public housing, supports for low income families, education and homeland security! (See Figure 1. Note that the breakdown in the figure is based on the CBO's January 2003 projection rather than on the most recent [March 2003] projection cited above.) Together with the Bush tax cuts, new military spending accounts for 83% of the ten-year costs of legislation enacted under the Bush administration. The remaining additional civilian spending went to new entitlement spending, primarily to a farm bill, compensation for 9/11 victims, an airline bailout and educational and other benefits for veterans and military retirees.

And all of that was before the Bush administration's guns 'n tax-cuts budget for FY 2004 reached Congress. If the Republican-controlled Congress enacts the current Bush budget proposal, loaded with more tax cuts for the well-to-do and a continued military buildup, budget deficits would grow to a whopping $2.1 trillion over the FY2002 to FY2011 period, says the CBO. Worse yet, the CBO's estimates (like the president's budget proposal) make no mention of the cost of the war in Iraq.

Big Deficits—Who Cares?

The Bush administration does not dispute that we have returned to an "era of large deficits." But Office of Management and Budget director Mitch Daniels says, "We ought not hyperventilate about this issue." Congressional Democrats are in fact having a hard time catching their breath as they beat the drum of fiscal responsibility. Kent Conrad, the ranking Democratic member of the Senate Budget Committee, warns that the Bush budget would post "the worst deficits in our nation's history." Federal Reserve chair Alan Greenspan, the Democrats' new patron saint, warned Congress that "If we do not … reaffirm our commitment to fiscal discipline, years of

FIGURE 1: THE PROJECTED SURPLUS: WHERE IT WENT

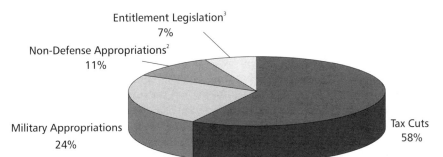

Entitlement Legislation[3]
7%

Non-Defense Appropriations[2]
11%

Military Appropriations
24%

Tax Cuts
58%

[1] Based on January 2001 CBO projection of the ten-year surplus FY 2001–2011, corrected for $2,577 billion due to overoptimistic revenue and cost estimates.
[2] Including Homeland Security.
[3] Entitlement legislation includes the farm bill, extended unemployment compensation, 9/11 victims compensation, the airline bailout, student loan changes, veterans education benefits, and dual benefits for military retirees and veterans, among others.
Source: Richard Kogan, "Are Tax Cuts a Minor or Major Factor in the Return of Deficits? What the CBO Data Show," Center on Budget and Policy Priorities, Feb. 12, 2003.

hard effort could be squandered."

The real charge against the Bush administration and its wealthy patrons, however, is not that they squandered a surplus built of our hard-earned fiscal discipline, but that they squandered it on themselves. Turning surpluses into deficits, even deficits as large as the 3% to 4% of Gross Domestic Product (GDP) that the Bush administration is likely to ring up this year and next, would not be a problem had the surplus been put to good use.

Consider just two examples. For $350 billion over ten years, no more than the tax cut that the Bush budgets lavished on the richest 1% of taxpayers, the administration could have covered 25% of the prescription drug costs of the entire Medicare population, according to budget analyst Richard Kogan with the Center on Budget and Policy Priorities. Likewise, $1.3 trillion, the cost of the 2001 Bush tax cut, is the amount of new spending the American Society of Civil Engineers recently found was necessary to bring U.S. infrastructure up to what it calls acceptable standards. That money could have made much-needed improvements in school buildings, sewers, airports, mass transit systems, roads, and other vital infrastructure.

The Next Budget

But precious little new social spending made its way into the Bush budgets, which have consistently turned butter into margarine. The Bush budget proposal for FY2004 is no different. It limits the growth of total discretionary spending to 4%, but that average masks large, damaging cuts to a whole host of domestic programs. To begin with, non-military discretionary spending (more or less everything outside of Social Security, Medicare, and the military) will increase at only a 2.3% annual rate through 2008, according to the CBO, barely keeping up with the expected rate of inflation. This does nothing to reverse the decline in non-military domestic discretionary spending from 4.7% of GDP in 1980 to 3.5% of GDP in 2002.

Key domestic spending programs are on the chopping block in the Bush budget proposal for FY2004, including funding for public housing, rural health programs, and community policing. Also singled out for cuts are infrastructure items such as roads and wastewater treatment facilities. The administration slashes employment and training programs by 11% even though the U.S. economy shed 2.3 million private sector jobs between January 2001 and January 2003. Even the Bush education budget would increase by less than the rate of inflation, while cutting spending on after-school programs and vocational training and eliminating four student aid programs. While the budget promises $400 billion for a Medicare prescription drug benefit, cuts in general Medicare funding in the Republican House budget would actually leave the program with a net increase of only $186 billion over the next ten years, far less than the amount necessary to fund any meaningful prescription drug benefit.

These budget cuts have already jeopardized the social safety net. But the long-term effects of the Bush policies are even more alarming. A recent study by the Center on Budget and Policy Priorities argued that the administration's tax-cutting agenda will endanger even our most basic entitlement programs. For example, over the next 75 years the Bush tax cuts would cost more than three times as much as the Social Security Administration's most recent estimate of the deficit in Social Security over the same time period!

The Bush budget does far better by military spending. After a 15% jump last year, military spending is still slated to increase by 4.7% a year through 2008. Military-related spending consumes the majority of the $782 billion in discretionary spending in the Bush FY2004 budget. Some $399 billion would go to the Pentagon (the Defense Department plus nuclear weapons programs in the Department of Energy). Homeland security gobbles up another $41.3 billion.

The Bush administration has requested an additional $75 billion in supplemental funding for this fiscal year to pay for its war with Iraq. But initial estimates of the cost of wars are notoriously low. The CBO puts the cost of a three-month ground war with a five-year occupation, its worst case scenario, at $272 billion. If the United States actually reconstructs Iraq, as the Bush administration promises, the costs run far higher. One estimate, by economist William Nordhaus of Yale, puts the cost of the war plus reconstruction as high as $755 billion; his worst-case estimate rises to nearly $2 trillion when negative impacts on the oil market and the macroeconomy are included. And alienated allies who picked up much of the tab for the Gulf War seem unlikely to bail the United States out this time around.

Despite earlier tax cuts and a slumping economy eating away at government revenues and the war with Iraq driving up expenditures, new tax cuts continue to be the signature of the Bush budget plan. This time, the Bush team wants $1.6 trillion in additional tax cuts over the coming decade. Some $624 billion would go to make permanent the $1.3 trillion tax giveaway to the wealthy Bush pushed through Congress in 2001. Another $726 billion would finance the Bush growth package proposed this January. Its centerpiece, the exclusion of dividends from taxation, would bestow 42% of its benefits on the richest 1% of taxpayers. Should his budget be adopted, the total cost of the Bush tax cuts, including those already enacted, would rise to $3.0 trillion over the years 2001 to 2013. Adding in the higher interest costs on the borrowing the government will have to do to make up for the revenue lost to those tax cuts, that cost reaches $3.7 trillion.

Tax cuts for the rich and military spending are the means that the Bush administration is using to constrict the flow of monies to programs that benefit working and low-income families. Giving to the rich, taking from the poor, and racking up large deficits is a policy combo straight out of the Reagan playbook.

But Bush's class-warfare budget is actually out of sync with how the United States has financed past wars. Large federal deficits have been a constant. But so too have been taxes levied against those most able to pay. For instance, in 1919, following World War I, the top tax bracket of the federal individual income tax jumped from 15% to 77%. During World War II, policy makers extended the income tax downward to apply to middle-income earners but also raised the top tax bracket. Even the President's father passed a tax increase during the first Persian Gulf War.

Not this time. Today we ask not one ounce of sacrifice from those best off in our society. Instead we spill red ink to pay for tax cuts for blue bloods and to finance an internationally-condemned war that spills the red blood of the people of a poor developing country who have already suffered through two decades of wars, political repression, and economic sanctions. That stain will remain with the Bush administration forever more.

Sources: Congressional Budget Office, "The Budget and Economic Outlook: Fiscal Years 2004–2013," January 2003; Congressional Budget Office, "An Analysis of the President's Budgetary Proposals for Fiscal Year 2004: An Interim Report," March 2003; Democratic Caucus of the Budget Committee, "Big Tax Cuts, Harmful Program Cuts, and Record Deficits: Summary and Analysis of President Bush's 2004 Budget," Feb. 7, 2003; Democratic Staff of the Senate Budget Committee, "Review & Analysis of the President's FY2004 Budget," February 27, 2003; Richard Kogan, "Are Tax Cuts A Minor or Major Factor in the Return of Deficits? What the CBO Data Show," (Center on Budget and Policy Priorities, February 12, 2003); Center on Budget and Policy Priorities, "House Republican Budget Contains large Cuts in Medicare, Medicaid, and Other Domestic Programs," March 17, 2003; Richard Kogan, "Costs of the Tax Cuts and of a Medicare Prescription Drug Benefit," (Center on Budget and Policy Priorities, June 14, 2002); Citizens For Tax Justice, "Revised Estimate Pegs Latest Bush Tax Cut Plan at $2.0 Trillion Over Decade," March 18, 2003.

TAX CUT TIME BOMB
Adria Scharf
March/April 2004

President George W. Bush and Congress planted a time bomb in the federal budget, and they're about to light the fuse. The largest parts of the tax cuts passed in 2001 and 2003 didn't activate immediately, but were designed to kick in later this decade. If they go forward, the cuts will likely cripple or destroy the social programs that form the cornerstone of the federal welfare state. Even worse, the Bush administration is now pushing to make permanent virtually all of the 2001 and 2003 tax cuts, which were originally set to expire by 2010.

In 2001, Bush sought and won the largest income tax rollback in two decades—it reduced tax rates on the top four income brackets and gave advance refunds of $300 to $600 to 94 million taxpayers. In 2003, despite the growing budget deficit, the administration secured a second tax cut—the third largest in U.S. history. The 2003 package shrank dividend and capital gains taxes and accelerated the 2001 rate cut for top income brackets. Combined, the 2001 and 2003 tax cuts will cost at least $824.1 billion between 2001 and 2010, even if Republicans don't succeed in renewing the provisions scheduled to expire, or "sunset," according to Citizens for Tax Justice (CTJ). If the cuts are extended, CTJ estimates they will cost more than $1 trillion between 2004 and 2014, with over 80% of the revenue loss hitting after 2009. (See Figure 1.)

FIGURE 1: ESTIMATED COSTS FROM BUSH TAX CUTS, 2004–2014

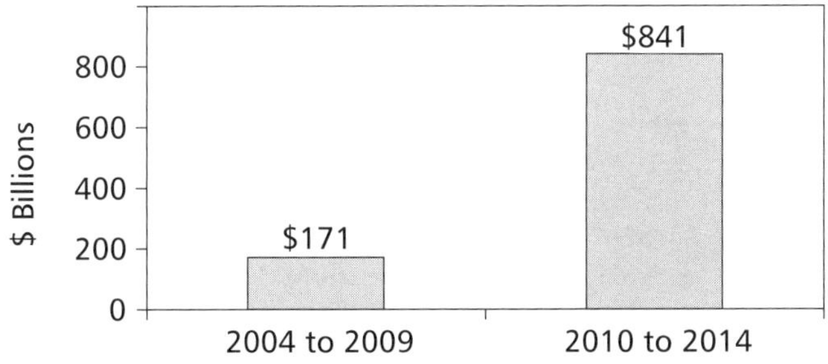

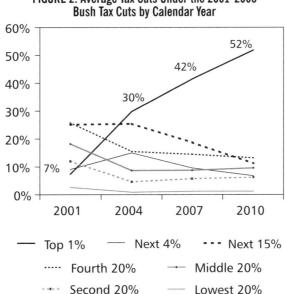

Source: Citizens for Tax Justice, December 17, 2003.

Aside from their sheer size, the 2001 and 2003 packages were notable for a couple of reasons: First, their major provisions were deliberately scheduled to hit later in the decade. Republican congressional leaders delayed the largest cuts to protect the bills from filibuster and deflect attention from their long-term effects on the budget and inequality. Second, they were frontloaded with tiny morsels for the middle class and backloaded with enormous benefits for the top 1%. (See Figure 2 and Table 1, which are conservative in that they assume expiring provisions will in fact "sunset.")

**FIGURE 2: Average Tax Cuts Under the 2001-2003
Bush Tax Cuts by Calendar Year**

Source: Citizens for Tax Justice, December 17, 2003.

TABLE 1: Average Tax Cuts Under the 2001-2003
Bush Tax Cuts by Calendar Year*

	2001	2005	2010
Top 1%	$3,221	$41,264	$85,002
Next 4%	$1,015	$3,913	$2,780
Next 15%	$742	$2,015	$1,225
Fourth 20%	$572	$971	$1,081
Middle 20%	$403	$563	$791
Second 20%	$266	$371	$508
Lowest 20%	$57	$77	$98

*with sunsets
Source: Citizens for Tax Justice, December 17, 2003.

Over the next 75 years, the cost of extending the 2001 and 2003 tax cuts would amount to $5.9 trillion, or 1.1% of gross domestic product (GDP), according to William G. Gale and Peter R. Orszag of the Brookings Institution. To put that figure into perspective, the expected costs of funding Social Security during that same period are just $3.8 trillion (or 0.7% of GDP). Gale and Orszag warn the new Bush budget plan will necessitate one of the following changes, or a "change of a similar magnitude," within the decade, and argue that even deeper cuts may be required:

- A 29% cut in Social Security benefits;

- A 70% cut in federal Medicaid benefits;

- A 49% cut in all domestic discretionary spending, or

- A 21% increase in payroll taxes.

Sources: William G. Gale and Peter R. Orszag, "Should the President's Tax Cuts be Made Permanent?" Brookings, Washington, D.C., February 24, 2004; "The Bush Tax Cuts: The Most Recent CTJ Data," Citizens for Tax Justice, December 17, 2003, <www.ctj.org>; "Details of the Administration's Budget Proposals," Citizens for Tax Justice, February 3, 2004, <www.ctj.org>.

Chapter 6

"DEREGULATION DREAMS"

IS THE DIGITAL ECONOMY UNREGULATABLE?
Phineas Baxandall
March/April 2002

Back in the 1950s, the Soviet Union proclaimed that computerization heralded the triumph of centralized economic planning over decentralized markets. Computers would allow planners to process unprecedented amounts of information and accurately forecast and fine-tune the economy. Success with computerization at individual plants and regional ministries only made Soviet officials more confident of its potential for the economy as a whole. Across the sea, U.S. officials fretted that the Soviets were right, that the Soviet economy was catching up to the West, and that computerization would show the world that markets were obsolete.

The Soviet vision of a computer-planned future may seem silly today, but it puts in perspective the recent free-market hype about the so-called "New Economy." Free-marketeers, no less that Soviet bureaucrats, tend to project their own fondest wishes onto technology itself. "Governments of the Industrial World, you weary giants of flesh and steel," cyberlibertarian John Perry Barlow demands, "on behalf of the future, I ask you of the past to leave us alone." The main effect of the "New Economy" has been to convince people that information technology and computer networks somehow make government regulation obsolete—more or less the Soviet dream in reverse.

Today, the bloom is off the rose of the "New Economy." With high-tech stock prices plummeting after March 2000 (the NASDAQ index lost over half its value within a year), few people still believe that a computer and an online stock account guarantee overnight riches. Dot-com millionaires no longer represent the glorious future, and chastened "New Economy" boosters have had to accept that the business cycle is not just an iron-age relic. Nonetheless, even in today's recession, we still hear that government regulation is an "Old Economy" dinosaur.

Three largely unexamined myths perpetuate this nonsense. First, the belief that information inherently resists regulation. Second, that the networked economy favors spontaneous markets over slow-footed government bureaucracies. And third, that new technologies have globalized the economy beyond the influence of national

117

governments. There is a grain of truth in each, but none of it leads to the conclusion that public regulation is either impossible or undesirable.

Myth #1: Information must be governed by "free markets" because "information must be free."

Free-market enthusiasts have missed the most novel thing about information goods as a commodity—that after the research and development is done, the cost of producing each unit is very low. Think of software giants. It costs just a few cents to burn each copy of WindowsXP or Excel onto a CD. For digitalized property such as databases, electronic music files (such as the "MP3s" exchanged on Napster), or password-protected information, there is virtually no cost for an additional copy. In economics lingo, the "marginal cost" of these goods is zero or close to zero.

Mainstream "neoclassical" economics argues that the most efficient price for a product is equal to its marginal cost. If the price is lower, people who do not value the product as much as its cost will buy it. If the price is higher, people who value the product more than its cost will forego it. Either way, there will be a "net welfare loss" to society. The neoclassical argument that competitive markets are efficient depends on the view that they push prices to this efficient level. But "zero marginal cost" goods turn these arguments on their head. In the words of Berkeley economist Brad DeLong, the "assumptions ... of the invisible hand fray when transported into tomorrow's information economy."

Take the analogy of paying for a bridge. The bridge is expensive to build, but once it is constructed there is virtually no additional cost for an additional individual to use it. If people are charged more than this miniscule cost, there will be a net welfare loss (since some people who would benefit from using the bridge will be prevented from using it by the artificial cost of the toll). Even mainstream economists are forced to conclude that a private toll is a less efficient way to pay for a bridge than a general tax. The same is true for information goods like digital music files. Once you pay the members of the band and the sound engineers, for example, pretty much all the costs of producing a Metallica song are accounted for, whether you create one digital sound file or millions. Therefore, charging people to download the file would cause a net welfare loss. "Even though economic theory is severely biased toward markets," concludes economist Michael Perelman, "according to the criteria of economics, information should not be treated as private property."

Following this logic, the Canadian government levies a small tax on recording media, such as blank CDs and tapes, and uses the revenue to fund Canadian artists who lose sales as a result of people recording their work for free. Germany and other European countries have explored attaching a fee to the sale of computers and other devices that can be used to copy recorded music. The revenue from this fee would then be distributed to recording companies to compensate them for royalties lost due to unauthorized copying of their copyrighted music. As economist Dean Baker of the

Economic Policy Institute argues, this approach has great advantages over prosecuting information "pirates" or adding elaborate mechanisms to disrupt copying: "While there are problems with the system devised by Germany, it should lead to vast economic gains compared to the systems being developed in the United States. The inefficiency associated with the traditional copyright is enormous in the Internet age."

The Internet itself did not result from "free markets" but centralized planning. In the early years of the Cold War, the U.S. Defense Department sought to establish communications networks that might survive a nuclear war. At the time, only the military and large universities had powerful computers, which researchers across the country wanted to use. Networking prevented them from sitting idle. In order to enable different computers to talk to each other, the Defense Department funded the development of communications standards called TCP/IP, adopting them in 1980.

The Defense Department then released the standards for free to the general public. Nobody has to pay to use these technical protocols to send email or post or view web pages. The U.S. government even pushed for the widespread adoption of the freely available TCP/IP standards, instead of alternate versions developed by private European companies that refused to share their inventions. The Web has grown so quickly and become such a rich and varied source of information largely because these open standards make it accessible to anyone with a computer and a modem.

Even outside of government, some of the fastest-growing parts of the "New Economy" have flourished by making technologies freely available. The most important email transport software (Sendmail), the most important internet server software (Apache), the most widely used programming language on the Web (Perl), the domain-name service for the entire Internet (BIND), and the fastest-growing computer operating system (Linux) are all examples of public domain (or "open-source") software.

Linux is the best known of these "open-source" products. Linus Torvalds, a Finnish computer-science student, invented the new computer operating system in 1991, based on the existing strengths of the UNIX system. But instead of applying for a patent, he posted the code on the Internet for other programmers to add to and improve. Many programmers were interested in the Linux project because UNIX had just been taken over by private firms like IBM. These companies kept their underlying code secret and designed their programs to lock users into their products. Programmers were also worried about the growing dominance of Microsoft's clumsy operating systems. By 1998, over 10,000 software developers from 31 different countries had contributed improvements or helped develop new versions of Linux. By the year 2000, the program boasted about 16 million users and a quarter of the market share. Major high-tech firms, like Intel, Oracle, Dell, Hewlett-Packard, IBM, and Compaq, have all made major commitments to use Linux or cater to Linux users.

A conventional argument for private ownership is that owners have greater incentive to produce things. People are more willing to cultivate a garden on a piece of ground they can fence off, more willing to improve a house when they own it, and more willing to work hard in a business if they share in the profits. But intellectual products can be shared with others without diminishing their value. In fact, computer programs and other information technology are often more valuable when many other people also have them. Many users, for example, do not buy Microsoft Word because they think it is the best word-processing program, but because they know others use the program and will be able to read their files. Likewise, Linux and similar "open-source" projects work so well because they have large numbers of users who identify glitches and devise improvements. They can expect that future versions of the operating system will include not only their contributions but also those of thousands of other contributors. Online communities of programmers voluntarily contribute their efforts to building better software because the product remains in the public domain.

Allowing others to reproduce a computer program does not take anything away from the owner. It merely refuses to help the owner get rich from artificially enforced scarcity. As Wired magazine puts it, "The central economic distinction between information and physical property is that information can be transferred without leaving the possession of the original owner. If I sell you my horse, I can't ride him after that. If I sell you what I know, we both know it." This feature of information goods might make redistribution from property owners to the public more politically appealing in the "New Economy" than in the "Old Economy." Seizing somebody's land or factory to help the poor deprives the old owners of what was theirs. Not so with computer software or digital audio files.

Myth #2: The "networked" economy favors spontaneous and flexible markets over slow-footed regulators.

To many free-marketeers, the Internet is like heaven on earth. It seems to exhibit all the ideal qualities of markets: decentralized, instantaneous, unregulated. The wild growth of online trading (at sites like E*Trade and Ameritrade) and auction sites (like eBay) seems to prove some kind of affinity between "free markets" and the digital age. A recent article in the *Wall Street Journal* urges us to "Think of the Internet as an economic-freedom metaphor for our time. The Internet empowers ordinary people and disempowers government."

While it is true that the 1990s saw a rollback in government regulation at the same time as a rapid growth of information technology, the new technology did not cause the tilt towards "free-market" capitalism. Businesses have certainly implemented new technologies in ways that make certain kinds of regulation more difficult. And politicians have often used the "New Economy" as a pretense for opposing social programs or regulatory policies. But these are ultimately political issues. New information technologies did not require the deregulation associated with the "New Economy," and a changing political tide could reverse the ways those technologies have been implemented.

As with all markets, the results of electronic production and commerce depend on what rules govern businesses: what businesses can own, what privileges and responsibilities come with ownership, what kinds of contracts are legally binding, how they will be taxed, etc. This institutional "architecture" of markets is especially important in information technologies.

Unlike traditional markets, whose rules have evolved over hundreds of years, the online architecture is new enough that we can see how it results from specific policies of governments and corporations. Such thinking challenges the notion that market outcomes are "spontaneous" at all.

People in power can use architecture to control the behavior of others, designing environments to encourage certain kinds of actions while discouraging others. If a local government wants to discourage motorists from driving fast down a street, one way is to legislate a speed limit and have police chase down cars that drive too fast. But another way is through the architecture of a speed bump, which changes behavior more automatically, without obvious laws or games of cat and mouse. Architecture can also be used to change behavior in more insidious ways. In the wake of late-1960s campus protests, for example, universities redesigned campuses with fewer open common areas, in order to discourage student demonstrations.

Just as the architecture of buildings manipulates the laws of physics to human ends, so does the architecture of cyberspace constrain online interactions to serve the ends of those who design or control it. America Online (AOL), for example, limits the number of people who can join one of its chat rooms to 23. The AOL rule can't even be broken in protest because the prohibition is enforced automatically by the software code itself. Attempts to be the 24th participant in the conversation are just met with an error message.

As Internet traffic moves increasingly from phone lines into the control of cable-TV companies, these companies will try to exert even greater control over the traffic they carry. Already some cable companies have tried to prevent Internet users from using "streaming video," which competes with the companies' own pay-per-view channels. Internet companies like Yahoo, which provide "portals" for reaching other websites, already steer people towards businesses that pay to have "banner" ads linking to their sites or to get top billing when people use a search engine. The logical next step is for media conglomerates to use their cable companies to make it faster and easier to reach their product content, to view trailers for their movies, and perhaps to charge users extra for any time spent out of their universe of "infotainment." The trend gives more power to large media conglomerates. The majority of Internet traffic has already been gobbled up by corporations like AOL Time Warner (which owns CNN.com) and Disney (which owns ESPN.com).

Stanford law professor Lawrence Lessig points out, however, that "the changes that make [Internet] commerce possible are also changes that will make regulation easy." For instance, business continues to struggle with how to authenticate who is logging on, and if they really are who they say. E-business has long favored a system of digital certificates that could authenticate a user's identity when surfing the web. Such a system could pose serious dangers—to reduce users' privacy or even threaten their civil liberties. But it could also mean greater abilities to implement public regulations. For example, states do not currently charge state sales tax on purchases made over the internet. Digital certificates could allow states (or even cities) to charge taxes for online purchases to the certificate holder.

Myth #3: As a result of the information revolution, the global economy can no longer be influenced by government.

New information technologies are often seen as having made governments impotent to influence anything on the Net, since web sites can relocate outside the legal jurisdiction of governments that wish to regulate them. The state of Missouri can make it illegal to host a gambling or pornography site from a computer within the state, but it can't stop people from logging onto such a site launched from another state or country. The Amazon.com site based in Germany may comply with that country's laws by refusing to carry Nazi literature, but cyber-Nazis in Germany can order Hitler's *Mein Kampf* from Amazon.com sites hosted in the United States or other countries.

But electronic finance is different. When a bank wires money, it relies on a centralized infrastructure guaranteed by governments to make sure that money is subtracted from one account and added to another. A system of mutual recognition and settlement between powerful institutions like central banks confirms that the person transferring the money actually has those funds and is not simultaneously promising them to banks all over the world. Globalized money will, for this reason, never fully conform to the libertarian fantasy. The same infrastructure that makes it possible to send money electronically across borders also makes it technically possible to restrict and tax these transfers.

Governments have done just that for over a century. It has been possible to wire funds more or less instantaneously since the invention of the telegraph. Even today, most capital transfers are communicated through faxes or telex machines and authenticated with pen-and-ink signatures. Today's system of capital transfers, however, has become centralized through national central banks. This system already assigns a unique identifying number to each capital transfer. Far from making regulation unfeasible, the more these finance systems are digital and networked, the more viable regulation will become.

A system of capital controls would make it possible to stop international money laundering, which the IMF estimates drains away 2–5% of the world's income, and to squelch corruption—especially in poorer countries where warlords or kleptocrats steal essential investment funds. A tiny transaction fee of the kind charged by the Securities and Exchange Commission (SEC) in the United States could discourage market volatility caused by trigger-happy investors seeking tiny profit margins on huge currency transactions. More ambitiously, a levy of one penny on every million dollars in international financial transfers would not discourage any productive investment, but would raise more money than the UN estimates is required to provide for basic health, nutrition, education, and water sanitation to the 1.3 billion people on the planet who live without.

Creating an international architecture of capital controls would not be easy. The big U.S. banks might be particularly resistant to capital controls. U.S. banks receive large quantities of international money partially due to the United States' weak laws on disclosure and taxation of foreign funds. Foreign investors, unlike U.S. citizens or residents, pay no tax on interest or capital gains and do not have to disclose the sources of their earnings to the IRS.

Just as the Great Depression made the federal government establish the agencies that regulate domestic finance (the SEC, the Federal Deposit Insurance Corporation, etc.), the September 11 destruction has brought more attention to the need for regulation of international finance. Some commentators have called for greater international scrutiny of secretive Saudi banks, the likely conduits of terrorist funds. Legislation signed into law in October 2001 bars U.S. banks, which often do business with overseas "paper" corporations, from dealing with a foreign bank unless the latter has a physical existence somewhere with at least one employee. The Treasury Department can now require banks to monitor accounts formally held by overseas banks, especially to determine who is the real owner of the account.

So far, it is not clear that these few, halting steps will lead to real change, but new wisdom has a way of gaining momentum as new practices become more common. Once a capital control system got under way, banks might find it to be in their interests to comply with regulations on international transactions, or face exclusion from the centralized payment systems that make this lucrative business possible. Who knows? They might even reassure their stockholders that, after all, information technology makes it inevitable.

Whatever the future of the Internet may bring, the way markets will operate in cyberspace will not result from some inexorable logic of technology itself. The logic of the Net will depend on the architecture built there—and who has the power to build it.

Thanks to Alexandra Samuelson for her useful input and suggestions on this article.

THE NEW OLD WALL STREET SETTLEMENT
Ten reasons the Wall Street fix is a farce
Nomi Prins
July/August 2003

You may have experienced a sense of déjà vu soaking in the media fanfare surrounding the recent Wall Street settlement, a $1.4 billion wrist-slap levied on the investment banking industry in the name of reform. That's because the headlines that accompanied the finalization of the "global" agreement were recycled versions of the ones that came out in December 2002, when the settlement was first publicized.

On April 28, the Securities and Exchange Commission (SEC), the New York Stock Exchange (NYSE), the National Association of Securities Dealers (NASD), and New York State Attorney General Eliot Spitzer settled "enforcement actions" with 10 top Wall Street banks and two star 1990s research analysts. The banks—including Citigroup-Salomon Brothers, JPM Chase, Goldman Sachs, Merrill Lynch, and Morgan Stanley—were charged with deliberately misleading investors with biased stock research that exaggerated the virtues of key client corporations.

The process leading up to the settlement started two years ago when Spitzer's office began investigating conflicts of interest on Wall Street. In April 2002, regulators at the SEC hopped on board with a joint investigation into the "undue influence of investment banking interest on securities research at brokerage firms."

The settlement makes three main changes to banking practices. First, it will insulate (or "firewall") research analysts from the influence of investment bankers by demanding that analyst pay be set with no input from the investment-banking department. Second, it requires that investment banks and brokerage firms provide independent research purchased from external sources to their clients (but only for the next five years—not exactly a permanent fix) and it makes analyst opinions public 90 days after they have been issued privately. Third, it bans firms from practicing hot IPO "spinning," or doling out initial public offering stock to the senior executives of client companies.

According to Spitzer's statement, the settlement "implements far-reaching reforms that will radically change behavior on Wall Street." But nothing in the settlement poses a serious threat to the status quo.

It's quite telling that no Wall Street firm has complained about the settlement. That's because it doesn't impact how they do business.

Here are the top 10 reasons this settlement is a smokescreen:

1. The fines are tiny. If you remove the $513 million thrown in for spurious investor research and education activities—banks will distribute research from independent firms that they select—you're left with less than a billion bucks in fines. Putting that into perspective, the top 10 Wall Street firms made $62 billion in fees alone over the four years in which their activities are in question. The fines amount to just 1.5% of fee revenue. And that's not to mention the $1 trillion in other revenues these banks garnered over the same period. The settlement fines are so miniscule they are unlikely to deter future wrongdoing.

2. Individual investors will see little of the settlement money. Spurred by class-action lawyers, Spitzer et al. established 10 different distribution funds for customers whose claims are "deemed appropriate" by the federal court at some future date. About $387.5 million of the $1.4 billion will go to the funds. But with thousands misled by brokers (brokers, not

just analysts), it will take years to divvy up that cash.

3. It is not a global settlement even though it was spun as such. It's a U.S. settlement, and about as global as the World Series. Even the original 2002 SEC press release put the word "global" in quotes. Though most of the named firms are international, their practices outside the United States don't fall under SEC jurisdiction. And foreigners who bought stock under misleading information won't receive compensation.

4. No bank admitted any wrongdoing. This is, unfortunately and consistently, par for the course with all SEC corporate corruption settlements. There is never an admission of any culpability.

5. Acting contrite is no substitute for being held to account. And banks are not even managing to act contrite. At an investor conference held days after the settlement announcement, the *New York Times* reported Morgan Stanley CEO Philip Purcell saying, "I don't see anything in the settlement that will concern the retail investor about Morgan Stanley. Not one thing." (He's right, but that's because the settlement doesn't say anything meaningful at all, not because Morgan Stanley was above the fray.) SEC chairman William Donaldson shot off an irate response, concerned that those remarks were "evidence [of] a troubling lack of contrition." It is totally hypocritical for Donaldson to accuse Purcell of not acting sorrier. If that's the best our new SEC head can do, we're in trouble. Plus, back to #4, why should he be sorry if he didn't admit any wrongdoing to begin with?

6. The hardship of being prohibited from spinning hot IPOs, in a dead stock market environment when nothing's hot anyway, is a non-starter. There is no such thing as a hot IPO right now. And, when IPOs become hot again, there are myriad simple ways to get around the ban. Just wait and see. As a ban, this IPO ruling is as robust as, well, a Wall Street firewall.

7. The increased insulation, or "firewalls," mandated by the settlement— like prohibiting investment bankers and analysts from joint business trips with clients or ensuring a few extra lawyers are present at potentially questionable internal meetings—are cosmetic changes.

Many top analysts are now switching to jobs as investment bankers or salespeople. As a result, they'll be able to say anything to customers, anyway. It just won't be called research. Wall Street firms are not about to physically relocate their analyst staffs to separate buildings. (And even that wouldn't be sufficient.) If you're on the same e-mail system, share the same limos home and get your food from the same cafeteria, you're connected.

8. This settlement does nothing to change the deeply institutionalized in-

centive systems (and cultures) within financial firms. As a managing director at one of the fine-paying firms put it, "Hey, it's not like junior analysts in training are now being told they'll get penalized for bringing in deals." Without a deeper revision of the system, there will always be someone at a high level who will find ways to ensure someone lower doesn't publicize negative views on a company with whom the firm is about to do a large deal.

9. The settlement scapegoats analysts while leaving senior executives and investment bankers unscathed. The central problem with Wall Street and conflicts of interest is not former Citigroup-Salomon Brothers' star telecom analyst, Jack Grubman, and is even less Merrill Lynch's Internet analyst Henry Blodget (paying $15 million and $4 million in fines respectively). These people were tools who played their roles in the whole system exceedingly well, while the media promulgated their cheerleading.

The settlement criminalizes analysts for extolling the virtues of their top client corporations, but does nothing to reform the more troublesome—and clandestine—behavior of senior executives and investment bankers who created the deals and issued the stock that analysts were paid to market.

Instead of penalizing analysts who don't even close investment-banking deals, the priority should be to pry apart and isolate corporate executives and investment bankers, and their corporate customers, starting at the top—with the board. Citigroup CEO Sandy Weill was on AT&T's board when Citigroup-Salomon's chief telecom analyst Grubman inflated AT&T's rating. AT&T CEO Michael Armstrong was also on Citigroup's board at the time (and still is). E-mails uncovered by Spitzer suggest that Weill had asked Grubman to upgrade AT&T's rating as a personal favor. Grubman upped AT&T's rating just before Citigroup bagged the deal to do an IPO for AT&T's wireless division. Citigroup reaped profits from doing and distributing the AT&T IPO, all the while duping investors.

Yet while Grubman was banned from ever working as an analyst again, and has to pay a multimillion dollar fine, Weill remains at Citigroup's helm, his wallet untouched by the settlement.

10. There has been no mention of bringing back the Glass-Steagall Act, which prohibited commercial banks from owning brokerages. The repeal of Glass-Steagall in November 1999 unleashed a spate of bank mergers that resulted in many firms combining investment, broker activities, and commercial banking under the same roof.

The New Deal-era act was passed in 1933 to resolve the rampant conflicts of interest and fraud in the 1920s that led to the 1929 crash. Though hacked at for years since, Glass-Steagall was the one piece of legislation that kept the same banks that merged companies, issued debt, and created stock IPOs from touting them to the public via retail brokerage arms and commercial bank accounts.

Real reform would reinstitute strong, Glass-Steagall-type separation between investment and commercial banking activities. And it would regulate conflicted senior investment banking and corporate relationships. Key to any real reform would be regulation of the widespread practice of loan-tying, or giving cheap credit to corporate clients in exchange for profitable banking business (like IPOs and mergers). Loan-tying is a prac-

---

Investment Banking Glossary

Firewall is a non-legal delineation between investment banking and brokerage activities (respectively the creation and the distribution of securities).

Brokers, or salespeople, facilitate the buying and selling of securities for investors. In that capacity, they work on the public side of the firewall. SEC laws dictate that they advise investors based on their specific needs and financial situation. But, often brokers get paid a higher commission to sell the securities their banks want sold.

Analysts study individual companies, often specializing in a particular industry, and make buy and sell recommendations. Investors may rely on these recommendations to make investment decisions. Analysts can act on both sides of the firewall but are not supposed to let their different roles collide. (The recent spate of scandals proved this to be an impossibility.) On the "public" side, they worked with brokers explaining the merits (but rarely drawbacks) of a stock being recommended to a customer. On the other side of the firewall, analysts worked with investment bankers. They met with corporations about to issue new stock or bonds, or merge or acquire other corporations, to glean information that could be used in the subsequent marketing of new deals or newly created securities. This is referred to as the "private" side of the wall, because all conversations take place in a "planning" stage, before the general public is made aware of the deals. The settlement will supposedly prohibit analysts from performing both private and public roles, except in the presence of intermediaries, like lawyers or compliance officers.

Investment Bankers may be lower down in the firm's hierarchy than the senior executives, but senior bankers are still quite powerful. They create the terms, nature, and timing of the deals between banks and corporations, thus facilitating mergers, acquisitions, or corporate restructurings. They also arrange underwriting agreements for corporations issuing securities. Investment bankers worked closely with stock analysts like Jack Grubman to ensure that when a deal got off the ground, there was enough positive publicity on the public side of the firewall—with the investor base—to ensure the highest degree of profit back to the corporation, and fees to the bank.

Senior Executives (like the CEO, CFO, or President) run the banks or large divisions within them. They are thus in the position of deciding which client firms receive favored status or service. Senior executives escaped the recent period of scandals, untarnished.

tice made easier by Glass-Steagall repeal. Citigroup became the largest issuer of Ford debt after Citigroup director and former Treasury secretary Robert Rubin joined Ford's board of directors. Because of Rubin's relationship with Ford, Citigroup gave the company preferential terms, offering to issue debt (in the form of bonds) for Ford more cheaply than other banks would. The net result was that Ford issued more debt because it was so cheap. Yet, under all that debt weight, Ford's stock price and ratings plummeted this past year, taking along jobs and pensions with them.

Of course, there's a good reason points eight, nine, and ten haven't been brought to light—they are remedies that would actually make a difference.

SUPREMES LIMIT PUNITIVE DAMAGES

In a little noticed ruling, the Supreme Court curbed juries' ability to punish corporate misdeeds.

Jamie Court
March/April 2004

Punitive damages are designed to punish wrongdoers for intentional malicious conduct. Awarded over and above compensatory damages, they're meant to teach a defendant a lesson and deter others from similar behavior.

Traditionally, punitive damages have served as juries' big stick against those corporations that place human life and safety at risk in pursuit of profits. But juries no longer wield much of a stick. In a widely overlooked decision, the U.S. Supreme Court recently reversed the long-standing practice of allowing juries to make independent decisions about how to punish corporate wrongdoing. The ruling will have far-reaching repercussions and may fundamentally shift the balance of power between individuals and corporations in society.

In Campbell v. State Farm (2003), the court overturned $145 million in punitive damages against the insurance giant. It ruled, 6-to-3, that punitive damages must be proportionate to the actual losses suffered by individual plaintiffs. The court did not set an outright cap on such damages, but noted that a ratio of more than 4-to-1 "might be close to the line of constitutional impropriety." In other words, if a wrongful injury or death results in lost wages and other losses totaling $500,000, then, under this ruling, punitive damages should not generally exceed $2 million.

In the past, juries have been free to consider how much profit a corporate defendant had made at the cost of human life and suffering. Some juries chose to correlate punitive damage awards to the size of the defendant's ill-gotten gains, and in doing so taught corporations important lessons.

- In 1999, a Los Angeles jury issued the biggest punitive damage verdict ever—$4 billion—against General Motors (GM). The plaintiffs had been trapped and burned when their automobile gas tanks exploded. In court it was revealed that GM had chosen not to warn the public about the gas-line defect because it judged it would be cheaper to pay out individual lawsuits than to recall the defective automobiles. Central to the case was an internal company memo by a GM engineer who calculated that the automaker would have to pay $2.40 per car in lawsuits, as compared to $8.59 per car to fix the problem. The victims' lawyers argued that installing a safer fuel system would have prevented 300 to 500 injuries each year.

- The Dalkon Shield IUD, a birth control device used during the 1970s, had a tendency to trap bacteria in the uterus—causing infections, spontaneous abortions, infertility and death. Despite receiving dozens of reports of spontaneous abortions, the manufacturer, A.H. Robbins Co., defended the product, and continued to do so even after the Food and Drug Administration banned the device in June 1974. Only after it incurred 11 punitive damage awards in the 1980s, totaling more than $24.8 million, did the corporation urge doctors and women to remove the device.

Product liability lawsuits like these, in which individuals recover damages against corporations for dangerous and defective products, are the legal cases that most commonly result in punitive damages. And they work: the suits change corporate decision making about product safety. A major 1987 Conference Board study of 232 risk managers at large American corporations found:

> Where product liability has had a notable impact—where it has most significantly affected management decision-making—has been in the quality of the products themselves. Managers say products have become safer, manufacturing procedures have been improved, and labels and use instructions have become more explicit.

Corporations are driven by the bottom line. The stick that deters them the best is the one that can hurt them the most: costly monetary damages. Under this new ruling, not only will punitive damages do less damage to a corporation's bottom line, but big business will be better able to anticipate the size of potential damages and treat them as a predictable cost of doing business.

The jury foreman in the GM case, Coleman Thorton, noted: "GM has no regard for the people in their cars, and they should be held responsible for it." Yet with the U.S. Supreme Court's new verdict, corporations that knowingly decide to maim or kill can rest assured they'll likely keep most of the profits they reap. Juries will no longer have the power to do what the jury in the GM case successfully did—punish a corporate defendant in a way that ensures it truly pays a price for its crimes.

Who's Behind the Attack on Consumers' Legal Rights?

Large corporations have invested heavily in a coordinated 25-year effort by right-wing think tanks, publishing houses, law firms, scholars, politicians, and public relations specialists to convince the public that lawsuits are injuring society. This "tort reform" movement is largely a corporate-led public-relations offensive. Its proponents portray the corporation as having humanlike frailties and sensitivities and argue that big business must be protected from the "litigation explosion," as if individuals' rights—including the right to sue and collect punitive damages—are illegitimate and dangerous. Because a major goal of tort reform is to restrict jury control over damages, last spring's Supreme Court ruling was quietly celebrated by the corporate interests underwriting this "movement."

A key force behind the attack on consumers' legal rights is a national anti-litigation network called "Citizens Against Lawsuit Abuse" (CALA). The Center for Justice & Democracy and Public Citizen issued a report in 2000 about CALA's corporate financing. It found "the money trail from many of these groups leads directly to large corporate donors, including tobacco, insurance, oil and gas, chemical and pharmaceutical companies, medical associations and auto manufacturers." Since the mid-1990s, CALA has been working with local business associations to "to ensure the election of pro-industry state judges and to ensure the defeat of judges who typically support plaintiffs' verdicts or have voted to strike down state tort law restrictions as unconstitutional." As governor of Texas, George W. Bush was one of Texas CALA's biggest boosters. (For more information, see "The CALA Files: The Secret Campaign by Big Tobacco and Other Major Industries to Take Away Your Rights," November 2000; <www.citizen.org>.)

Corporate defense attorney Phillip K. Howard is another key figure in the tort reform effort. In 2002 he formed an organization called "Common Good" to "overhaul America's lawsuit culture." The group calls the legal system "a tool for extortion," claiming that "anyone can sue for almost anything." Howard has written two books on this theory, gives regular speeches, and is now on a radio tour. His law firm, Covington & Burling, has routinely and vigorously defended a "Who's Who" of America's largest corporations, from pharmaceutical giants to the tobacco industry. The firm has funneled millions of tobacco dollars into tort reform groups. Covington & Burling has also sought to limit attorneys' contingency fees, which would rob many people of their only access to legal representation. (For more, see "The Truth About Common Good and Phillip K. Howard" at <www.consumerwatchdog.org/corporate>.)

Yet "despite all the rhetoric about litigiousness, empirical research shows that Americans are not all that litigious," according to Deborah R. Hensler, director of the Rand Institute for Civil Justice. The institute conducted a comprehensive study of injured people in the 1980s that found only 2% sought recovery through lawsuits.

The legal system is far from perfect. Litigation can be time-consuming, expensive, and ineffective. Still, the judicial branch is the only branch of government where individuals can directly confront and punish corporate misconduct. Corporations have bought off the legislative branch and funded presidential campaigns, but they can't buy juries—which is precisely why the tort reform movement is so intent on tying juries' hands.

DEREGULATION OBSESSION

Past deregulation has made a mess of the telecommunications industry. What does the
Wall Street Journal think further deregulation will accomplish?

Nomi Prins
May/June 2004

Broadband Fiasco

Local phone carriers are once again challenging the FCC's "unbundling" requirements, which force them to lease the use of their networks to rivals at below-market rates. Consequently, the regional Bells have been slow to upgrade to fiber. Their big concern is not getting a fair return on investment if a state regulator, rather than the market, gets to set the prices they can charge.... After leading the technology boom in the 1990s, the U.S. now ranks 11th world-wide in high-speed Internet use per capita, behind the likes of Germany, Canada—even Italy.... The telecom industry has lost in excess of half a million jobs since 2001, and market capitalization is down $2 trillion from its peak in the late 1990s. We don't for a moment lay all this to [FCC Chairman Michael] Powell, who ... has tried mightily to deregulate the market. Mr. Powell actually opposed the FCC rules.... But thanks to a lack of White House leadership, ... the Bush Administration has ended up enforcing what is essentially Al Gore's telecom policy.

—The *Wall Street Journal*, Feb. 11, 2004

The *Wall Street Journal's* editors got their way. On March 2, the D.C. Circuit Court of Appeals voted to uphold Powell's proposal (voted down by the FCC last year 3-2) to remove the requirement that states set and regulate lease rates for the use of Bell phone lines by competing phone companies like AT&T and MCI. The court also ruled that the Bells do not have to lease their new fiber-optic lines to competing high-speed Internet providers.

Despite all evidence to the contrary, the Journal's editors still view telecom deregulation as a Holy Grail that will pour forth the benefits of robust competition. Somehow, the resulting field of goliath players will entice smaller players into the telecom game. Then, all the scrawny geeks in the playground will rise up and beat the bullies into submission. It's a beautiful concept. Too bad corporate America doesn't work that way.

In reality, the fallout from deregulation is nearly always more consolidation, not more competition. And in no sector is this more apparent than in telecommunications, where a small set of mega-carriers has come to dominate the industry's landscape.

The 1996 Telecommunications Act forced the local phone companies, at the time the seven Baby Bells plus GTE, to open their lines to competing telecom providers. The idea was that competitors would enter the market and provide services over those lines at lower rates to consumers. (Competitors would have to pay a fee to the Bells to use their lines.) In return, the Baby Bells could apply for long distance licenses to augment their local business.

But, in practice, the Bells still made it hard for competitors to get involved, and true competition in local phone service barely happened. Instead, the four remaining, consolidated Baby Bells (Verizon, SBC, BellSouth, and Qwest) trounced their rivals and muscled into long distance and wireless networks. Now the Baby Bells want to monopolize high-speed broadband Internet access as well, by completely restricting the use of their new fiber-optic networks to keep competitors out of that business.

Broadband Access

The *Journal's* editors complain that the United States ranks a mere 11th worldwide in high-speed Internet use per capita because other governments have deregulated more. This is just false. "The real reason is that the Bells don't want to spend money on installing 'last mile' connectivity to potential users," according to Om Malik, author of Broadbandits. (The term "last mile" refers to the connection from the fiber-optic network to the homes or workplaces of end users.)

Additionally, foreign governments hold significant ownership stakes in their once- nationalized telecoms. France Telecom is 56% government owned; Deutsche Telekom, 43%. The South Korean government subsidized broadband service, a fact the Journal editors neglect to mention when citing the country's 78% rate of home broadband usage. In the United States, not only is there no federal ownership of phone companies, there is no policy or subsidy ensuring that consumers can get a high-speed Internet connection regardless of geographic locale or proximity to central hubs. The Bells just don't consider it profitable to build last-mile infrastructure outside of upscale urban areas with dense clusters of potential broadband customers. As a result, the industry has neglected poor and rural communities—"electronic redlining."

The Big Eat the Small

The *Journal* supports FCC Chairman Michael Powell's wish to close entry to the Bell networks, both the old copper phone networks as well as the new fiber ones. It contends further deregulation would usher in a "flourishing telecom sector" which would play an important role in "reviving the economy." Evidently, too much regulation caused private investment in broadband to dwindle. Not, say, the fact that the sector vaporized trillions of dollars of capital in just a few years—think WorldCom and Global Crossing. Or the fact that a glut of fiber was created during the late 1990s without the companion creation of last-mile connectivity.

The *Journal's* editors believe that restricting competitors' use of broadband networks will magically create cheap service for all. This is ludicrous. Big telecom companies already control capital, legislators, and regulators. The sector is second only to finance in political contributions. Small competitors either get bought out, depleted financially, or shut out of a game that's stacked against them.

If the Appeals Court's decision stands, the Bells will be able to keep competition out of their broadband business. The result will be closed and content-controlled networks, higher rates, and less incentive to upgrade services for captive customers. Once fully in control of the networks, these firms will be able to control who provides content via those networks by negotiating deals with select content providers. ("Imagine a situation where typing www.amazon.com directs you to Barnes & Noble's website instead because it's affiliated with the broadband provider," warns Chris Murray of Consumers Union.) Also, the more consumer market share these firms have in the absence of any rate regulation, the more they'll charge consumers. This is what happened with cable TV companies, whose unregulated rates have increased 45% since 1996.

Instead of spending time protecting the public from the sight of Janet Jackson's nipples, Congress and the FCC should design a system that provides all citizens low-cost broadband access. To do so, they need to maintain open entry to the Baby Bells' lines—just the opposite of what the Journal suggests—regulate consumer broadband costs, and force the Bells to invest in last-mile infrastructure. If the goals are competition, innovation, and efficient distribution of services and costs, we need more regulation protecting Internet access, not less. We need a guaranteed, universally open network, like highways and postal routes. It was, after all, the government that originally subsidized the Internet's creation. It wasn't a corporate gift.

Chapter 7

RHETORIC AND REALITY OF "GLOBALIZATION"

HOW HAS NAFTA AFFECTED TRADE AND EMPLOYMENT?
Ellen Frank
January/February 2003

Dear Dr. Dollar:

Free-traders claim that free trade will increase U.S. exports, providing more jobs for Americans. So I would expect that NAFTA increased U.S. exports and reduced our trade deficit. I would also expect to see employment increase both in our country and in our trading partners. Has that in fact happened?
—Lane Smith, Ronkonkoma, New York

Since the North American Free Trade Agreement (NAFTA) between the United States, Mexico, and Canada went into effect, trade within North America has increased dramatically. Exports from the United States to Mexico have risen 150% and exports to Canada are up 66%. This much is beyond dispute.

NAFTA's effects on employment, on the other hand, are hotly debated. Clinton administration officials estimated in the late 1990s that expanded trade in North America had created over 300,000 new U.S. jobs. Economic Policy Institute (EPI) economists Robert Scott and Jesse Rothstein contend, however, that such claims amount to "trying to balance a checkbook by counting the deposits and not the withdrawals."

This is because NAFTA and other trade agreements have also increased U.S. imports from Canada and Mexico—and by quite a lot more than exports. Since 1993, America's trade deficit with its North American trading partners (exports minus imports) has ballooned from $16 billion to $82 billion annually. As Scott points out, "increases in U.S. exports create jobs in this country, but increases in imports destroy jobs because the imports displace goods that otherwise would have been made in the U.S. by domestic workers."

Employment in virtually all U.S. manufacturing industries has declined since NAFTA went into effect. Counting jobs that actually left the United States plus those that would have been created if not for rising imports, EPI estimates that NAFTA caused a net loss of 440,000 U.S. jobs. In fact, during the 1990s, the overall U.S. trade deficit quadrupled, resulting in a net loss of 3 million jobs, according to EPI president Jeff Faux.

Of course, in a large and complex economy, trade is only one of many factors that affect job creation, and its influence is difficult to isolate. As trade expanded during the 1990s, for example, the United States also experienced an investment boom that created jobs faster than rising imports destroyed them; overall, the number of jobs in the United States has risen by 28 million since 1994.

Any free-trade booster worth her lobbying fees would argue that the boom itself resulted from liberalized trade. Lower trade and investment barriers, the story goes, unleash entrepreneurial talents, spurring innovation and productivity gains. Old jobs lost are offset by new jobs gained, and falling wages by cheaper prices on imported goods. Moreover, free-traders contend, any reckoning of NAFTA's impact should tote up new jobs and factories in Mexico against shuttered plants in the United States.

So what about NAFTA's effect on Mexico? In a study for the Interhemispheric Resource Center, analysts Timothy Wise and Kevin Gallagher conclude that NAFTA has given Mexico "trade without development." Since NAFTA weakened barriers to U.S. investment in Mexico, foreign investment into the country tripled and exports grew rapidly. But the development promised by free-trade advocates never materialized. Mexican employment did grow during the early years of NAFTA, but in recent years, it has declined as mobile manufacturers have sought even cheaper labor in Asia. Mexican manufacturing wages fell 21% during the 1990s and poverty worsened.

Wise's and Gallagher's findings echo the conclusions of Harvard development specialist Dani Rodrik. Poor countries that turn to trade as a cure for poverty find themselves ensnared in the "mercantilist fallacy": they can't all export their way to riches, since one country's exports are another's imports. Someone has to buy all this stuff. The United States, with its annual trade deficit approaching $500 billion, is the world's buyer and its manufacturing industries suffer as a result. But poor countries don't fare much better. They face increasing competition from low-wage manufacturers in other poor countries, and world markets are now saturated with cheap apparel and electronics, driving prices and wages down.

The result is one thing that almost everybody who studies trade now agrees upon. Whatever else they have wrought—more jobs, fewer jobs, more or less poverty—globalized trade and production coincide with greater inequality both within and between countries. The reasons for this are complex—globalization weakens unions, strengthens multinationals, and increases competition and insecurity all around—but the data are clear. Markets do not distribute wealth equitably.

Sources: Robert Scott and Jesse Rothstein, "NAFTA and the States: Job Destruction is Widespread," <www.epinet. org>; Jeff Faux, "Why U.S. Manufacturing Needs a 'Strategic Pause in Trade Policy,'" Testimony before the Senate Committee on Commerce, *Sciences and Transportation*, June 21, 2001; Timothy Wise and Kevin Gallagher, "NAFTA: A Cautionary Tale," FPIF Global Affairs Commentary, 2002; Dani Rodrik, *The New Global Economy and Developing Countries: Making Openness Work* (Overseas Development Council, 1999).

OFFSHORING BY THE NUMBERS

New numbers suggest that offshoring accounts for a very small percentage of jobs lost to mass layoffs.

Angel Chen and Adria Scharf
July/August 2004

Offshoring has attracted a lot of attention lately from the presidential candidates, the media, economists, and workers. From all the talk, you'd think that offshoring represents the single largest threat to U.S. jobs. But according to new Bureau of Labor Statistics (BLS) data, a small fraction—just 2.5%—of jobs lost to mass layoffs in a recent period involved the relocation of work overseas.

The Department of Labor's BLS only began tracking overseas relocation of work in January and included the statistics for the first time in a quarterly report on layoffs released in June. Of the 182,456 private-sector nonfarm workers who lost their jobs in mass layoffs between January and March of 2004, 4,633 of these job separations (or 2.54% of the total) involved the movement of work from within the United States to locations outside of the country. (These figures exclude layoffs caused by vacation and seasonal factors. See Table 1.) Of the 34 reported cases of mass layoffs in which work was relocated overseas, 62% involved juggling work within companies, while 38% involved shifting work to a different company.

The BLS estimates are minuscule in comparison to other widely cited figures on international outsourcing. For example, Goldman Sachs estimates that about 300,000 to 500,000 jobs were offshored in the last three years, and Cambridge, Mass.-based

TABLE 1: EXTENDED MASS LAYOFFS AND SEPARATIONS, FIRST QUARTER 2004

	Number of Mass Layoff "Events"		Job Separations from Mass Layoffs	
Total in private nonfarm sector, excluding seasonal and vacation events	869		182,456	
Overseas relocations	34	3.9%	4,633	2.5%
Within company	21	2.4%	2,976	1.6%
Different company	13	1.5%	1,657	0.9%

Note: Questions on movement of work were not asked of employers when the reason was either seasonal work or vacation period.

Source: Bureau of Labor Statistics (June 10, 2004).

Forrester Research projects 3.3 million jobs will move abroad by 2015.

Why the disparity? Without question, the BLS figures understate the magnitude of the trend. Because the bureau only tracks layoffs in large companies in which 50 or more people are laid off for more than 30 days, its data do not reflect job losses in small establishments, smaller-scale layoffs, or layoffs in the public sector or agriculture. (According to one study, mass layoffs account for only about one in five layoffs.) Moreover, neither the BLS nor anyone else tracks a major dimension of offshoring: the creation of new jobs abroad that do not directly result in layoffs at home (e.g., when a growing company decides to open its new call center in Mumbai rather than in Cleveland).

In sum, the BLS data capture only part of the offshoring phenomenon. So it would be a mistake to take these figures as an assurance that offshoring fears are overblown. We would do better to join Brian Deese and John Lyman of the Center for American Progress in calling for "much better data" on the subject.

Still, the low percentage of work lost to overseas relocations as a portion of all mass layoffs suggests that other factors are playing far more significant a hand in the job loss picture (See Table 2). As a proportion of total job separations, "company reorganization" and "labor disputes" are the two most significant reasons that em-

TABLE 2: REASON FOR LAYOFF

	Number of Mass Layoff "Events"	Job Separations from Mass Layoffs
Total, private nonfarm	1,204	239,361
Bankruptcy	28	8,422
Business ownership change	31	4.217
Contract cancellation	29	4,238
Contract completed	170	51,795
Environment-related	0	0
Financial difficulty	84	15,755
Import competition	14	1,182
Labor dispute	4	21,293
Natural disaster	0	0
Product line discontinued	8	1,675
Reorganization in company	162	26,982
Seasonal work	332	56,478
Slack work	146	16,999
Vacation period	3	427
Weather-related	15	1,382
Other	56	11,004
Not reported	115	15,656

Note: Data on automation, material shortage, model changeover, and plant or machine repair are omitted because they do not meet BLS or state agency disclosure standards. All data in this table are preliminary.
Source: Bureau of Labor Statistics (June 10, 2004).

ployers cite for issuing mass layoffs, other than seasonal cycles and contract comple-tion—a reminder that ordinary downsizing and the ongoing war on workers merit at least as much attention and concern as the offshoring phenomenon.

Sources: Brian Deese and John Lyman. "The Offshoring Numbers Game," Center for American Progress, June 28, 2004; "Extended Mass Layoffs Associated With Domestic And Overseas Relocations, First Quarter 2004," Bureau of Labor Statistics, June 10, 2004; "Putting Layoffs in Context," Employment Policy Foundation, April 9, 2001.

ASK DR. DOLLAR: PROTECTIONISM
Ellen Frank
July/August 2004

Dear Dr. Dollar:

Supposedly, countries should produce what they are best at. If the United States makes computers and China produces rice, then the theory of free trade says China should trade its rice for computers. But if China puts tariffs on U.S.-made computers and builds up its own computer industry, then it will become best at making them and can buy rice from Vietnam. Isn't it advantageous for poor countries to practice protectionism and become industrial powers themselves, rather than simply producing mono-crop commodities? I'm asking because local alternative currencies like Ithaca Hours benefit local businesses, though they restrict consumers to local goods that may be more expensive than goods from further away.

—Matt Cary, Hollywood, Fla.

The modern theory of free trade argues that countries are "endowed" with certain quantities of labor, capital, and natural resources. A country with lots of labor but little capital should specialize in the production of labor-intensive goods, like hand-woven rugs, hand-sewn garments, or hand-picked fruit. By ramping up production of these goods, a developing country can trade on world markets, earning the foreign exchange to purchase capital-intensive products like computers and cars. Free trade thus permits poor countries (or, to be more precise, their most well-off citizens) to consume high-tech goods that they lack the ability to produce and so obtain higher living standards. "Capital-rich" countries like the United States benefit from relative-ly cheap fruit and garments, freeing up their workforce to focus on high-tech goods. Free trade, according to this story, is a win-win game for everyone.

The flaw in this tale, which you have hit upon exactly, is that being "capital-rich" or "capital-poor" is not a natural phenomenon like having lots of oil. Capital is cre-ated—typically with plenty of government assistance and protection.

Developing countries can create industrial capacity and train their citizens to manufacture high-tech goods. But doing so takes time. Building up the capacity to manufacture computers, for example, at prices that are competitive with firms in developed countries may take several years. To buy this time, a government needs to keep foreign-made computers from flooding its market and undercutting less-established local producers. It also needs to limit inflows of foreign capital. Studies show that when foreign firms set up production facilities in developing countries, they are unlikely to share their latest techniques, so such foreign investment does not typically build local expertise or benefit local entrepreneurs.

The United States and other rich countries employed these protectionist strategies. In the 1800s, American entrepreneurs traveled to England and France to learn the latest manufacturing techniques and freely appropriated designs for cutting-edge industrial equipment. The U.S. government protected its nascent industries with high tariff walls until they could compete with European manufacturers.

After World War II, Japan effectively froze out foreign goods while building up world-class auto, computer, and electronics industries. Korea later followed Japan's strategy; in recent years, so has China. There, "infant industries" are heavily protected by tariffs, quotas, and other trade barriers. Foreign producers are welcome only if they establish high-tech facilities in which Chinese engineers and production workers can garner the most modern skills.

Development economists like Alice Amsden and Dani Rodrik are increasingly reaching the conclusion that carefully designed industrial policies, combined with protections for infant industries, are most effective in promoting internal development in poor countries. "Free-trade" policies, on the other hand, seem to lock poor countries into producing low-tech goods like garments and agricultural commodities, whose prices tend to decline on world markets due to intense competition with other poor countries.

In the contemporary global economy, however, there are three difficulties with implementing a local development strategy. First, some countries have bargained away their right to protect local firms by entering into free-trade agreements. Second, protectionism means that local consumers are denied the benefits of cheap manufactured goods from abroad, at least in the short run.

Finally, in many parts of the world the floodgates of foreign-made goods have already been opened and, with the middle and upper classes enjoying their computers and cell phones, it may be impossible to build the political consensus to close them. This last concern bears on the prospects for local alternative currencies. Since it is impossible to "close off" the local economy, the success of local currencies in bolstering hometown businesses depends on the willingness of local residents to deny themselves the benefits of cheaper nonlocal goods. Like national protectionist polices, local currencies restrict consumer choice.

Ultimately, the success or failure of such ventures rests on the degree of public support for local business. With local currencies, participation is voluntary and attitudes toward local producers often favorable. National protectionist polices, however, entail coerced public participation and generally fail when governments are corrupt and unable to command public support.

DOLLAR ANXIETY
Real Reasons to Worry

The advantages of imperial finance have propped up the U.S. economy—but they may not last.

John Miller
January/February 2005

The value of the dollar is falling. Does that mean that our economic sky is falling as well? Not to sound like Chicken Little, but the answer may well be yes. If an economic collapse is not in our future, then at least economic storm clouds are gathering on the horizon.

It's what lies behind the slide of the dollar that has even many mainstream economists spooked: an unprecedented current account deficit—the difference between the country's income and its consumption and investment spending. The current account deficit, which primarily reflects the huge gap between the amount the United States imports and the amount it exports, is the best indicator of where the country stands in its financial relationship with the rest of the world.

At an estimated $670 billion, or 5.7% of gross domestic product (GDP), the 2004 current account deficit is the largest ever. An already huge trade deficit (the amount exports fall short of imports) made worse by high oil prices, along with rock bottom private savings and a gaping federal budget deficit, have helped push the U.S. current account deficit into uncharted territory. The last time it was above 4% of GDP was in 1816, and no other country has ever run a current account deficit that equals nearly 1% of the world's GDP. If current trends continue, the gap could reach 7.8% of U.S. GDP by 2008, according to Nouriel Roubini of New York University and Brad Setser of University College, Oxford, two well-known finance economists.

Most of the current account deficit stems from the U.S. trade deficit (about $610 billion). The rest reflects the remittances immigrants send home to their families plus U.S. foreign aid (together another $80 billion) less net investment income (a positive $20 billion because the United States still earns more from investments abroad than it pays out in interest on its borrowing from abroad).

The current account deficit represents the amount of money the United States must attract from abroad each year. Money comes from overseas in two ways: foreign investors can buy stock in U.S. corporations, or they can lend money to corporations or to the government by buying bonds. Currently, almost all of the money must come from loans because European and Japanese investors are no longer buying U.S. stocks. U.S. equity returns have been trivial since 2000 in dollar terms and actually negative in euro terms since the dollar has lost ground against the euro.

In essence, the U.S. economy racks up record current account deficits by spending more than its national income to feed its appetite for imports that are now half again exports. That increases the supply of dollars in foreign hands.

At the same time, the demand for dollars has diminished. Foreign investors are less interested in purchasing dollar-dominated assets as they hold more of them (and as the self-fulfilling expectation that the value of the dollar is likely to fall sets in). In October 2004 (the most recent data available), net foreign purchases of U.S. securities—stocks and bonds—dipped to their lowest level in a year and below what was necessary to offset the current account deficit. In addition, global investors' stock and bond portfolios are now overloaded with dollar-denominated assets, up to 50% from 30% in the early '90s.

Under the weight of the massive current account deficit, the dollar has already begun to give way. Since January 2002, the value of the dollar has fallen more than 20%, with much of that dropoff happening since August 2004. The greenback now stands at multiyear lows against the euro, the yen, and an index of major currencies.

Should foreign investors stop buying U.S. securities, then the dollar will crash, stock values plummet, and an economic downturn surely follow. But even if foreigners continue to purchase U.S. bonds—and they already hold 47% of U.S Treasury bonds—a current account deficit of this magnitude will be a costly drag on the economy. The Fed will have to boost interest rates, which determine the rate of return on U.S. bonds, to compensate for their lost value as the dollar slips in value and to keep foreigners coming back for more. In addition, a falling dollar makes imports cost more, pushing up U.S inflation rates. The Fed will either tolerate the uptick in inflation or attempt to counteract it by raising interest rates yet higher. Even in this more orderly scenario of decline, the current expansion will slow or perhaps come to a halt.

Imperial Finance

You can still find those who claim none of this is a problem. Recently, for example, the editors of the *Wall Street Journal* offered worried readers the following relaxation technique—a version of what former Treasury Secretary Larry Summers says is the sharpest argument you typically hear from a finance minister whose country is saddled with a large current account deficit.

First, recall that a large trade deficit requires a large surplus of capital flowing into your country to cover it. Then ask yourself, would you rather live in a country that continues to attract investment, or one that capital is trying to get out of? Finally, remind yourself that the monetary authorities control the value of currencies and are fully capable of halting the decline.

Feel better? You shouldn't. Arguments like these are unconvincing, a bravado borne not of postmodern cool so much as the old-fashioned, unilateral financial imperialism that underlies the muscular U.S. foreign policy we see today.

True, so far foreigners have been happy to purchase the gobs of debt issued by the U.S. Treasury and corporate America to cover the current account deficit. And that has kept U.S. interest rates low. If not for the flood of foreign money, Morgan Stanley economist Stephen Roach figures, U.S. long-term interest rates would be between one and 1.5 percentage points higher today.

The ability to borrow without pushing up interest rates has paid off handsomely for the Bush administration. Now when the government spends more than it takes in to prosecute the war in Iraq and bestow tax cuts on the rich, savers from foreign shores finance those deficits at reduced rates. And cash-strapped U.S. consumers are more ready to swallow an upside-down economic recovery that has pushed up profit but neither created jobs nor lifted wages when they can borrow at low interest rates.

How can the United States get away with running up debt at low rates? Are other countries' central banks and private savers really the co-dependent "global enablers" Roach and others call them, who happily hold loads of low-yielding U.S. assets? The truth is, the United States has taken advantage of the status of the dollar as the currency of the global economy to make others adjust to its spending patterns. Foreign central banks hold their reserves in dollars, and countries are billed in dollars for their oil imports, which requires them to buy dollars. That sustains the demand for the dollar and protects its value even as the current account imbalance widens.

The U.S. strong dollar policy in the face of its yawning current account deficit imposes a "shadow tax" on the rest of the world, at least in part to pay for its cost of empire. "But payment," as Robert Skidelsky, the British biographer of Keynes, reminds us, "is voluntary and depends at minimum on acquiescence in U.S. foreign policy." The geopolitical reason for the rest of the capitalist world to accept the "seignorage of the dollar"—in other words, the advantage the United States enjoys by virtue of minting the reserve currency of the international economy—became less compelling when the United States substituted a "puny war on terrorism" for the Cold War, Skidelsky adds.

The tax does not fall only on other industrialized countries. The U.S. economy has not just become a giant vacuum cleaner that sucks up "all the world's spare investible cash," in the words of University of California, Berkeley economist Brad DeLong, but about one-third of that money comes from the developing world. To put this contribution in perspective: DeLong calculates that $90 billion a year, or one-third of the average U.S. current account deficit over the last two decades, is equal to the income of the poorest 500 million people in India.

The rest of the world ought not to complain about these global imbalances, insist the strong dollar types. That the United States racks up debt while other countries rack up savings is not profligacy but a virtue. The United States, they argue, is the global economy's "consumer of last resort." Others, especially in Europe, according to U.S. policymakers, are guilty of "insufficient consumption": they hold back their economies and dampen the demand for U.S. exports, exacerbating the U.S. current account deficit. Last year U.S. consumers increased their spending three times as quickly as European consumers (excluding Britain), and the U.S. economy grew about two and half times as quickly.

If the United States Was an Emerging Market

If the United States was a small or less-developed country, financial alarm bells would already be ringing. The U.S. current account deficit is well above the 5%-of-GDP standard the IMF and others use to pronounce economies in the developing world vulnerable to financial crisis.

Just how crisis-prone depends on how the current account deficit affects the economy's spending. If the foreign funds flowing into the country are being invested in export-producing sectors of the economy, or the tradable goods sectors, such as manufacturing and some services, they are likely over time to generate revenues necessary to pay back the rest of the world. In that case, the shortfall is less of a problem. If those monies go to consumption or speculative investment in non-tradable (i.e., non-export producing) sectors such as a real estate, then they surely will be a problem.

By that standard, the U.S. current account deficit is highly problematic. Economists assess the impact of a current account deficit by comparing it to the difference between net national investment and net national savings. (Net here means less the money set aside to cover depreciation.) In the U.S. case, that difference has widened because saving has plummeted, not because investment has picked up. Last year, the United States registered its lowest net national savings rate ever, 1.5%, due to the return of large federal budget deficits and anemic personal savings. In addition, U.S. investment has shifted substantially away from tradable goods as manufacturing has come under heavy foreign competition toward the non-traded goods sector, such as residential real estate whose prices have soared in and around most major American cities.

Capital inflows that cover a decline in savings instead of a surge in investment are not a sign of economic health nor cause to stop worrying about the current account deficit.

Global Uprising

Not surprisingly, old Europe and newly industrializing Asia don't see it that way. They have grown weary from all their heavy lifting of U.S. securities. And while they have yet to throw them overboard, a revolt is brewing.

Those cranky French are especially indignant about the unfairness of it all. The editors of Le Monde, the French daily, complain that "The United States considers itself innocent: it refuses to admit that it lives beyond its means through weak savings and excessive consumption." On top of that, the drop of the dollar has led to a brutal rise in the value of the euro that is wiping out the demand for euro-zone exports and slowing their already sluggish economic recoveries.

Even in Blair's Britain the Economist, the newsweekly, ran an unusually tough-minded editorial warning: "The dollar's role as the leading international currency can no longer be taken for granted. ... Imagine if you could write checks that were accepted as payment but never cashed. That is what [the privileged position of the dollar] amounts to. If you had been granted that ability, you might take care to hang to it. America is taking no such care. And may come to regret it."

But the real threat comes from Asia, especially Japan and China, the two largest holders of U.S. Treasury bonds. Asian central banks already hold most of their reserves in dollar-denominated assets, an enormous financial risk given that the value of the dollar will likely continue to fall at current low interest rates.

In late November, just the rumor that China's Central Bank threatened to reduce its purchases of U.S. Treasury bonds was enough to send the dollar tumbling.

No less than Alan Greenspan, chair of the Fed, seems to have come down with a case of dollar anxiety. In his November remarks to the European Banking Community, Greenspan warned of a "diminished appetite for adding to dollar balances" even if the current account deficit stops increasing. Greenspan believes that foreign investors are likely to realize they have put too many of their eggs in the dollar basket and will either unload their dollar-denominated investments or demand higher interest rates. After Greenspan spoke, the dollar fell to its lowest level against the Japanese yen in more than four years.

A Rough Ride From Here

The question that divides economists at this point is not whether the dollar will decline more, but whether the descent will be slow and orderly or quick and panicky. Either way, there is real reason to believe it will be a rough ride.

First, a controlled devaluation of the dollar won't be easy to accomplish. Several major Asian currencies are formally or informally pegged to the dollar, including the Chinese yuan. The United States faces a $160 billion trade deficit with China alone. U.S. financial authorities have exerted tremendous pressure on the Chinese to raise the value of their currency, in the hope of slowing the tide of Chinese imports into the United States and making U.S. exports more competitive. But the Chinese have yet to budge.

Beyond that, a fall in the dollar sufficient to close the current account deficit will slaughter large amounts of capital. The Economist warns that "[i]f the dollar falls by another 30%, as some predict, it would amount to the biggest default in history: not a conventional default on debt service, but default by stealth, wiping trillions off the value of foreigners' dollar assets."

Even a gradual decline in the value of dollar will bring tough economic consequences. Inflation will pick up, as imports cost more in this bid to make U.S. exports cheaper. The Fed will surely raise interest rates to counteract that inflationary pressure, slowing consumer borrowing and investment. Also, closing the current account deficit would require smaller government deficits. (Although not politically likely, repealing Bush's pro-rich tax cuts would help.)

What will happen is anyone's guess given the unprecedented size of the U.S. current account deficit. But there is a real possibility that the dollar's slide will be anything but slow or orderly. Should Asian central banks stop intervening on the scale needed to finance the U.S. deficit, then a crisis surely would follow. The dollar would drop through the floor; U.S. interest rates would skyrocket (on everything from Treasury bonds to mortgages to credit cards); the stock market and home values would collapse; consumer and investment spending would plunge; and a sharp recession would take hold here and abroad.

The Bush administration seems determined to make things worse. Should the Bush crew push through their plan to privatize Social Security and pay the trillion-dollar transition cost with massive borrowing, the consequences could be disastrous. The example of Argentina is instructive. Privatizing the country's retirement program, as economist Paul Krugman has pointed out, was a major source of the debt that brought on Argentina's crisis in 2001. Dismantling the U.S. welfare state's most successful program just might push the dollar-based financial system over the edge.

The U.S. economy is in a precarious situation held together so far by imperial privilege. Its prospects appear to fall into one of three categories: a dollar crisis; a long, slow, excruciating decline in value of the dollar; or a dollar propped up through repeated interest rates hikes. That's real reason to worry.

Sources: "Dollar Anxiety," editorial, *Wall Street Journal*, 11/11/04; D. Wessel, "Behind Big Drop in Currency: U.S. Soaks Up Asia's Output," *WSJ*, 12/2/04; J. B. DeLong, "Should We Still Support Untrammeled International Capital Mobility? Or are Capital Controls Less Evil than We Once Believed," *Economists' Voice*, 2004; R. Skidelsky, "U.S. Current Account Deficit and Future of the World Monetary System" and N. Roubini and B. Setser "The U.S. as A Net Debtor: The Sustainability of the U.S. External Imbalances," 11/04, Nouriel Roubini's Global Macroeconomic and Financial Policy site <www.stern.nyu.edu/globalmacro>; Rich Miller, "Why the Dollar is Giving Way," *Business Week*, 12/6/04; Robert Barro, "Mysteries of the Gaping Current-Account Gap," *Business Week*, 12/13/04; D. Streitford and J. Fleishman, "Greenspan Issues Warning on Dollar," *L.A. Times*, 11/20/04; S. Roach, "Global: What Happens If the Dollar Does Not Fall?" Global Economic Forum, Morgan Stanley, 11/22/04; L. Summers, "The U.S. Current Account Deficit and the Global Economy," The 2004 Per Jacobsson Lecture, 10/3/04; "The Dollar," editorial, *The Economist*, 12/3/04; "Mr. Gaymard and the Dollar," editorial, *Le Monde*, 11/30/04.

Chapter 8

THE PROFITS OF WAR

IS IT OIL?
Arthur MacEwan
May/June 2003

Before U.S. forces invaded Iraq, the United Nations inspection team that had been searching the country for weapons of mass destruction was unable to find either such weapons or a capacity to produce them in the near future. As of mid-April, while the U.S. military is apparently wrapping up its invasion, it too has not found the alleged weapons. The U.S. government continues to claim that weapons of mass destruction exist in Iraq but provides scant evidence to substantiate its claim.

While weapons of mass destruction are hard to find in Iraq, there is one thing that is relatively easy to find: oil. Lots of oil. With 112.5 billion barrels of proven reserves, Iraq has greater stores of oil than any country except Saudi Arabia. This combination—lots of oil and no weapons of mass destruction—begs the question: Is it oil and not weapons of mass destruction that motivates the U.S. government's aggressive policy towards Iraq?

The U.S. "Need" for Oil?

Much of the discussion of the United States, oil, and Iraq focuses on the U.S. economy's overall dependence on oil. We are a country highly dependent on oil, consuming far more than we produce. We have a small share, about 3%, of the world's total proven oil reserves. By depleting our reserves at a much higher rate than most other countries, the United States accounts for about 10% of world production. But, by importing from the rest of the world, we can consume oil at a still higher rate: U.S. oil consumption is over 25% of the world's total. (See the accompanying figures for these and related data.) Thus, the United States relies on the rest of the world's oil in order to keep its economy running—or at least running in its present oil-dependent form. Moreover, for the United States to operate as it does and maintain current standards of living, we need access to oil at low prices. Otherwise we would have to turn over a large share of U.S. GDP as payment to those who supply us with oil.

Iraq could present the United States with supply problems. With a hostile government in Baghdad, the likelihood that the United States would be subject to some sort of boycott as in the early 1970s is greater than otherwise. Likewise, a government in Baghdad that does not cooperate with Washington could be a catalyst to a reinvigoration of the Organization of Petroleum Exporting Countries (OPEC) and the result could be higher oil prices.

Such threats, however, while real, are not as great as they might first appear. Boycotts are hard to maintain. The sellers of oil need to sell as much as the buyers need to buy; oil exporters depend on the U.S. market, just as U.S. consumers depend on those exporters. (An illustration of this mutual dependence is provided by the continuing oil trade between Iraq and the United States in recent years. During 2001, while the two countries were in a virtual state of war, the United States bought 284 million barrels of oil from Iraq, about 7% of U.S. imports and almost a third of Iraq's exports.) Also, U.S. oil imports come from diverse sources, with less than half from OPEC countries and less than one-quarter from Persian Gulf nations.

Most important, ever since the initial surge of OPEC in the 1970s, the organization has followed a policy of price restraint. While price restraint may in part be a strategy of political cooperation, resulting from the close U.S.-Saudi relationship in particular, it is also a policy adopted because high prices are counter-productive for

FIGURE 1: YEARS OF RESERVES AT CURRENT ANNUAL PRODUCTION RATES*.

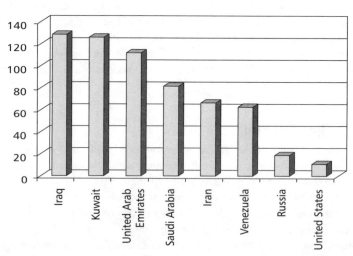

*The number of years it would take to use up existing reserves at current production rate. Past experience, however, suggests that more reserves will be found. In the 1980s, the world's proven reserves expanded by 47%, even as the consumption continued apace. With a more rapid rate of economic growth in the 1990s, and thus with the more rapid rate of oil consumption, the world's reserves rose by almost 5%. *Source:* BP Statistical Review of World Energy 2002 <www.bp.com/centres/energy2002>

FIGURE 2: OIL CONSUMPTION 2001

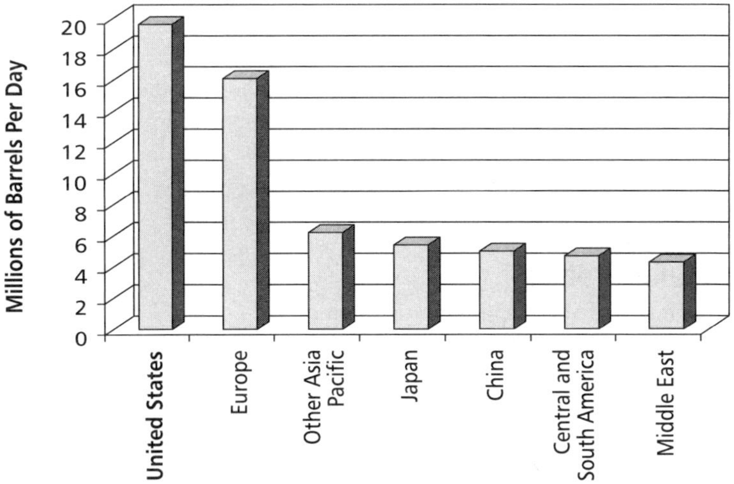

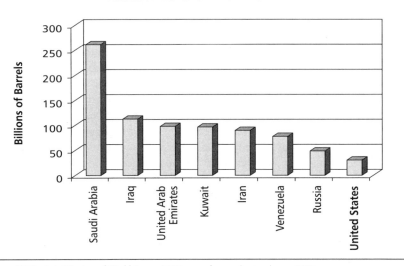

FIGURE 3: PROVEN OIL RESERVES 2001

Source: BP Statistical Review of World Energy 2002 <www.bp.com/centres/energy2002>

OPEC itself; high prices lead consumers to switch sources of supply and conserve energy, undercutting the longer term profits for the oil suppliers. Furthermore, a sudden rise in prices can lead to general economic disruption, which is no more desirable for the oil exporters than for the oil importers. To be sure, the United States would prefer to have cooperative governments in oil producing countries, but the specter of another boycott as in the 1970s or somewhat higher prices for oil hardly provides a rationale, let alone a justification, for war.

The Profits Problem

There is, however, also the importance of oil in the profits of large U.S. firms: the oil companies themselves (with ExxonMobil at the head of the list) but also the numerous drilling, shipping, refining, and marketing firms that make up the rest of the oil industry. Perhaps the most famous of this latter group, because former CEO Dick Cheney is now vice president, is the Halliburton Company, which supplies a wide range of equipment and engineering services to the industry. Even while many governments—Saudi Arabia, Kuwait, and Venezuela, for example—have taken ownership of their countries' oil reserves, these companies have been able to maintain their profits because of their decisive roles at each stage in the long sequence from exploration through drilling to refining and marketing. Ultimately, however, as with any resource-based industry, the monopolistic position—and thus the large profits—of the firms that dominate the oil industry depends on their access to the supply of the resource. Their access, in turn, depends on the relations they are able to establish with the governments of oil-producing countries.

From the perspective of the major U.S. oil companies, a hostile Iraqi government presents a clear set of problems. To begin with, there is the obvious: because Iraq has a lot of oil, access to that oil would represent an important profit-making opportunity. What's more, Iraqi oil can be easily extracted and thus produced at very low cost. With all oil selling at the same price on the world market, Iraqi oil thus presents opportunities for especially large profits per unit of production. According to the *Guardian* newspaper (London), Iraqi oil could cost as little as 97 cents a barrel to produce, compared to the UK's North Sea oil produced at $3 to $4 per barrel. As one oil executive told the *Guardian* last November, "Ninety cents a barrel for oil that sells for $30—that's the kind of business anyone would want to be in. A 97% profit margin—you can live with that." The *Guardian* continues: "The stakes are high. Iraq could be producing 8 million barrels a day within the decade. The math is impressive—8 million times 365 at $30 per barrel or $87.5 billion a year. Any share would be worth fighting for." The question for the oil companies is: what share will they be able to claim and what share will be claimed by the Iraqi government? The split would undoubtedly be more favorable for the oil companies with a compliant U.S.-installed government in Baghdad.

Furthermore, the conflict is not simply one between the private oil companies and the government of Iraq. The U.S.-based firms and their British (and British-Dutch) allies are vying with French, Russian, and Chinese firms for access to Iraqi oil. During recent years, firms from these other nations signed oil exploration and development contracts with the Hussein government in Iraq, and, if there were no "regime change," they would preempt the operations of the U.S. and British firms in that country. If, however, the U.S. government succeeds in replacing the government of Saddam Hussein with its preferred allies in the Iraqi opposition, the outlook will change dramatically. According to Ahmed Chalabi, head of the Iraqi National Congress and a figure in the Iraqi opposition who seems to be currently favored by Washington, "The future democratic government in Iraq will be grateful to the United States for helping the Iraqi people liberate themselves and getting rid of Saddam.... American companies, we expect, will play an important and leading role in the future oil situation." (In recent years, U.S. firms have not been fully frozen out of the oil business in Iraq. For example, according to a June 2001 report in the *Washington Post*, while Vice President Cheney was CEO at Halliburton Company during the late 1990s, the firm operated through subsidiaries to sell some $73 million of oil production equipment and spare parts to Iraq.)

The rivalry with French, Russian and Chinese oil companies is in part driven by the direct prize of the profits to be obtained from Iraqi operations. In addition, in order to maintain their dominant positions in the world oil industry, it is important for the U.S. and British-based firms to deprive their rivals of the growth potential that access to Iraq would afford. In any monopolistic industry, leading firms need to deny their potential competitors market position and control of new sources of supply; otherwise, those competitors will be in a better position to challenge the leaders. The British Guardian reports that the Hussein government is "believed to have offered the French company TotalFinaElf exclusive rights to the largest of Iraq's oil fields, the Majoon, which would more than double the company's entire output at a single stroke." Such a development would catapult TotalFinaElf from the second ranks into the first ranks of the major oil firms. The basic structure of the world oil industry would not change, but the sharing of power and profits among the leaders would be altered. Thus for ExxonMobil, Chevron, Shell and the other traditional "majors" in the industry, access to Iraq is a defensive as well as an offensive goal. ("Regime change" in Iraq will not necessarily provide the legal basis for cancellation of contracts signed between the Hussein regime and various oil companies. International law would not allow a new regime simply to turn things over to the U.S. oil companies. "Should 'regime change' happen, one thing is guaranteed," according to the *Guardian*, "shortly afterwards there will be the mother of all legalbattles.")

Oil companies are big and powerful. The biggest, ExxonMobil, had 2002 profits of $15 billion, more than any other corporation, in the United States or in the world. Chevron-Texaco came in with $3.3 billion in 2002 profits, and Phillips-Tosco garnered $1.7 billion. British Petroleum-Amoco-Arco pulled in $8 billion, while Royal

Dutch/Shell Group registered almost $11 billion. Firms of this magnitude have a large role affecting the policies of their governments, and, for that matter, the governments of many other countries.

With the ascendancy of the Bush-Cheney team to the White House in 2000, perhaps the relationship between oil and the government became more personal, but it was not new. Big oil has been important in shaping U.S. foreign policy since the end of the 19th century (to say nothing of its role in shaping other policy realms, particularly environmental regulation). From 1914, when the Marines landed at Mexico's Tampico Bay to protect U.S. oil interests, to the CIA-engineered overthrow of the Mosadegh government in Iran in 1953, to the close relationship with the oppressive Saudi monarchy through the past 70 years, oil and the interests of the oil companies have been central factors in U.S. foreign policy. Iraq today is one more chapter in a long story.

The Larger Issue

Yet in Iraq today, as in many other instances of the U.S. government's international actions, oil is not the whole story. The international policies of the U.S. government are certainly shaped in significant part by the interests of U.S.-based firms, but not only the oil companies. ExxonMobil may have had the largest 2002 profits, but there are many additional large U.S. firms with international interests: Citbank and the other huge financial firms; IBM, Microsoft, and other information technology companies; General Motors and Ford; Merck, Pfizer and the other pharmaceutical corporations; large retailers like MacDonald's and Wal-Mart (and many more) depend on access to foreign markets and foreign sources of supply for large shares of their sales and profits.

The U.S. government (like other governments) has long defined its role in international affairs as protecting the interests of its nationals, and by far the largest interests of U.S. nationals abroad are the interests of these large U.S. companies. The day-to-day activities of U.S. embassies and consular offices around the world are dominated by efforts to further the interests of particular U.S. firms—for example, helping the firms establish local markets, negotiate a country's regulations, or develop relations with local businesses. When the issue is large, such as when governments in low-income countries have attempted to assure the availability of HIV-AIDS drugs in spite of patents held by U.S. firms, Washington steps directly into the fray. On the broadest level, the U.S. government tries to shape the rules and institutions of the world economy in ways that work well for U.S. firms. These rules are summed up under the heading of "free trade," which in practice means free access of U.S. firms to the markets and resources of the rest of the world.

In normal times, Washington uses diplomacy and institutions like the International Monetary Fund, the World Bank, and the World Trade Organization to shape the rules of the world economy. But times are not always "normal." When governments have attempted to remove their economies from the open system and break with the "rules of the game," the U.S. government has responded with overt or covert military interventions. Latin America has had a long history of such interventions, where Guatemala (1954), Cuba (1961), Chile (1973) and Nicaragua (1980s) provide fairly recent examples. The Middle East also provides several illustrations of this approach to foreign affairs, with U.S. interventions in Iran (1953), Lebanon (1958), Libya (1981), and now Iraq. These interventions are generally presented as efforts to preserve freedom and democracy, but, if freedom and democracy were actually the goals of U.S. interventions the record would be very different; both the Saudi monarchy and the Shah of Iran, in an earlier era, would then have been high on the U.S. hit list. (Also, as with maintaining the source of supply of oil, the U.S. government did not intervene in Guatemala in 1954 to maintain our supply of bananas; the profits of the United Fruit Company, however, did provide a powerful causal factor.)

The rhetorical rationale of U.S. foreign policy has seen many alterations and adjustments over the last century: at the end of the 19th century, U.S. officials spoke of the need to spread Christianity; Woodrow Wilson defined the mission as keeping the world safe for democracy; for most of the latter half of the 20th century, the fight against Communism was the paramount rationale; for a fleeting moment during the Carter administration, the protection of human rights entered the government's vocabulary; in recent years we have seen the war against drugs; and now we have the current administration's war against terrorism.

What distinguishes the current administration in Washington is neither its approach toward foreign affairs and U.S. business interests in general nor its policy in the Middle East and oil interests in particular. Even its rhetoric builds on well established traditions, albeit with new twists. What does distinguish the Bush administration is the clarity and aggressiveness with which it has put forth its goal of maintaining U.S. domination internationally. The "Bush Doctrine" that the administration has articulated claims legitimacy for pre-emptive action against those who might threaten U.S. interests, and it is clear from the statement of that doctrine in last September's issuance of The National Security Strategy of the United States of America that "U.S. interests" includes economic interests.

The economic story is never the whole story, and oil is never the whole economic story. In the particular application of U.S. power, numerous strategic and political considerations come into play. With the application of the Bush Doctrine in the case of Iraq, the especially heinous character of the Hussein regime is certainly a factor, as is the regime's history of conflict with other nations of the region (at times with U.S. support) and its apparent efforts at developing nuclear, chemical, and biological weapons; certainly the weakness of the Iraqi military also affects the U.S. government's willingness to go to war. Yet, as September's Security Strategy document makes clear, the U.S. government is concerned with domination and a major factor driving that goal of domination is economic. In the Middle East, Iraq and elsewhere, oil—or, more precisely, the profit from oil— looms large in the picture.

An earlier version of this article was prepared for the newsletter of the Joiner Center for War and Social Consequences at the University of Massachusetts-Boston.

IN HARM'S WAY
The Working Class on the War Front and the Home Front
Rodney Ward
May/June 2003

> "Old man Bush wasn't half the president his son is. When the father was president, I only took a 15% pay cut. Now that his idiot son is president, I get to take a 40% pay cut. Way to go, George!"
>
> —a US Airways Fleet Services union activist

> "I've had enough of being fired at from all directions. I just want to go home."
>
> —a U.S. Marine, speaking to *BBC News*

First, the obvious: In Iraq, a U.S. and allied military made up of working-class soldiers has fought against a working-class Iraqi military. But the war tears at the lives of working people in the United States as well. As Martin Luther King observed about an earlier war, the bombs raining down on the "enemy" also jeopardize the futures and livelihoods of people in poor and working-class communities in the United States.

On any number of dimensions, the war in Iraq is hurting working people back home. The U.S. soldiers who return will find their benefits slashed by Congress and their prospects limited by continuing economic stagnation. The massive cost of the war and occupation robs resources from those who can least afford it and exacerbates federal and state budget crises. In turn, the social safety net is unraveling further just as wartime anxiety pushes the economy back toward recession.

The Bush administration is using wartime insecurity as a pretext to strip union rights from many federal workers and to intensify the criminalization of immigrant communities. In the private sector, entire industries—most notably, the airlines—are using the moment as an opportunity to bludgeon unions and savagely restructure their workplaces. As the shooting in Iraq winds down, an unwelcome occupation begins that will drain more resources away from meeting urgent human needs; just as important, it will prolong an atmosphere of crisis that gives cover for those whose agenda is to weaken the union movement and workers' rights.

Working Warriors

The modern U.S. military is vaunted as an all-volunteer force, but the truth is more complex. Conscription was ended in 1973 as a result of antiwar protest at home and, more important, among soldiers. Since then, the Department of Defense has built a voluntary military, primarily on a system of economic incentives. The military targets communities that have been devastated by disinvestment for recruitment, and military service has become a primary economic opportunity structure for working-class communities, disproportionately so for people of color.

Oskar Castro of the Youth and Militarism Project of the American Friends Service Committee (AFSC) points out that "most people didn't sign up because they were gung-ho warriors. Most people signed up for the college money and wonderful career opportunities, leadership skills and respect" that military recruiters offer—attractive promises to a young person whose alternatives are a dead-end job or unemployment. Researchers at the Rand Corporation found that low personal or family income and unemployment (particularly long term) increase the chances that someone will enlist. Not surprisingly, the military "seems to resemble the makeup of a two-year commuter or trade school outside Birmingham or Biloxi," note *New York Times* reporters David Halbfinger and Steven Holmes. As a result, close observers of military enlistment like the Central Committee for Conscientious Objectors refer to today's recruitment strategy as a "poverty draft."

Half of the 3.2 million soldiers in the U.S. military are reservists. In addition to the emotional trauma soldiers and their loved ones experience during a wartime mobilization, reservists also endure significant economic hardships. As they are activated from civilian jobs, many face dramatic pay cuts and disruption of health benefits. Tod Ensign of Citizen Soldier, an advocacy group for soldiers, explains, "Take an EMT making $42K driving an ambulance, enough to support a wife and two or three kids in a working-class suburb of New York City. They will earn $18K–22K once activated. Setting aside the risk of war, these people are taking heavy hits, often 30% to 50% cuts in pay!" Though some unionized workers have contractual pay protections in the event of reserve call-up, most reservists are out of luck. Civilian bills at best stay the same; with one parent absent, child care costs may go up. One New York City reservist explained that activation would mean his family would lose their home.

And when the war is over, the GIs will return home to find that politicians— many of whom used privilege to avoid military service themselves— are mouthing support while actually pulling the rug out from under soldiers' futures. On March 20, the Congress overwhelmingly passed a resolution to "express the gratitude of the Nation to all members of the United States Armed Forces." Then, early the next morning, the House of Representatives voted to cut funding for veterans' health care and benefit programs by nearly $25 billion over the next ten years. The cuts are designed to accommodate the massive tax cuts the Bush administration has been pursuing—while the war diverts the public's attention. The government track record on ignoring postwar problems like Agent Orange, post-traumatic stress disorder, and

Gulf War Syndrome does not bode well for the soldiers fighting the current war. Says the AFSC's Castro, "Even the military doesn't support the troops. Families are not supported. When it comes to dollars and cents, the military doesn't put its money where its mouth is."

Speaking of money, Defense Secretary Donald Rumsfeld's strategy for the Iraq war was based on the cost-cutting lean, just-in-time production model favored by corporate restructuring consultants. Rumsfeld apparently quashed the logistics plans of experienced officers, pressuring them to stage far fewer personnel and much less hardware in the Gulf than they considered adequate. Observers of the impact of lean restructuring in the corporate world report that increased workplace injuries are a major result. One wonders what impact importing this model into the battlefield will have on soldiers and civilians.

Union Busting as Homeland Security

Meanwhile, on the home front, both public- and private-sector workers are suffering a savage assault. The fiscal crisis brought about by war spending, recession, and tax cuts for the wealthy is squeezing public workers at all levels, resulting in wage freezes and elimination of entire departments. Thousands of public-sector workers are losing their jobs. Treasury Department worker Renee Toback reports that her department was told their budget would be "taxed" to pay for the war in Iraq.

At the same time, the Bush administration has stripped thousands of federal workers in the hastily cobbled-together Department of Homeland Security of union rights in the name of national security. The Department of Defense is developing plans to do the same. Are fearful employees with no voice on the job in the best position to protect national security? No. But it's no surprise that the administration's agenda prioritizes union busting over public safety. AFL-CIO Organizing Director Stewart Acuff says, "The most outrageous thing they [the Bush administration] said was that they had to remove union rights from the Department of Homeland Security when all of the people who answered the call on September 11, all of the firefighters and cops who died trying to save people, were union members! And 90% of the people who cleaned up in the aftermath were union members as well." Against this backdrop, the administration has also called for the privatization of as many as 800,000 non-postal federal jobs. If Bush succeeds, this move would replace large numbers of union jobs with non-union ones at lower pay and with less accountability; it would strike a huge blow at the strength of public-sector unions. (Naturally, Bush also plans to privatize Iraqi health care and education.)

Diane Witiak, an American Federation of Government Employees (AFGE) spokeswoman, describes the current atmosphere: "If you dare to oppose the administration, you're almost considered a traitor. We resent that the administration considers unionization and patriotism incompatible. In fact, [unionization is] essential. [The administration] will go back to the old cronyism and favoritism that the Civil

Service Act corrected. It's only a matter of time before Bush starts with the private sector!"

Much as Witiak predicted, the administration is using the national-security pretext to erode the rights of some private-sector workers as well. Last year, Homeland Security director Tom Ridge called the president of the west coast longshore union. He claimed a strike would harm national security and threatened dockworkers with replacement by military personnel. Ultimately, it was management that locked out the dockworkers, but Bush invoked the Taft-Hartley Act and threatened to prosecute International Longshore and Warehouse Union members who engaged in any kind of work slowdown or other industrial action.

More broadly, efforts are under way in Congress to ban strikes by airline workers and to pass a number of other anti-worker measures. Among these are expansion of the restrictive Railway Labor Act's jurisdiction to include certain industries now under the umbrella of the National Labor Relations Act, making it harder for workers in these sectors to win union recognition and severely limiting their right to strike. Another legislative initiative would eliminate "card-check," the system of conducting a union recognition election once a certain number of representation petition cards have been signed by workers at a particular facility. In recent years, card-check has been the chief mechanism of successful union organizing drives. The AFL-CIO's Acuff points out that "the direction the government is moving in will indeed have a chilling effect on mobilizations, collective activity, demonstrations and direct action, all necessary parts of contract and bargaining campaigns and union strength. This administration, by law and by culture, is trying to stigmatize or make illegal the kinds of activity that are necessary to build union workplace strength."

What Does a Terrorist Look Like?

Wartime is always dangerous for immigrant communities. When the towers collapsed on September 11, they crushed the movement to give undocumented immigrants amnesty. Since then, immigrants have been subject to a dramatically stepped-up campaign by the federal government to find and deport them. Rachael Kamel, AFSC education director, points to "growing attempts to criminalize immigrant workers—all now justified in the name of security." As the next episode in the now-permanent war on terror, the war in Iraq only serves to extend the period in which such policies appear legitimate.

For example, the Social Security Administration (SSA) sends so-called no-match letters to employers when it finds that a worker's Social Security number does not match SSA records. These letters serve to intimidate workers, since employers can threaten to turn them in to the Immigration and Naturalization Service (INS). The number of no-match letters has increased 800% since 9/11. Similarly, special registration of immigrants from a select list of countries, mostly in the Middle East and Southern Asia, has snared thousands of people with minor visa infractions, many of whom face deportation. (Of bizarre note is the case of Iraqi exile Katrin Michael. She met with President Bush on March 14 to recount the gas attack she survived, and then found herself on the INS deportation list the next week, according to a *Washington Post* story.)

All of this has a powerful impact on worker organization because, for the past decade, immigrant workers have been the bedrock of aggressive labor organizing campaigns in economically strategic states like California, Texas and New York. Last year in Los Angeles, 60 workers active in organizing the Koreatown Assi Supermarket were placed on indefinite suspension after their names appeared on no-match letters. And the same Homeland Security rules that stripped newly-federalized airport screeners of union rights also banned immigrant workers in those positions. As a result, 7,000 immigrant airport security screeners—some of whom had just succeeded in winning union representation—have been fired.

Shock and Awe for Airline Workers?

Amid official and unofficial repression against public sector workers and immigrant communities, the economy appears stalled and is likely heading for a double-dip recession. The World Bank is already estimating that the Iraq war will reduce worldwide economic growth by one-half of a percentage point during the first six months of this year.

When the economy is weak, the industries most affected make cuts wherever they can, and workers bear the brunt of industry restructuring. The airline industry continues to be the crucible of this restructuring; as such, it provides an instructive case study. Before the war, the industry's Air Transport Association predicted 70,000 layoffs (100,000 if a terrorist attack accompanied the war) in addition to the thousands already cut since September 11, as well as $4 billion in additional losses. Editorials intoned about "Airline Apocalypse."

True to their word, airlines began shedding employees by the thousands as soon as the bombs started to fall on Baghdad. Continental laid off 1,200, with more to come, Northwest, 4,900, while United and American (possibly in Chapter 11 bankruptcy reorganization by the time you read this) plan to get rid of thousands more. Jeff Matthews, the Aircraft Mechanics Fraternal Association's national contract coordinator at Northwest, told Reuters: "Northwest is using the Iraq conflict as an excuse to justify mass layoffs planned before the conflict started. The number of planned layoffs is far larger than would be justified based on the number of planes Northwest is removing from service." One United employee and Marines veteran describes wartime layoffs as United's own campaign of "shock and awe."

All of these airlines have succeeded in, or are in the process of, extracting concessions on levels unheard of in the history of the industry. Of particular importance has been US Airways' use of the war as leverage to terminate the defined-benefit pension plan for its pilots. At a time when defined-benefit plans are underfunded by about

$300 billion in the United States, this is alarming. Representative Bernie Sanders (I-Vt.) warned in the *Wall Street Journal* that "this could set a horrible precedent by making it easier for companies to renege on the retirement promises they made to their workers." Nomi Prins, author of the forthcoming book Money for Nothing, points out, "The poor stock market is offering a convenient excuse for companies that already desired to reduce future plan benefits."

The airlines cite the war as a major reason for the concessions they demand. United mechanic Jennifer Salazar-Biddle remarked, "The crisis is real, but the graft is unbelievable." In fact, executive compensation in the midst of the industry's crisis has shocked and awed even Republicans. Responding to reports of the doubling of Delta CEO Leo Mullin's compensation package, Sen. John McCain (who champions eliminating airline workers' right to strike) exclaimed, "You ought to be ashamed of yourself." Nonetheless, a new bailout is in the works for the airline industry. The bailout bill does include a cap on executive compensation, but at 2002 levels—a good example of closing the barn doors after the escape. It also requires the airline companies to reduce operating costs, a provision that will primarily bleed workers. The only bone the bill offers airline workers is a meager extension of their unemployment benefits.

Chain of Change

Wars have always had a deep impact on working people. In addition to the slaughter of war, wars have often undermined the strength of working class organization. Government repression tied to World War I all but destroyed the Industrial Workers of the World and the Socialist Party. Workplace regimentation in World War II played an important role in the long-term bureaucratization of unions, replacing militant shop floor activity with safer routinized grievance and arbitration procedures.

On the other hand, soldiers returning from war have also played an important role in reviving struggles at home. At the end of World War II and during the Vietnam War, opposition to the war surfaced among GIs, along with discussions of soldiers' rights to free speech and even to unions. Soldiers returning from Vietnam played an important role in the antiwar movement as well as rebellions within a variety of unions, most notably the wave of auto-worker wildcat strikes from 1969 to 1972. African-American soldiers returning from both of these wars parlayed their wartime experiences into civil-rights activism.

There are some hopeful signs that workers will fight back against the current wave of assaults on their rights. Transportation Security Administration (TSA) employees are continuing to organize themselves with AFGE in spite of TSA director James Loy's directives to the contrary. AFGE succeeded in securing a one-year moratorium on the de-unionization of the Department of Homeland Security. Federal workers in Seattle and dozens of other localities have begun a campaign of public rallies to protest privatization.

Time will tell how working people in the military will respond to what they are enduring today. One thing is clear, though: The immediate impact of the war has been to strengthen the hands of corporations and weaken unions and other worker organizations while placing thousands of working people in harm's way. In the long term, whether grassroots activists can turn this tide will depend on how they understand and address the class dimensions of this and future wars.

Sources: Soldiers & Veterans: Citizen Soldier <www.citizen-soldier.org>; Military Families Speak Out <www.mfso.org>; Veterans for Common Sense <www.veteransforcommonsense.org>; National Gulf War Resource Center <www.ngwrc.org>; Immigrant Rights: National Network for Immigrant and Refugee Rights <www.nnirr.org>; Labor: US Labor Against War <www.uslaboragainstwar.org>; Dept. of Homeland Security Workers <www.dhsworkers.org>; Association of Flight Attendants <www.afanet.org>; Airline Mechanics Fraternal Association <www.amfanatl.org>; See also: David Cortright, Soldiers in Revolt: The American Military Today (Anchor Press/Doubleday, 1976); Kim Moody, An Injury To All (Routledge, 1997).

THE REAL WINNERS
A rogue's gallery of war profiteers
Todd Tavares
July/August 2003

Even as bombs were raining down on Baghdad, a short list of private beneficiaries was being drawn up behind closed doors. As the invasion entered its final phase, the United States Agency for International Development (USAID) and the Army Corps of Engineers (funded through the Pentagon) began doling out contracts. Citing security concerns and time constraints, they hand picked the companies that would be allowed to bid for the contracts (American firms only, thank you), and in some cases they awarded colossal sums with no bidding at all.

USAID, whose mission is to further "America's foreign policy interests in expanding democracy and free markets while improving the lives of the citizens of the developing world," invited 21 firms to bid on eight contracts worth $1.7 billion. Many of the contract details have not been revealed to American taxpayers or the Iraqi people. A look at the past records of the companies that received contracts reveals that most have long histories of project work with USAID, specialize in privatization, and maintain strong political connections. These are the firms that benefited most from the reconstruction largesse. In fact, they may be the war's real winners

Where two figures are given for award amount, the low number is money allocated to begin work and the high number is the estimated final cost.

Stevedoring Services of America (SSA)

Seattle-based private operator of port facilities.
Awarded: $4.8 million (initially)
For: Seaport Administration (to assess Umm Qasr port facilities; develop improvement plan; hire port pilots; facilitate cargo-handling services; coordinate transport shipments from Umm Qasr)

Stevedoring Services of America is the largest marine and rail-cargo handler in the United States and the largest terminal operator in the world, with annual revenue of $1 billion. A notorious union-buster, SSA is the dominant member of the Pacific Maritime Association (PMA), the stevedoring trade association responsible for paying longshore workers. Joseph Miniace, the PMA president alleged to have been installed by SSA, worked for years to break union power by outsourcing and automating the ports. It was the International Longshore and Warehouse Union's (ILWU) effort to resist his changes and maintain full unionization that prompted the PMA to lock out port workers in September 2002.

After USAID gave SSA the Iraq contract, its security office discovered that the firm did not have the necessary security clearance. Instead of revoking the contract and awarding it to a company with the correct clearance credentials, USAID waived the requirement.

International Resources Group (IRG)

Washington, D.C.-based private consulting firm.
Awarded: $7.1 million minimum (90 day initial contract, renewable for two additional 1-year terms)
For: Personnel Support (to provide technical expertise for reconstruction)

USAID contacted International Resources Group to discuss the post-war reconstruction contract in January 2003, well before the U.S. and allied invasion began, according to the *Washington Post*. Granted, the agency and the consulting conglomerate have a longstanding relationship—since 1978, USAID has awarded IRG over 200 contracts amounting to hundreds of millions of dollars. About one-third of the company's total business is done for USAID. Its other projects are funded by government agencies, foreign states, the World Bank, and the Asian Development Bank. IRG also does extensive energy-related consulting work in the private sector, notably for large oil firms. Its contract to provide personnel services for the reconstruction of Iraq was "sole sourced," meaning the job was simply handed to IRG. No other bids were solicited.

Abt Associates, Inc.

Cambridge, Massachusetts-based government and business consulting firm; employee owned and for-profit.

Awarded: $10 million to $43.8 million (12 month contract)

For: Public Health (supporting the Iraqi Ministry of Health; delivering health services; providing medical equipment and supplies; training and recruiting health staff; providing health education and information; and determining the specific needs of the health sector and vulnerable populations such as women and children)

One of the largest for-profit research and consulting firms in the world, Abt's clients include governments, international organizations, business and industry, foundations, and nonprofit associations. One of its specialty areas is privatization. The firm offers client states "technical assistance to facilitate policy reforms in countries moving from command economies to market-oriented economies." The firm helped privatize government-owned pharmaceutical industries in Kazakhstan and worked on other privatization efforts in the former Soviet Union involving health, financing, and service delivery activities. Abt has also undertaken privatization projects in Central America, the Caribbean, African and Asia. USAID has a history of funding these "market-based reforms."

Creative Associates International, Inc. (CAII)

Washington, D.C.-based private for-profit international consulting firm.

Awarded: $1 million to $62.6 million (12-month contract)

For: Primary and Secondary Education (to increase enrollment and quality; provide necessary supplies; retain students and increase baseline indicators)

Since 1977, Creative Associates International has assisted "the stabilization of post-conflict environments" in many countries—including such casualties of U.S.-sponsored conflict as Angola, El Salvador, Guatemala, and Nicaragua, according to its website. Ninety percent of its business is funded by USAID. In March, CAII snagged an agency grant of $6 million to produce textbooks for students in Afghanistan. It won the bid over the previous bid-holder, the University of Nebraska at Omaha (UNO). UNO had insisted the textbooks be produced by Afghans themselves in order to employ residents of Kabul and provide a small measure of self-sufficiency to the Afghan people. CAII promptly transferred the printing to Indonesia, resulting in job losses in Kabul.

Research Triangle Institute (RTI)

Research Triangle Park, North Carolina-based nonprofit research and development organization.
Awarded: $7.9 million to $167.9 million (12 month contract)
For: Local Governance (strengthening of management skills and capacity of local administrations and civic institutions; training programs in communications, conflict resolution, leadership skills and political analysis)

Research Triangle Institute does a strange mix of business through its 12 offices. The 2,100-person firm helps transfer NASA research to the private sector, "commercializing" NASA's technologies and "bringing them to markets." It also receives Defense Department funding. RTI was recently awarded a USAID grant for $60 million to implement Pakistan's "Education Sector Reform Action," a plan for reforming Pakistan's education system, increasing literacy, and increasing public-private partnerships in the education sector. In Iraq the firm will provide local governance support through a project dubbed the "Iraq Sub-National Governance and Civic Institution Support Program." Little detailed information about the program has been made public.

Bechtel Group

San Francisco-based, private for-profit engineering and construction firm; one of the largest in the world.
Awarded: $34.6 million to $680 million (18 month contract)
For: Capital Construction (to repair and rehabilitate water, power, and sewage infrastructure; repair and upgrade Umm Qasr seaport; repair hospitals, schools, ministry buildings, irrigation and transportation links)

The construction giant now in control of repairing the water and irrigation systems of Iraq is a renown water privatizer. A Bechtel subsidiary privatized the water of Cochabamba, Bolivia in the late 1990s, making it unaffordable to the poor. Massive protests ensued, in which at least six people were killed and hundreds injured by the police. When the Bolivian government canceled the company's contract, the firm sued for loss of potential profit.

The $13.3 billion family-owned conglomerate has strong connections to the current and previous Republican administrations. In fact, a revolving door between Bechtel and Washington has been spinning around for decades. Caspar Weinberger was a Bechtel executive before he became Secretary of Defense under Reagan. Former CIA Director William Casey also rose from the Bechtel ranks.

Current Bechtel board member George Shultz was president and director of the company from 1974 until he became Secretary of State under Reagan in 1982. Earlier this year, the good Mr. Schultz cheered loudly for the Iraq war, not only in op-ed pieces, but also as a member of the Committee for the Liberation for Iraq (CLI), an eclectic mix of warmongers—Democrat and Republican—lobbying for combat. The

CLI included former Senator Bob Kerrey, former House speaker Newt Gingrich, and Senators John McCain (R-Ariz.) and Joseph Lieberman (D-Conn.).

In February 2003, President Bush appointed company CEO (and Republican Party loyalist) Riley Bechtel to the Export Council, a group dedicated to expanding the U.S. export market. Other senior executives of Bechtel who double as government advisors include Senior Vice President Jack Sheehan, who advises the Pentagon through the Defense Policy Board, and Senior Vice President Daniel Chao, who serves on the advisory committee of the U.S. Export-Import Bank.

Bechtel is also a major campaign contributor—its employees gave $1.3 million to federal candidates and party committees between 1999 and 2002 (59% to Republicans, 41% to Democrats).

Another interesting plotline in the story of Bechtel's contract coup is the company's relationship with the current head of USAID, Andrew Natsios. As chairman of the Massachusetts Turnpike Authority in 2000-2001, Natsios worked closely with Bechtel on Boston's "Big Dig" construction project—Bechtel was and is the project's principle contractor. In the 1980s, Bechtel estimated the Big Dig's price tag would be $2.5 billion. Since then the cost has ballooned by more than 560% to over $14 billion due in large part to Bechtel mismanagement and the lack of state oversight of its work. When Natsios took over the Turnpike Authority, he promised to rein in the overruns. He worked with Bechtel to renegotiate its Big Dig contract, and succeeded in reducing their management fees. But Natsios permitted the Bechtel team to continue to review and evaluate their own work, basically changing little. During Natsios' tenure, the cost estimate of the Big Dig continued to rise. A few months after he left for his post at USAID, $300 million more in cost overruns were announced. Natsios denies allegations that he gave preferential treatment to Bechtel for the Iraq reconstruction contract.

Kellogg Brown and Root (KBR) (A Halliburton subsidiary)
KBR is the engineering and construction wing of the Houston, Texas-based petroleum and gas service firm; Halliburton is publicly traded on NYSE (HAL).
Amount: Unlimited
For: Repair of Petroleum Infrastructure (putting out oil fires, contingency planning)

The contract to extinguish and repair the oil infrastructure of Iraq is the true gem of the reconstruction spoils. For starters it is a "cost plus" contract in which the government pays the total cost of work done, plus a profit. The Army Corps of Engineers predicts the total value will amount to $7 billion over two years with KBR taking 7% (about $490 million) as profit. The contract also gives KBR the right to produce and sell oil inside the country of Iraq. Remarkably, this was a closed-door handout granted to KBR without bidding.

It seems odd that the Halliburton subsidiary would be chosen for the plum contract, given that a recent KBR contract in the Balkans resulted in $2 million in fines to resolve claims the firm committed fraud. And KBR recently admitted to the SEC that they had bribed Nigerian officials to avoid paying their fair share of taxes. This is not exactly the type of organization you'd think the administration would want heading the "we're here to help you" parade in a newly occupied country.

But Halliburton is not only a darling of Republican fundraisers—95% of their $700,000 donations between 1999 and 2002 went to Republican candidates—the company also has an intimate relationship with vice president Dick Cheney, a relationship that helps explain the firm's good fortune. As Secretary of Defense under George H. W. Bush, Cheney hired then-Brown and Root to consult the army about privatizing army jobs. Brown and Root would later win a contract to provide worldwide logistics for the Army Corps of Engineers. When Cheney became Halliburton CEO (1995-2000), the company became the 18th largest Pentagon contractor, up from 73rd. Cheney also helped change tax payments of $302,000,000 in 1998 to tax refunds of $85,000,000 in 1999 in part by quintupling its offshore subsidiaries. Since he left Halliburton to run for vice president, Cheney has continued to receive deferred compensation from his former company of between $100,000 and $1,000,000 per year.

Qualcomm, Inc.
San Diego-based, publicly traded wireless-communications technology firm.
Awarded: Nothing

Although it has not yet been decided who will build the cell-phone network in post-war Iraq, it seems likely that it will be built to the specifications of GSM technology—the Middle East and European standard. For Qualcomm, which produces and collects royalties from chip sales of a rival system (CDMA), Iraq's adoption of GSM would represent a tremendous loss. Upon learning of the GSM plans, a Qualcomm lobbyist went to Rep. Darrel E. Issa (R-Calif.), the recipient of $5,500 in Qualcomm campaign contributions. Together the wireless technology firm and the congressman drafted a letter advocating use of CDMA technology in Iraq, had it signed by 41 lawmakers, and sent it to USAID and Defense Secretary Donald Rumsfeld.

The letter argued that CDMA is technologically superior and that the money spent on reconstruction should benefit American firms, not the European firms that developed GSM. Unfortunately for Qualcomm, the use of GSM would isolate Iraq from neighboring countries. And in terms of American benefits, many firms make GSM handsets and at least one owns royalty-gaining GSM patents. The only real beneficiary of a CDMA system in Iraq would be Qualcomm itself.

Rep. Issa introduced a bill that would mandate the use of Qualcomm's technology to the House of Representatives at the end of March. It is not expected to pass.

Sources: Financial Times May 6, 2003; *New York Times* April 9, 2003, April 11, 2003; <www.citizenworks. org>;<www.corpwatch.org>. Campaign contribution information is from Open Secrets <www.opensecrets. org>. USAID contracts and updates can be found at <www.usaid.gov/iraq/activities.html>.

OPERATION IRAQI PLUNDER

The United States spends Iraq's money—with little accountability.

Lorenzo Nencioli
July/August 2004

A s the war in Iraq looks increasingly like an imperialist quagmire, so does the Bush administration's handling of Iraqi oil wealth.

Shortly after the U.S. invasion in March 2003, the Coalition Provisional Authority (CPA) appropriated billions of dollars of Iraqi wealth, including frozen Iraqi assets in the United States and abroad and new oil revenues. The funds were to be spent on reconstructing Iraq; they are in addition to the $18.4 billion in U.S. taxpayer dollars that Congress appropriated last year for Iraq reconstruction.

Expenditure of these funds has been beset by secrecy, nepotism, and an absence of minimally acceptable accounting practices. As a result, the Iraqi people may never know how the U.S. occupiers have spent their wealth. They do know that their money is being monitored under at best a far more casual regime than the already weak accounting standards that track U.S. dollars spent in Iraq.

In May 2003, the United Nations and other international bodies formed an oversight body, the International Advisory and Monitoring Board (IAMB), to audit the CPA's expenditures of Iraqi oil revenues via the Development Fund for Iraq (DFI). The DFI was created by the United Nations as the main repository of Iraqi oil revenue; since last May, the fund has taken in over $20 billion and has committed over $17 billion for various projects and purchases, from school renovations to combat boots and body armor.

The IAMB and a number of nonprofit organizations in Iraq maintain that the board's attempts to oversee those expenditures have been thwarted by an uncooperative and secretive CPA. "It has been impossible to tell with any accuracy what the CPA has been doing with Iraq's money," notes the U.K.-based agency Christian Aid, whose June 2004 report estimates that $4 billion of Iraqi oil revenue has been not been accounted for by the CPA. Another group that has closely monitored the CPA, Iraq Revenue Watch, cautioned as early as last fall that, in its estimate, over $7 billion of DFI money was being spent without any independent management or supervision. Both groups, as well as the IAMB, have noted that the CPA does not meter Iraqi oil extraction—a standard industry practice—making it impossible to accurately track production or to determine how much oil has been smuggled prior to refining and shipping.

Despite the fog surrounding CPA business practices, there is at least one clear example of how the CPA has been spending Iraqi oil revenue: it used DFI money to award three no-bid contracts worth $1.4 billion to Halliburton Corp. Although Congress has prohibited the awarding of noncompetitive contracts with federal funds, the DFI was under no similar legal constraint—and its administrators in the CPA evidently did not see a need to apply the same standard to the outlay of Iraqi funds. Halliburton, the energy services company once headed by Vice President Dick Cheney, has recently come under fire for a number of potentially criminal business practices, including overcharging the federal government by $61 million for fuel delivery services.

Such bloated contract awards are particularly galling given the many Iraqi construction companies that were waiting for their fair share of DFI contracts. Though these companies charge about a tenth of what their American counterparts do, according to Christian Aid, the CPA allowed Iraqi companies to compete only for contracts of under $500,000, and not until this past April—eleven months after the authority took power and two months before it left.

With such questionable contract awards receiving little scrutiny from the Bush administration, the IAMB audit of the CPA is critical. But both Christian Aid and Iraq Revenue Watch have criticized the CPA for its slow pace in turning over financial reports to the IAMB. Though the United Nations elected to transfer operating authority over the DFI to the new Iraqi interim government and to extend the IAMB's monitoring mandate past the June handover of sovereignty, Stuart Halford of Christian Aid told me via e-mail that the extended mandate would mean little: "The CPA are not around to be held accountable for what they spent the money on, and they granted themselves immunity while they were there anyway."

It's unlikely that a proper audit based on full disclosure will ever be carried out. With the U.S. military occupying a country that is home to the world's second largest quantity of known oil reserves, the potential for further corruption in the oil industry-friendly Bush administration is acute. As Halford told me via e-mail: "Many people said this war was all about oil. Well, the CPA's lack of proper accounting about Iraq's oil revenue"—not to mention the long list of well-connected U.S. corporations to whom that revenue has been funneled—"certainly won't dissuade many who follow that argument."

IRAQI LABOR CONFRONTS NEW RULERS, OLD RULES

Iraqi workers defy a ban on union organizing and win support from U.S. unions.

David Bacon
September/October 2004

When the U.S. occupation of Iraq began 18 months ago, Iraqi workers lost no time in reorganizing their country's labor movement. Labor activity spread from Baghdad and the Kurdish north to the southern port of Um Qasr, with intensive activity centered in the oil and electrical installations around Basra, where workers have organized three general strikes.

After years of repression under Saddam Hussein, many in Iraq's labor movement hoped that conditions would improve with Hussein's removal. Instead, the occupation authorities moved quickly to prevent a labor upsurge. When the Coalition Provisional Authority (CPA) took power in March 2003, it kept in place and continued to enforce Saddam Hussein's 1987 law banning unions from the public enterprises that employ the majority of Iraqi workers. To this, CPA head Paul Bremer added a ban on pronouncements that "incite civil disorder, rioting or damage to property." The phrase "civil disorder" can be and has been applied to strike organizing; leaders of two new labor organizations—the Iraqi Federation of Trade Unions and Iraq's Union of the Unemployed—have been detained a number of times.

U.S.–Iraq Labor Solidarity

Labor repression by the CPA and the Iraqi interim government has provoked U.S. unions to speak out against the war and occupation more vocally than they've responded to any foreign policy since Ronald Reagan's wars in Central America. U.S. unions first learned of Bremer's hostility toward labor last fall, when a U.S. Labor Against the War (USLAW) delegation to Iraq brought back accounts of the mass suppression of basic worker's rights. (USLAW is a network of U.S. unions and labor councils encompassing hundreds of thousands of members working actively to oppose the war.) In January, AFL-CIO president John Sweeney condemned the CPA's enforcement of the 1987 law and called on the CPA "to allow Iraqi workers to associate together and participate collectively in rebuilding the economy."

Throughout the spring, USLAW raised money for Iraq's new unions. This June in Geneva, Neil Bisno, secretary- treasurer of Service Employees International Union Local 1199P, delivered two $5,000 checks to the IFTU and Iraq's other new labor federation, the Workers Councils and Unions of Iraq. U.S. labor opposition to the occupation has grown so strong that two of the AFL-CIO's largest unions, SEIU and the American Federation of State, County, and Municipal Employees (AFSCME), passed resolutions this summer calling for the withdrawal of U.S. troops and respect for the rights of Iraqi workers. The California Labor Federation, with one-sixth of all U.S. union members, followed suit. Opposition to the Iraq war and support for that country's new labor movement have become election issues for thousands of U.S. workers, adding fuel to the labor movement's efforts to unseat George W. Bush.

Back in Iraq, however, the National Endowment for Democracy, a U.S. government-funded organization with ties to the CIA, is proffering funds for a range of U.S.-sponsored "labor programs." NED is renowned for meddling in the politics of countries in the global South (most recently, it funded anti-Aristide groups in Haiti leading up to the coup in February). Some USLAW activists fear that NED funding of training programs and financial assistance for Iraqi workers could co-opt unions into supporting the military occupation and perhaps also endanger the more progressive parts of the country's labor law, like guarantees of healthcare, housing, and education.

Public-Sector Pay Cuts

Low wages are the main driver of Iraq's labor protests. For several months following the arrival of U.S. troops, Iraq's public-sector workers received emergency salaries ranging from roughly $60 to $120 monthly, about what they had earned before the war. Last September, the CPA lowered the base to $40 and eliminated housing and food subsidies.

Iraqi longshoremen working for the port authority in Um Qasr saw their pay lowered still further when their profit-sharing arrangement, which had given them 2% of unloading fees, was terminated. When authorities decided in October to pay them in Iraqi dinars instead of dollars—another sizeable loss—the longshore workers began organizing a union.

On the day they were set to vote on the officers for their new union, port director Abdel Razzaq told them the election was cancelled because of the 1987 prohibition. In November, he fired three port workers for union organizing.

Dockers struck briefly in January over the low wage scale, blocking anyone from entering the main gate to the port. They grew angrier when managers decided to pay them in old banknotes worth only 75% of the value of new ones. In the melee that ensued, Razzaq's office was occupied, and the demonstration ended only when he was rescued by occupation troops. Workers say he has been protected by a private militia ever since.

On hearing about the firing of the Um Qasr longshoremen, San Francisco's International Longshore and Warehouse Local 10 condemned the action. "You are not alone," President Henry Graham told them. "If dockworkers in the rest of the world hear about your situation, you can count on their support." Local 10 and other west-coast dock unions stopped work on March 20 to coincide with worldwide demonstrations on the anniversary of the Iraq invasion.

Privatization Threat

Iraqi workers and unions charge that the United States is suppressing wages in order to attract the foreign investors that Washington sees as essential to its plans for a privatized Iraqi economy. The Bush administration sees the country as a free-market beachhead into the Middle East and South Asia. Over a year ago, it put Thomas Foley, a Bush campaign fundraiser, in charge of private-sector development at the CPA. Under his direction, the CPA enacted major changes to the Iraqi economic system, permitting 100% foreign ownership of businesses, except for the oil industry, and allowing foreign investors to repatriate 100% of the profits they make in the country. Foley drew up a list of state enterprises to be sold off, including cement and fertilizer plants, phosphate and sulfur mines, pharmaceutical factories, and the country's airline. While sales have been delayed, the CPA's goal—the free-market reengineering of the country's economy—is now firmly encoded in law. Iraq's new constitution forbids the interim government from reversing the CPA's privatization measures.

Privatized Military Training and Operations

Military training and operations is perhaps the smallest, but in many ways the most troubling, arena in which privatization is taking place.

Around the world, including Guantanamo Bay, Cuba; Colombia; Afghanistan; and Iraq, new private-sector teams of skilled former military personnel are offering their services to a range of clients, including governments, the United Nations, nongovernmental organizations, warlords, and drug kings.

In Iraq, private firms represent the second largest contributor of forces to the war effort, according to the Guardian. Numbering about 10,000, private contractor employees are believed to exceed the number of British troops on the ground. They provide training and operations, food catering, engineering, consulting, and security. Many are armed.

Blackwater Security Consulting, whose four employees were killed and mutilated by an angry crowd in Fallujah in March, is a North Carolina-based company headed by former U.S. Navy SEALs. The four employees were guarding a convoy delivering U.S. government food. Blackwater is one of over a dozen security companies hired by the Pentagon to guard key installations, protect the Coalition Provisional Authority, and train the Iraqi army and police. Other security firms in Iraq include Virginia-based Custer Battles; the British companies Erinys and Global Risk; and DynCorp of Reston, Virginia. The United States awarded DynCorp, now owned by the multibillion dollar Computer Sciences Corporation, a contract for as much as $250 million to provide up to 1,000 civilian advisors to organize civilian law enforcement in post-war Iraq.

The presence of contractors in Iraq is unprecedented in its scale, but their involvement

The threat of privatization and the influx of U.S. contractors have led to more labor unrest. Workers fear that new corporate owners would cut costs by laying off workers. Companies with fat reconstruction contracts are already trying to perform work previously done by Iraqis. Iraq has no unemployment benefits or welfare system, and the unemployment rate is estimated to be between 50% and 70%. So the loss of a stable job in a state enterprise condemns a family to hunger and misery. One obvious advantage to having a union is that it gives workers more of a voice in decisions about privatization and contracting.

Conflict over reconstruction work boiled over last October in a two-day wildcat strike at the Bergeseeya Oil Refinery near Basra. Kellogg, Brown & Root (KBR), a division of Halliburton Corp., had been given a no-bid contract to repair oil facilities. KBR brought in a Kuwaiti construction company, Al Khoorafi, with Indian and Pakistani workers. To protect their jobs, Iraqi workers threw them out of the worksite and protested outside the company's offices. Today, Iraqi workers continue to perform the reconstruction work at this site.

At Southern Oil Company, the Basra-based firm with sites all over southern Iraq, workers organized a union and banned foreign workers following the Bergeseeya action. KBR tried to get them to accept its foreign staff but local workers refused to budge. "Iraq will be reconstructed by Iraqis. We don't need any foreign interference," reflects a long-term trend. Over 9,000 contract employees worked in the Persian Gulf War theatre in 1990, and 1,400 went to Bosnia as part of U.S. peacekeeping forces in 1997. In the late 1990s, the United States and United Kingdom hired DynCorp to oversee withdrawal of Serb forces from Kosovo.

The pitfalls of privatized training of foreign military forces are illustrated in Deborah Avant's research on Military Professional Resources Inc. (MPRI) in Croatia. MPRI is a northern Virginia firm founded in 1986 by several high-ranking retired American military officers. By the late 1990s, it employed 350 people full time and could call upon a database of over 7,000 potential employees, all with significant experience in the U.S. armed forces. In 1994, Croatia hired MPRI to educate its military leaders in western-style civilian-military relations. The Pentagon vetted the operation, granting the firm an export license and extensively briefing MPRI personnel before their departure to Croatia. This way, the United States was able to remain formally neutral while influencing and monitoring events on the ground. Observers believe that the firm's training activities and support enabled the Croatians to launch a bloody ethnic cleansing offensive in Slovenia and the Krajina region that resulted in the displacement of more than 150,000 Serbs.

All this raises important questions: How will such firms be held accountable to civilian and democratic goals? What happens when the firm's interest diverges from the home government's interest? Because sending contractors instead of military personnel into conflict zones is more politically palatable, and often invisible to the public, will it give the national security apparatus a way to get around the constraints of Congress? These dilemmas should spark a public debate on the advisability of selling advanced western military training on the private market.

union head Hassan Jum'a said.

Soon, Southern Oil Company workers began challenging the company's wage schedules. They surveyed prices and proposed a monthly minimum of $85. Workers threatened to strike and shut off oil production, and said they'd join the armed resistance if occupation troops were called in. The CPA Oil Minister immediately flew to Basra, where he agreed to return to the higher wage scale, with extra pay for working in risky or isolated locations prone to attack by the armed opposition.

In January, unrest spread to the Najibeeya, Haartha, and Az Zubeir electrical generating stations, where workers mounted a wildcat strike, stormed the administration buildings, declared the September 2003 wage schedule void, and vowed to shut off power if salaries were not raised. Again the ministry agreed to return to the old scale.

Following another walkout in February at the Basra Oil Pipeline Company, the Southern Oil Company wage schedule eventually spread to most worksites in the oil sector. Workers then took the fight back to the power stations, where they threatened again to stop electrical generation, a move with the potential to halt all other industries.

Samir Hanoon, vice president of the Iraqi Federation of Trade Unions in Basra, warned that if the ban on unions wasn't lifted, "we will take other actions—protests, demonstrations, and total shut-downs." The U.S. installation of the interim administration of Iyad Allawi at the end of June did not improve worker salaries or respect for labor rights. Hanoon's warning has gone unheeded by Baghdad's new authorities, much as it was by the CPA. And since the transitional law prevents Allawi's government from changing the 1987 law and the prohibition on "civil disorder," militant labor action is likely to continue, and to result in the same kinds of arrests of union leaders that took place last December.

THE CASE AGAINST PRIVATIZING NATIONAL SECURITY
Ann Markusen
May/June 2004

In the past 20 years, this country has undergone a transformation in the way it prepares for, conducts, and mops up after war. The Pentagon has overseen a large-scale effort to outsource all aspects of its operations to private corporations. But despite the claims of privatization proponents, there's scant evidence that private firms perform better or at lower cost than public-sector agencies. More troubling, as corporations cash in on lucrative contracts, they encroach on the political process, driving up military spending and influencing military and foreign policy.

The Growing "Shadow Pentagon"
National defense is one of the most heavily outsourced activities in the U.S. federal government. From 1972 to 2000, private contractors' share of all defense-related jobs climbed from 36% to 50%. While the country's public-sector defense workforce remains large—about 2.2 million in 2000—its "shadow workforce," the true number of people supported by federal government spending and mandates, is far larger. (See Table 1.)

Of the dozens of major military contract firms in the United States today, Lockheed Martin, Boeing, and Northrop Grumman are the largest three—they divvied up $50 billion of the $209 billion the Pentagon awarded in prime contracts in 2003, according to defense analyst William Hartung—but lesser-known info-tech and engineering companies like Computer Sciences Corporation, BDM International, and Science Applications International Corporation are emerging as major Department of Defense (DOD) suppliers, each with billions of dollars in defense business annually.

Despite the popular image of a defense contract as a contract for building large weapons systems like aircraft, missiles, or tanks, contracts for services are actually more typical. Service workers—not production workers—accounted for nearly three out of four contract-created jobs in 1996, up more than 50% since 1984. A growing

TABLE 1: ESTIMATED FULL-TIME EQUIVALENT FEDERAL CIVIL SERVICE, CONTRACT, AND GRANT JOBS BY CATEGORY, 1996

Federal Agency	Civil Service Jobs	Contract Jobs	Grant Jobs*	Ratio of Civil Service to Contract + Grant Jobs
Defense	778,900	3,634,000	53,000	1:4.7
Energy	19,100	633,000	40,200	1:37
NASA	20,100	350,600	26,900	1:19
Total Defense-Related	818,100	4,617,600	120,100	1:5.8
All Other Federal	1,073,900	1,017,400	2,292,900	1:3.1

*Jobs created by money given as a grant rather than a contract for performance of services. The grant category includes research grants to universities.

Source: Paul Light, The True Size of Government, Washington, DC: Brookings Institution Press, 1999.

legion of contracted employees install, maintain, trouble-shoot, operate, and integrate military hardware. Similarly, research and development work is increasingly farmed out. (Navy technical centers outsourced 50% of research, development, test, and evaluation work by 1996, up from 30% in 1970.) And other, lower-skill, service contract firms perform a panoply of other functions, from base maintenance and catering and support, to security detail and military training.

Economic Expectations

According to economic theory, it's competition, not privatization per se, that is expected to produce cost savings and performance improvements. Competition is key because private contractors are profit-seeking firms whose first loyalties are to their shareholders. Without competition, and in the absence of close monitoring, the corporations have every incentive to raise prices and hide information about their products and services. Defense economists suggest competition should generate efficiencies, but only under certain conditions: four or more firms competing for a given job, ongoing competition over time, clarity by the government buyer about task and performance requirements, and active, sustained government monitoring.

That's the theory. In the real world of military contracting, these conditions are rarely met. Most contracts that are opened to competing bids have fewer than three bidders. Once signed, contracts last for long periods, insulating firms from ongoing competitive pressures. The bidding process itself may be distorted in that firms "low-ball" bids, knowing they can negotiate add-ons later. And with the dramatic consolidation of the industry in the mid-1990s, and the shrinking number of large prime contractors, collusion among firms is a recurrent problem.

Several Pentagon contracts are "cost-plus," meaning the companies recoup their costs, including a portion of overhead, and are guaranteed a percentage of the costs as profit—a recipe for cost inflation. For example, Halliburton subsidiary Kellogg Brown & Root was given a 10-year multibillion dollar contract to provide logistical support services to U.S. troops overseas. The contract guarantees the firm will receive 1% of total costs as profit. In addition, KBR is eligible for a bonus payment of up to 2%. The firm has a long record of cost overruns in Kosovo, and its performance to date in Iraq has been weak. KBR admitted to overcharging the government by $61 million for gasoline, and its own internal audit of its Iraq operations reveals serious problems including a failure to control subcontractor costs and widespread loss of supplies and equipment, according to the *Wall Street Journal*.

The Evidence on Expected Gains from Privatization

Given the colossal sum of government dollars doled out in defense contracts, you'd think Congress and the Pentagon would carefully track cost and performance outcomes. But Pentagon records are sketchy and largely hidden from public view. Even the U.S. General Accounting Office (GAO), the investigative arm of Congress, has had difficulty prying data from the Pentagon. What's more, the few assessments that do exist focus on competitions between public and private bidders (where a government agency bids for work in competition with a private entity), and not private-private competitions, or the 50% of DOD purchases that are sole-sourced, simply given to a contractor with no competitive bidding process at all.

Some have estimated that the DOD saves 20% to 30% from public-private competitions, but those approximations are based on savings estimates at the initial bidding stage. In other words, they look at the promise of savings, not actual savings over time—a poor measure, since cost overruns are common and contracts are often renegotiated or otherwise changed after they're awarded.

The few existing studies of longer-term outcomes—conducted mainly by the Center for Naval Analysis (CNA), a federally funded research and development center, and the GAO—offer mixed results.

A CNA study of surface ships found that readiness was about the same whether the work was done in a public Navy yard or a private yard; a study of Navy maintenance work over time found that for a period of around two years, the contractors' performance was worse than that of the Navy in-house team, but that overall, the contractors performed better than the Navy team.

CNA insists that public-private competitions do generate bids and plans which would, if implemented, save the Pentagon money. But CNA analyses are emphatic that "competition produces the savings and not outsourcing per se." Its simulations suggest that 65% of total savings should in theory be achieved simply by the exercise of competing, even if no private firm receives a contract.

GAO is less sanguine about the potential for cost savings. The agency investigated some of the Pentagon's savings estimates and concluded that they were overstated because "DOD has not fully calculated either the investment costs associated with undertaking these competitions or the personnel separation costs likely to be associated with implementing them." DOD had assumed it would cost just $2,000 per position to conduct a competition, but in actuality the costs run from $7,000 to $9,000. In a later review of the Pentagon's claim that it had saved $290 million through public-private competition in 1999, the GAO concluded that it was difficult to determine how much had actually been saved. A large part of the problem, again, is that the DOD does not systematically track or update its savings estimates once contracts are underway.

GAO also cautions that savings from outsourcing come chiefly from cuts in personnel costs. We cannot know whether these cuts normally take the form of wage and benefit reductions, the use of temporary workers, cuts to the full-time workforce, or some combination, because private-sector firms refuse to share personnel information, calling it proprietary.

The large role of labor-cost savings in Pentagon outsourcing should give policy-makers pause. It's troubling that the Pentagon does not monitor the pay and working conditions of its "shadow employees." If private prison administrators are required to share employment data with evaluators, why shouldn't Pentagon contractors face the same requirement?

In sum, the jury's still out on whether outsourcing military work produces efficiencies, and little is known about how savings that are achieved may result from cutting wages. Furthermore, no study has included the cost of competent oversight in the outsourcing calculus, or looked systematically at performance outcomes.

Corruption and Policy Influence

Beyond efficiency and performance concerns, the increasing reliance on for-profit firms for national defense creates deeper political and institutional problems—namely, the capture of public decision-making by private military interests.

Through lobbying, advertising, and heavy campaign contributions, the private defense sector calls for weapons systems and defense initiatives that generate lucrative contracts. Since the end of the Cold War, private military contractors have formed a powerful lobby to protect obsolete Cold War weapons systems. For example, during the Reagan years, strenuous lobbying overcame even the highly mobilized and scientifically well-informed opposition to the B-1 bomber and the Star Wars program, two of the most costly weapons programs in the postwar period. In the 1990s, lobbyists undermined important initiatives to control the export of conventional arms, and recently the aerospace industry—led by Lockheed Martin—pushed hard to bring Poland, Hungary, and the Czech Republic into NATO in the expectation that these countries would then upgrade their militaries with costly new hardware. In general, the defense industry's leverage in Congress makes it difficult for the nation to shift resources toward peacekeeping missions, negotiated settlements, and the use of economic development in place of regional warfare.

As John Donahue summarizes in *The Privatization Decision*:

> In any contractual relationship between government and private business, a key question becomes who is representing the broader public interests. Unless there are sturdy provisions to prevent it—and even if all parties are immune to corruption—the natural outcome is an alliance between private-sector suppliers and government officials at the taxpayers' expense.

Less visible than the congressional lobbyists and trade groups, but just as significant, contractors employ their superior technical expertise to sell Pentagon procurement managers and top military leaders on pricey and risky new projects. Sitting on Pentagon advisory committees helps, as does the firms' insulation from public scrutiny. The quickening pace of privatization in research and development has left the government without the expertise to assess and monitor contractors' proposals.

What's Driving Defense Privatization?

The political, intellectual, and financial impetus for government privatization began in the 1970s and received its major political boost from the Reagan administration, which shrank government even as it increased defense expenditures by 50% in real terms. The Clinton administration's reversal of the Carter-Reagan military buildup had the unintended consequence of unleashing a hungry pro-privatization lobby onto the political scene—the mid-1990s reduction of the defense budget sent private contractors scrambling for new markets. At the same time, a raft of mergers consolidated the industry into a powerful handful of giant firms, all focused on developing new streams of government revenue. Their efforts on Capitol Hill dovetailed with and drew life from the 20-year ideological assault on public-sector provision of goods and services. During the Clinton years, insiders also adopted and capitalized on the "reinventing government" agenda spearheaded by Vice President Al Gore at the federal level.

Since the 1990s, private business groups, DOD advisory boards and key managers, and both the Clinton and Bush administrations have heightened calls to privatize national-security activity. For Pentagon managers, privatization offers a means of coping with a "go it alone" defense doctrine that deploys U.S. armed forces around the world with little international support.

Advocacy groups heavily populated by large defense contractors issue a stream of pronouncements and publications urging privatization. They recommend outsourcing functions outright rather than relying on public-private competitions (which give public agencies a chance to bid for projects), and back the wholesale privatization of complex business areas that currently involve large numbers of government employees.

One such task force, the Defense Science Board Task Force on Outsourcing and Privatization, issued studies in 1996 claiming that $10 billion to $30 billion could be saved through privatizing DOD's support and maintenance services.

Needless to say, they offered inadequate evidence to support these multibillion-dollar savings estimates. The panel that released the first study was headed by the CEO of military contractor BDM International.

At about the same time, Business Executives for National Security (BENS), a group founded in 1982 as a watchdog organization to monitor the Pentagon on weapons costs and nuclear, chemical, and biological warfare, transformed itself into an outspoken advocate of outsourcing. In 1996, BENS launched a high-profile commission to "promote outsourcing and privatization, closing unneeded military bases and implementing acquisition reform" with a self-described membership of "business leaders, former government officials and retired military officers." The commission published op-eds and position papers claiming the Pentagon civilian workforce is bloated. It decried what it misleadingly described as the bleeding away of private-sector defense jobs. (BENS used 1988 as its baseline; the year was an anomaly that included a spike in Reagan-era defense contracts.) It also claimed the Pentagon lags behind private corporations in outsourcing, and that the United States lags behind Europeans in privatization. Neither assertion is borne out by the evidence.

Under Clinton, Secretary of Defense William Cohen and other top DOD officials echoed BENS' calls for a "Revolution in Military Business Affairs." Dr. Jacques Gansler, President Clinton's undersecretary of defense for acquisition and technology, frequently spoke out in favor of outsourcing and a business approach:

> To meet the challenge of modernization, the Department of Defense ... must do business more like private business.... My top priority, as Under Secretary of Defense, is to make the Pentagon look much more like a dynamic, restructured, reengineered, world-class commercial sector business.

In February 2001, just after George W. Bush took office, a defense reform conference organized by the Aerospace Industries Association of America and Boeing, Lockheed Martin, Northrop Grumman, Raytheon, TRW, Inc., and BAE Systems met to set the agenda for the new administration. It attracted 500 participants and drew up a "Blueprint for Action" to slash bureaucracies, reduce "cycle times" and restore operational and financial strength to the defense industrial base. Also in February 2001, a BENS initiative, "Improving the Business End of the Military," identified activities the DOD can discontinue and "replace with world class business models," turning entire functions (housing, communications, power utilities, logistics systems) over to the private sector.

Since George W. Bush took office, the military budget has grown from $300 billion to $400 billion, not counting the $200 billion in supplemental expenditures for Iraq and Afghanistan. The spending hike has set off a feeding frenzy among contractors, some of which have seen double-digit growth in profits.

The Bush administration is intensifying efforts to transfer work from inside the Pentagon to private contractors. The DOD is expected to put 225,000 jobs up for competition between public employee groups and private companies by the end of

Bush's first term. Many more jobs have been displaced through direct outsourcing. The Bush push appears to be driven by a combination of ideology and political calculation, reinforced by defense-sector campaign contributions and the accelerating revolving door between the Pentagon and private contractors.

But this strategy poses serious risks and may threaten the possibility of society exercising democratic control over the evolution and use of military force. George Washington University political scientist Deborah Avant stresses that privatizing security "almost inevitably redistributes power over the control of violence both within governments and between states and non-state actors." In the United States, the private delivery of services has strengthened the executive branch, diminished the control of Congress, and reduced transparency. And, she warns, the process is cumulative—as private security companies are integrated into military efforts, the companies gain greater influence over foreign and military policy-making.

This article was adapted from a longer article published in the journal *Governance*, Vol. 16, No. 4 (October, 2003).

Sources: Deborah Avant, The Market for Force: Private Security and Political Change, manuscript under review, 2004; "The Revolution in Business Affairs: Realizing the Potential," Conference Summary, CNA Corporation, Alexandra, VA: 1998; John Donahue, *The Privatization Decision: Public Ends, Private Means,* New York: Basic Books, 1989; William D. Hartung, "Making Money on Terrorism," *The Nation,* February 5, 2004; Paul Light, The True Size of Government, Washington, DC: Brookings Institution Press, 1999.

Chapter 9

PLUNDERING THE PLANET

WHO'S TO BLAME FOR CLIMATE CHANGE?
Ben Boothby
March/April 2003

It's now an indisputable fact that the global climate is changing. Scientists have warned for decades that "greenhouse gases," mainly carbon dioxide (CO_2), were building up in the atmosphere and trapping the sun's heat. Over the course of the 20th century, as fossil-fuel pollution expanded, the amount of CO_2 in the atmosphere rose by about 30%, increasing temperatures and causing extreme weather patterns worldwide. The greenhouse danger is now so undeniable that even George W. Bush's "blue ribbon" scientific panel on climate change admitted that global temperatures are on the rise.

If we hope to combat global warming, we need to drastically reduce the levels of CO_2 released into the atmosphere. Scientists consider even the targets set by the Kyoto Protocol (the international agreement to limit greenhouse gas emissions) inadequate compared to the urgency of the problem. But the Bush administration reneged on the United States' commitment even to these minimal standards, on the pretext that the agreement "exempts 80 percent of the world including major population centers, such as China and India."

Bush's scapegoats, however, are hardly responsible for the climate-change crisis. China accounted for just 7% of the world's CO_2 emissions over the course of the 20th century; India, for only 2%. The United States, in contrast, accounted for more than 30% of the total. (See Figure 1.) Moreover, emissions levels in the United States continue to surge, rising every year between 1991 and 2000, the latest year for which data is available. According to the Department of Energy, the country's fossil-fuel-related CO_2 emissions increased by more than 2.7 percent between 1999 and 2000. In contrast, China reduced its emissions by almost 2.2% in 2000, its third straight year of reductions.

The United States' ruling elite has never been as big about taking responsibility for its actions (e.g., slavery, support for dictatorships, etc.), as it has been about posturing as a world leader. So it comes as no surprise that the United States remains number one in CO_2 emissions (in both total and per capita terms) year after year. (See Figure 2.) If any country is in a position—technologically and economically—to "lead by example" towards a sustainable future, it is the United States. Yet the U.S. government has steadfastly refused to adopt common-sense measures like raising fuel efficiency standards, reducing automobile use, lessening dependence on coal and petroleum, or promoting alternative-energy technologies.

Instead, less-developed countries with far fewer resources than the United States

FIGURE 1: PERCENTAGE OF WORLD CARBON EMISSIONS, 1900–1999

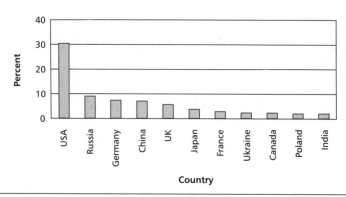

Source: World Resources Institute, "The U.S., Developing Countries, and Climate Protection: Leadership or Stalemate?" June 2001 <www.wri.org/wri/>.

FIGURE 2: PER CAPITA CARBON EMISSIONS, 1999

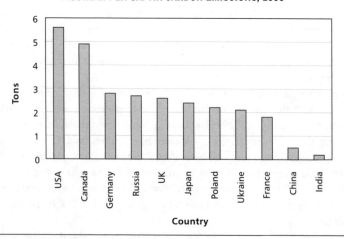

Source: World Resources Institute, "The U.S., Developing Countries, and Climate Protection: Leadership or Stalemate?" June 2001 <www.wri.org/wri/>.

are leading in the reduction of greenhouse-gas emissions. "China's actions are nothing short of remarkable," notes a 2001 report by the World Resources Institute. "The world's most populous country reduced its emissions ... by 19 percent from 1997 to 1999. This is simply unprecedented, especially considering that China's economy grew rapidly over the same period." Now that India, too, has ratified the Kyoto Protocol, it seems that Bush will just have to find himself some new scapegoats.

NATIONAL ENERGY PLAN?
Adria Scharf and Thad Williamson
March/April 2004

One huge political obstacle stands in the way of weaning the U.S. economy from fossil fuels: the all-but-certain opposition of leading energy corporations and other industries with vested interests in the status quo. Corporate interests have aggressively attacked environmentalists (starting with Rachel Carson) and environmental legislation at every turn over the past five decades, their opposition all too often proving deadly to even modest environmental reform proposals. (See "Industry Attacks on Dissent," *Dollars & Sense*, March/April 2002.)

During the current Bush administration, large corporate interests have gone from simply influencing energy-related policies to literally making them. Within days of taking office, George W. Bush appointed the National Energy Policy Development Group (NEPD), a task force headed by Vice President Dick Cheney, with the mandate to define the nation's energy policy for the new century. With the former CEO of the oil-services firm Halliburton at its helm, the task force consulted in secret with the captains of the nation's oil, nuclear, and coal industries, refusing to this day to name the meeting attendees or release minutes from the talks. The group issued its recommendations in May 2001. Its "National Energy Plan" takes as a given that over the next 20 years, U.S. oil consumption will increase by 33%, natural gas consumption by well over 50%, and demand for electricity by 45%. Rather than lay out a strategy to reduce the country's rapacious appetite for fossil fuels, the report focuses on how to feed the beast, making no real attempt to reduce aggregate fossil-fuel consumption, seriously raise energy efficiency, or aggressively build non-carbon alternatives (other than nuclear energy). In fact, the plan makes virtually no mention of promising forms of alternative energy like wind power.

Instead, it proposes the United States acquire more energy by drilling in the Arctic National Wildlife Refuge (ANWR) and offshore areas, building new electricity plants, burning more coal, and by continuing to import petroleum, both from our current suppliers—Saudi Arabia, Canada, Mexico, Venezuela—and, increasingly, from countries in the Caucasus, Central Asia, and Africa. The report recommends repeatedly that defense and trade policy be structured to ensure U.S. access to new oil supplies—and to commercial opportunities in the energy sector—in these regions.

"Big energy companies all but held the pencil for the White House task force as government officials wrote a plan calling for billions of dollars in corporate subsidies, and the wholesale elimination of key health and environmental safeguards," according to Natural Resources Defense Council (NRDC) president John H. Adams. The NRDC, which forced the Department of Energy to release some task-force documents by court order, concluded that oil industry representatives essentially wrote whole sections of the national energy policy. Bush's "Executive Order 13211," which requires government agencies to prepare "statements of energy effects" before implementing any policy that might affect energy supply, distribution, or use, was "nearly identical in structure and impact to [an American Petroleum Institute] draft, and nearly verbatim in a key section." A Bush proposal to weaken the Clean Air Act originated from a lobbyist for the electricity firm Southern Company, a major Bush donor.

Senate Democrats staved off ANWR drilling in 2003 by threatening to filibuster. But Bush has accomplished other key plan recommendations—including the expansion of drilling in Alaska's ecologically sensitive, federally managed outer continental shelf—through executive orders. Senate Republicans aim to pass the major remaining components of the legislation as stand-alone bills and amendments this session.

The political obstacles to major climate-change reform transcend the particulars of any single administration. Al Gore's attempts to pass a modest carbon tax are instructive. Long an advocate of taxing fossil fuels, Gore tried and failed to pass a carbon tax in the Senate in 1991. One of the first initiatives put forward by the new Clinton-Gore administration in 1993 was a small tax on fossil fuels, called a BTU tax, meant to force down fossil-fuel consumption and generate revenue. Despite Gore's strong support, the $73 billion five-year tax proposal was quickly trampled by both parties. Democrats and Republicans alike simply did not, and do not, see the tax as politically palatable. By 1998, in public statements about the Kyoto Protocol, a chastened Al Gore assured the legislature, and the oil and auto lobbies, that no carbon tax would be used to lower carbon emissions under the Kyoto accord. Gore said the administration had "completely ruled out new taxes of any kind as a means of meeting our obligations."

In short, there is a mismatch between the dramatic changes in our energy use needed if climate change is to be addressed rationally, and the capacity of the existing political-economic system to deliver such change. Environmentalists and others who are serious about achieving real policy change to address the global-warming threat must be equally serious about forthrightly challenging the power structures that make sane environmental policies all but impossible to achieve.

Sources: Natural Resources Defense Council <www.nrdc.org>; Report of the National Energy Policy Development Group <www.whitehouse.gov/energy>.

TOWARD A GLOBAL ENERGY TRANSITION

What would it take to reverse climate change?

Ross Gelbspan
March/April 2004

In 1998, Hurricane Mitch killed 10,000 people in Central America. Last May, the worst flooding in memory in Sri Lanka killed about 300 people, left another 500 missing, and left 350,000 homeless. The president of Tuvalu, an island nation in the Pacific threatened by rising sea levels, calls climate change "a form of slow death." These are just a few recent natural disasters that scientists fear may be linked to global warming.

To avert climate catastrophe, humanity needs to cut its use of fossil fuels by at least 70% in a very short time. That is the consensus of more than 2,000 scientists from 100 countries reporting to the U.N.-sponsored Intergovernmental Panel on Climate Change in the largest and most rigorously peer-reviewed scientific collaboration in history.

The urgency of the threat is spelled out in two other recent peer-reviewed studies corroborating the U.N. panel's findings. The first, written in 2001 by researchers at the Hadley Center, Britain's principle climate research institute, estimated that the climate will change 50% more quickly than scientists had previously believed. Earlier computer models had assumed a relatively static biosphere. But when researchers factored in the warming that has already taken place, they found that the rate of change is compounding. They project that most of the world's forests will begin to die off and emit, rather than absorb, CO_2 by around 2040.

The other study is equally troubling. Several years ago, a team of 11 researchers published a study in Nature suggesting that unless the world gets half its energy from non-carbon (that is, non-fossil fuel) sources by 2018, a doubling—and possible tripling—of pre-industrial carbon dioxide (CO_2) levels later in this century will be inevitable. A follow-up study, published in Science in November 2002, calls for a crash program to develop a carbon-free energy economy. Using conservative projections of future energy use, the researchers concluded that within 50 years, the world will need to generate at least three times more energy from alternative sources than it currently produces from fossil fuels in order to avoid a catastrophic build-up of atmospheric CO_2.

The science is taken very seriously outside the United States. In other countries, hardly anyone debates whether human activities are affecting the climate. Policymakers in Europe are in agreement about the urgency of the climate threat. Holland has completed a plan to cut emissions by 80% in the next 40 years. The United Kingdom has committed itself to 60% reductions in 50 years. Germany is planning for 50% cuts in 50 years.

By contrast, the White House has become the East Coast branch office of ExxonMobil and Peabody Coal, and climate and energy policy has become the pre-eminent case study in the contamination of the U.S. political system by money.

Two years ago, U.S. President George W. Bush reneged on a campaign promise to cap carbon emissions from coal-burning power plants. He then unveiled his administration's energy plan, which is basically a shortcut to climate hell. (See "National Energy Plan?" p. 26.) In a truly Orwellian stroke, the White House excised all references to the dangers of climate change on the Environmental Protection Agency's website in mid-2003. Finally, Bush withdrew the United States from the Kyoto climate negotiations, and the administration's chief climate negotiator declared that the United States would not engage in the Kyoto process for at least 10 years.

A Strategy to Reverse CO_2 Emissions

A plan that could actually stabilize the climate does exist. Provisionally called the World Energy Modernization Plan, it was developed by an ad hoc group of about 15 economists, energy policy experts, and others who met at the Center for Health and the Global Environment at Harvard Medical School three years ago.

The plan addresses a stark reality: The deep oceans are warming, the tundra is thawing, the glaciers are melting, infectious diseases are migrating, and the timing of the seasons has changed. All this has resulted from only one degree of warming. The U.N.-sponsored Intergovernmental Panel on Climate Change (IPCC) expects the earth to warm another three to 10 degrees later in this century.

To date, no other policy proposals have adequately addressed either the scope or the urgency of the problem. While some of its particulars may require revamping, the World Energy Modernization Plan reflects an appropriate scale of action, given the magnitude of the crisis.

The plan calls for three interacting strategies. One is a subsidy switch: industrial countries would eliminate government subsidies for fossil fuels and establish equivalent subsidies for renewable, non-carbon energy technologies. Another is a clean-energy transfer fund—a pool of money on the order of $300 billion a year to provide renewable energy technologies to developing countries. The last element is a progressively more stringent fossil-fuel efficiency standard that would rise by 5% per year.

While each of these strategies can be viewed as a stand-alone reform, they are better understood as a set of interactive policies that could speed the energy transition far more rapidly together than if they were implemented piecemeal.

Subsidy Switch

The United States now spends more than $20 billion a year to subsidize fossil fuels through corporate tax write-offs and direct payments to oil, gas, and coal companies (for research and development, and oil purchases for the Strategic Petroleum Reserve, for example). Subsidies for fossil fuels in industrial countries total an estimated $200 billion a year.

Under this proposal, industrial countries would withdraw those subsidies from fossil fuels and establish equivalent subsidies for renewable energy sources. A small portion of U.S. subsidies must be used to retrain or buy out the nation's approximately 50,000 coal miners. But the lion's share of the subsidies would go to aggressive development of fuel cells, wind farms, and solar systems. The major oil companies would be forced to re-tool and retrain their workers to stay afloat in the renewable energy economy.

Fund to Help Poor Countries Go Green

The second element of the plan involves the creation of a new $300-billion-a-year fund to help transfer renewable energy technologies to the global South. Developing countries such as China, Mexico, Thailand, and Chile contain some of the world's smoggiest cities. Many would love to go solar, but virtually none can afford to.

One attractive source of revenue to fund the transfer lies in a so-called "Tobin tax," named after its developer, Nobel prize-winning economist James Tobin. This tax would be levied on banks and other agents that conduct international currency transactions. Tobin conceived his tax as a way of damping volatility in capital markets by discouraging short-term trading and encouraging longer-term capital investments. But it would also generate enormous revenues. Today currency swaps by banks and speculators total $1.5 trillion per day. A tax of a quarter-penny on a dollar would net $300 billion a year, which could go for wind farms in India, fuel-cell factories in South Africa, solar equipment assemblies in El Salvador, and vast, solar-powered hydrogen-producing farms in the Middle East.

If a Tobin tax proves unacceptable, a fund of the same magnitude could be raised from a tax on airline travel or a carbon tax in industrial countries, although both these sources are more regressive.

Regardless of its revenue source, the fund would be allocated according to a United Nations formula. Climate, energy use, population, economic growth rates, and other factors would determine each developing country's allocation.

Recipient countries would negotiate contracts with renewable energy vendors to ensure domestic ownership of new energy facilities and substantial employment of local labor in their construction and operation. Although not explicitly mentioned in the initial version of the plan, it would be important for governments to be required to include representatives of ethnic and indigenous minorities, universities, nongovernmental organizations (NGOs), and labor unions in making decisions about the procurement and deployment of new energy resources.

An international auditing agency would monitor transactions to ensure equal access for all energy vendors and to review contracting procedures between banks, vendors, and recipient governments.

Individual countries would decide how to use their share. For example, if India received $5 billion in the first year, it could pick its own mix of wind farms, small-scale solar installations, fuel cell generators, and biogas facilities.

In this hypothetical example, the Indian government would entertain bids for these clean energy projects. Vendors might include large or small private companies, state-owned entities, and even nonprofit organizations. As these contractors met specified development and construction goals, they would be paid directly by the banks. And the banks would receive fees for administering the fund.

As developing countries acquired technology, the fund could simply be phased out, or the money in it could be diverted to other global needs.

If funded by a Tobin tax, it would transfer resources from speculative, nonproductive finance-sector transactions to the industrial sectors of developing nations for productive, job-creating, wealth-generating projects. A clean-energy transfer fund of this sort could have a massive impact on developing and transitional economies, similar to the Marshall Plan's effect on Europe after World War II.

Strict International Efficiency Standards

Third, the plan calls on the parties to the Kyoto talks to adopt a simple and equitable fossil-fuel efficiency standard that becomes 5% more stringent each year.

This mechanism, if incorporated into the Kyoto Protocol, would harmonize and guide the global energy transition in a way that the current ineffectual and inequitable system of international emissions trading cannot.

The system of international emissions trading at the heart of the Kyoto Protocol is based on the concept that a country that exceeds its allowed quantity of carbon emissions can buy emission credits from a country that emits less than its allowed quantity. The United States, for instance, can pay Costa Rica to plant more trees to absorb carbon dioxide, and subtract the resulting reduction from its own allowance.

This system of international "cap and trade," as it is called in the jargon of the Kyoto negotiators, has significant failings: It's not enforceable and is plagued by irreconcilable equity disputes between the countries of the North and South. (See box "Cap and Trade: Environmental Colonialism?")

International carbon trading cannot be the primary vehicle to propel a worldwide energy transition. Alone, it simply will not succeed in reversing—or even slowing—global CO_2 emissions at anywhere near an adequate rate. Even if all the problems with monitoring, enforcement, and equity could be resolved, emissions trading would at best be a fine-tuning instrument to help countries meet the final 10 to 15% of their obligation to reduce CO_2 emissions. We simply can't finesse nature with accounting tricks.

Instead, the parties to the Kyoto talks should increase their fossil-fuel energy efficiency by 5% every year until the global 70% reduction is attained. That means a country would either produce the same amount of goods as in the previous year with 5% less carbon fuel, or produce 5% more goods with the same amount of carbon fuel use as the previous year. During the first few years under the proposed efficiency standard, most countries would likely meet their goals by implementing low-cost improvements to their existing energy systems. After a few years, however, more expen-

Cap and Trade: Environmental Colonialism?

The global South has long contended that the Kyoto cap and trade system is unjust. Under Kyoto, each country's emissions cap is based on its 1990 emission levels—but developing countries argue that only a per-capita allocation of emission rights is fair. What's more, they argue, provisions in the Kyoto Protocol allow industrial nations to buy limitless amounts of cheap emission reductions in developing countries and to bank them indefinitely into the future. As the late Anil Agarwal, founder of the Centre for Science and Environment in New Delhi, has pointed out, when developing nations eventually become obligated to cut their own emissions (under a subsequent round of the Kyoto Protocol), they will be left with only the most expensive options. Agarwal considered this a form of environmental colonialism.

sive technology would be required to meet the progressively higher standard, making renewable energy sources more cost effective in comparison to fossil-fuel efficiency measures. The growing demand would create mass markets and economies of scale for renewables.

Given both fossil-fuel efficiency improvements and the growing use of alternatives, emissions reductions would outpace long-term economic growth, benefiting the environment.

Every country would begin at its current baseline for emission levels, which would reduce the inequities inherent in the cap-and-trade system.

This approach would be far simpler to negotiate than the current protocol, with its morass of emissions trading details, reviews of the adequacy of commitments, and differentiated emission targets for each country. It would also be easier to monitor and enforce. A nation's compliance would be measured simply by calculating the annual change in the ratio of its carbon fuel use to its gross domestic product. That ratio would have to change by 5% a year. Although this plan does not include an enforcement mechanism, one would be devised.

The approach has a precedent in the Montreal Protocol, under which companies phased out ozone-destroying chemicals. That protocol was successful because the companies that made the destructive chemicals were able to produce their substitutes with no loss of competitive standing within the industry. The energy industry must be restructured in the same way. Several oil executives have said in private conversations that they could, in an orderly fashion, decarbonize their energy supplies—but only if the governments of the world regulate the process to require all companies to make the transition in lockstep. A progressive fossil-fuel efficiency standard would provide that type of regulation.

A Regulated Transition

Even from the perspective of capitalist financial institutions, this plan should make perfect sense. Recently, Swiss Re-Insurance said it anticipates losses from climate impacts to reach $150 billion a year within this decade. Munich Re, the world's largest reinsurer, estimates that within several decades, losses from climate impacts will reach $300 billion a year. Climate change will destroy property; raise health care costs; ruin crops; and damage energy, communications and transportation infrastructures. It will likely wound the insurance and banking sectors in the process. Last year, the largest re-insurer in Britain said that unchecked climate change could bankrupt the global economy by 2065. And its effects hit poor countries hardest—not because nature discriminates against the poor, but because poor countries can't afford the kinds of infrastructure needed to buffer its impacts.

By contrast, a worldwide energy transition would create a dramatic expansion of the overall wealth in the global economy. It would raise living standards in the South without compromising those in the North. Rewiring the planet with clean energy in time to meet nature's deadline will generate a staggering number of new jobs for the global labor force. By blocking a transition to clean energy, the coal and oil industries are hindering a huge surge in new jobs all over the world.

This transition cannot be accomplished by unregulated free markets. A global energy conversion will require the world's governments to put in place a strong regime of mandatory regulation to control the economic activity of some of the world's largest and most powerful corporations. Without a binding structure of regulation to level the corporate playing field, competing energy companies will undercut today's voluntary initiatives by selling artificially cheaper oil and coal products. This would turn any investment in solar, wind, and hydrogen into money losers. On the other hand, energy firms that submit to the strong new regulations would gain a new $300-billion-a-year market.

A meaningful solution to the climate crisis could potentially be the beginning of a much larger transformation of our social and economic dynamics. This proposal is ambitious. But the alternative—given the escalating instability of the climate system and the increasing desperation caused by global economic inequities—is truly too horrible to contemplate.

Adapted with permission from Foreign Policy In Focus (FPIF) <www.fpif.org>, a joint project of the Interhemispheric Resource Center and the Institute for Policy Studies. A longer version of this article was prepared for the PetroPolitics conference co-sponsored by FPIP and the Sustainable Energy and Economy Network (SEEN), a project of the Institute for Policy Studies. For more information, and to read the web version of the article online, see <www.PetroPolitics.org>.

FLATTENING APPALACHIA

New mining techniques explode mountains and cause acres of land to collapse. The coal industry calls it economic development, and paid-off politicians agree.

Chris Sturr and Amy Offner
July/August 2003

Just after midnight on October 11, 2000, a Martin County Coal computer operator noticed a problem at Kentucky's largest "slurry impoundment"—one of the 200 waste reservoirs that catch the liquid run-off from Appalachian coal mines. The 2.2-billion-gallon impoundment was gushing black sludge into an underground mine, exploding its walls and sending the sludge back out into the Tug Fork and Big Sandy rivers. By the time workers stopped the leak, 300 million gallons of sludge had contaminated local water supplies and killed much of the aquatic life in nearby waterways. Officials from the Environmental Protection Agency (EPA) said it was a miracle that no human life was lost in the flood.

The Martin County sludge disaster was the nation's worst-ever black water spill, with a volume 22 times that of the Exxon Valdez oil spill. But it is just one of a series of environmental crises produced by new mining technologies on the rise since the 1990s: mountaintop removal and longwall mining.

As the name suggests, mountaintop removal uses enormous explosive power to blast the top off a mountain—sometimes the top 1,000 feet of a 3,000-foot peak. The rubble, or "overburden," is dumped into adjacent streams and valleys, diverting water flows, wreaking havoc on ecosystems, and exacerbating floods. Afterwards, the barren, rocky landscapes cannot absorb rain, so coal companies contain liquid run-off with structures—dams, sediment ponds, drainage ditches, and slurry impoundments—that can poison communities when they leak or overflow.

In states like Pennsylvania, another new technique called "longwall mining" removes entire seams of underground coal, causing what companies euphemistically term "a gentle lowering of the earth"—or what residents describe as man-made earthquakes. As coal companies hollow out tunnels up to 1,000 feet wide and two miles long, the earth above commonly sinks as much as four feet, damaging buildings, roads, streams, and wetlands. "Our first loss was our spring," explained Laurine Williams, whose Pennsylvania farm was damaged by longwall mining. "After many years of supplying excellent water for the house, our spring went dry when all of the wells down the valley went dry." Williams' pasture developed cracks 15 feet long and nearly three feet wide. "We couldn't tell how deep," she said, "because they appeared to be bottomless."

Today, longwall mining accounts for nearly 60% of Pennsylvania's coal production, and bears significant responsibility for the state's 2,500 miles of streams polluted by acid mine drainage. Meanwhile, mountaintop removal has buried at least 750 miles of West Virginia's streams and destroyed 300,000 acres of hardwood forest.

Some Appalachian counties have seen 20% of their landmass exploded, while coal companies place few if any limits on future "removals": in Whitesville, West Virginia, planned blast sites overlook elementary and high schools.

Economic Rationales, Real and Imagined

These exceptionally destructive mining techniques have become the strategies of choice in states like West Virginia, Kentucky, and Pennsylvania for a simple reason: they are the only profitable ways to mine dwindling, hard-to-reach coal reserves. By the industry's own estimates, at the current rate of production, West Virginia's coal may be gone in as few as 26 years. The long-term depletion of coal means that many companies are now scraping out seams once considered inaccessible or unprofitable.

The only way to mine these areas and turn a profit, the companies have found, is to eliminate the workers—and that is what mountaintop removal and longwall mining do. In West Virginia, the state most ravaged by mountaintop removal, these operations employ just 2,000 people; the state's total employment in mining has fallen from 100,000 in the late 1940s to 15,700 in 2000. Techniques that may simply be too dangerous to involve a lot of human beings—like blowing up mountains—are also incredibly efficient at extracting coal without them. In 2000, coal companies mined 170 million tons from West Virginia's mountains. Between 1983 and 1998, as Pennsylvania replaced most traditional underground mining with longwall mining, the state's coal production increased by 64% while the number of coal miners fell by 81%.

Of course, when coal companies publicly promote these techniques, they don't say that they're desperate to cut costs and are willing to wreck the environment to do it. "They say the flattened, remote areas [left by blasts] are great spots for developing jails, shopping malls, airports and schools," writes Vivian Stockman of the Ohio Valley Environmental Coalition, a group fighting mountaintop removal. Hydrogeologist and activist Rick Eades examined companies' claims that mining would promote economic development, and according to Stockman, he concluded that at the current rate of development, "it would take 3,700 years to develop the rest of the permitted mountaintop removal sites."

While the companies promise low-road economic development in the future, Stockman points to the current economic reality. "The counties with a lot of mountaintop removal are some of the poorest in an already poor state, with lousy schools and roads," she notes. "But that's King Coal's 'prosperity' for you."

The Department of Energy Production

Although most people living near mines have not profited from them, state and national politicians have. The coal industry gave $3.9 million in political contributions during the 2000 election cycle. In West Virginia, coal companies donated $115,600 to Democratic Governor Bob Wise's campaign, and another $120,340 to cover 20% of the cost of his inauguration. In return for their regular payments, coal companies have enjoyed near-immunity from state and federal regulations.

In Pennsylvania, for instance, streams and wetlands are protected by environmental regulations that are supposed to apply equally to mining and other industries. Yet according to Stephen Kunz, an ecologist who studies longwall mining, "Information routinely produced for applications for housing, shopping centers, highways, utilities, and other kinds of construction or development is not being required during the review of coal mine applications." The state Department of Environmental Protection (DEP) does not demand resource inventories, impact assessments, or procedures for monitoring and mitigating environmental damage. As Kunz explains, the DEP "acts more like a Department of Energy Production."

In West Virginia, the DEP issued a 2001 permit for Massey Energy—whose subsidiary, Martin, spilled the 300 million gallons in Kentucky—to build a 5-billion-gallon slurry disposal at the headwater of the Coal River. When the federal Surface Mine Board heard a citizen appeal on June 26, DEP officials didn't show, and evaded subpoenas by fleeing their offices. Thanks to such maneuvers, Massey has become the sixth-largest coal producer in the United States, collecting $32 million in profits during 2002.

As Massey board member James H. "Buck" Harless explains, it's not just state agencies that are helping the coal industry. "We were looking for friends," he told the *Wall Street Journal* in 2001, "and we found one in George W. Bush." The Bush energy plan suggests using executive orders of the president to speed energy production and power line construction; in fact, when he released the plan, Bush signed one such order requiring federal agencies to "fast track" permit approvals for coal-fired power plants.

Dollar for dollar, the Bush administration has given the coal industry excellent returns on its election-year investment. In exchange for $3.4 million in coal contributions to the GOP in 2000, the Bush administration allotted $2 billion over 10 years to the "Clean Coal Technology Program," a research initiative undertaken with the coal industry to make the dirtiest of all fuels "clean." The result: in February 2003, Bush released his "Clear Skies Plan," which proposes no reduction in mercury and carbon dioxide emissions from coal, and if implemented, will be less effective than simply enforcing the Clean Air Act. While spearheading all this "research," the Bush administration also had time to knock down key provisions of the Clean Water Act which banned companies from dumping mountaintop removal waste into waterways. Today, not only can companies legally destroy wetlands and streams, but the Bush administration's new permitting procedures allow them to do so with no public notice and minimal review by federal authorities.

The withering of state and federal regulations is ultimately the reason that mountaintop removal and longwall mining are considered efficient, inexpensive techniques. Today, coal is the cheapest fossil fuel per unit of energy, and produces more than half the country's electricity. But that is only because coal companies have pushed intolerable costs onto mining communities and the larger public. When the coal industry does not pay for destroyed infrastructure and ecosystems, mining communities do—either in cash or in ravaged landscapes and devastated local economies. Outside Appalachia, coal produces low-cost electricity, but also one-third of the country's mercury and carbon dioxide emissions—essentially forcing Americans to pay for electricity with their health. These are tremendous costs to pay for anything, and incomprehensible sacrifices to make for corporate profits. If the coal industry were held responsible for the true cost of coal, it would become a very expensive fuel—and coal companies might have to start peddling solar panels.

Sources: Coal Age, <www.coalage.com>; Stephen Kunz, "Wetlands and Longwall Mining," <http://www.rayproffitt.org/longwall/longwall. htm>; National Mining Association "2002 Coal Producer Survey," <www.nma.org>; National Resources Defense Council, "The Bush Record," <www.nrdc.org>; Ohio Valley Environmental Coalition, <www.ohvec.org>; Sierra Club, Pennsylvania Chapter, Coal and its Consequences, (Summer 2001).

THE BAD NEIGHBOR
Alcoa's Dirty Dealing in Central Texas
Esther Cervantes
July/August 2004

Earlier this year, the Aluminum Company of America (Alcoa) broke ground on the $83 million Three Oaks lignite mine outside Austin. The mine will provide coal to Alcoa's massive facility near the town of Rockdale: an aluminum smelter plus the three power plants that fire it. In addition to the lignite, Alcoa intends to remove groundwater from the new mine (as well as from its existing mine at Sandow, near Rockdale) and ship it to the city of San Antonio, more than 100 miles away. In a company report celebrating the Rockdale smelter's first 50 years, manager Geoff Cromer thanks the facility's neighbors for "the strong support we have received from the community"—but that's less than half the story. The "several hundred people" who "took time from their jobs" to attend numerous public hearings and "provide comment in support of Alcoa and this project" were far outnumbered by those who struggled against it for four years.

The protesters are an unlikely bunch—mostly cattle ranchers and suburban commuters, a population that has lived in the shadow of the Rockdale facility for decades without complaint. But when the company decided to expand its profit-making repertoire by selling the area's groundwater to a distant city, Alcoa's neighbors rebelled. In their effort to block the new mine and stop the water deal, they also dug up the dirt on Alcoa's 30-plus years of evading the Texas Clean Air Act at Rockdale. In spite of the protests, mining at Three Oaks is slated to begin in September; at the same time, though, Alcoa will have to announce how it will finally comply with clean air regulations.

Coal and Water

East of Austin the austere limestone hills over the Edwards aquifer give way to gently rolling scrubland—a patchwork of both bedroom communities of former ranchers and the oak, cedar, and tall grass-studded ranches of those who have yet to yield to the economic imperative of the commute.

In the 1970s the city of San Antonio bought 10,000 acres of this land, in Lee and Bastrop counties, and later leased mining rights to 4,000 more from Phillips Petroleum. San Antonio's municipally owned energy provider, City Public Service (CPS), hoped to fuel a new power plant with the lignite coal that lay under this domain. Public protest and, eventually, the offer of cheaper, cleaner coal from Wyoming changed the plan. CPS's new lands lay idle for years.

Though CPS never mined its lignite, other central Texas landowners have found use for the area's dirty brown coal. Since 1952, Alcoa has mined the Sandow deposit near Rockdale. Three power plants run day and night on the fuel, producing enough energy each year to light the city—or run an aluminum smelter.

The equipment Alcoa uses to extract the lignite would delight anyone who celebrates humankind's will to dominate the environment—or who has ever liked Tonka toys. Nate Blakeslee of the *Texas Observer* describes the draglines as two mechanical shovels, each 20 stories high with a 150-ton capacity bucket. Smaller (though still huge) shovels work inside the 100-foot-deep pit. Looking indeed like toys by comparison, dump trucks, bulldozers, and pickups dart around, lifting and hauling coal.

The draglines move enough earth each year to fill the Panama Canal; the resulting landscape dispels any impression that this is a game. Aerial photographs show a stark contrast between the stretches of mine that Alcoa has backfilled and the surrounding land it has never touched. The untouched land is a lush, deep green prairie dotted with stands of mature cedar and oak. The "reclaimed" land, planted almost exclusively with coastal bermuda grass, shows instead a sere khaki.

Alcoa officials like to point out that the company's land reclamation has won awards from the Texas Railroad Commission (TRC) and the U.S. Department of the Interior. But one shudders to imagine the competition for those awards: the TRC cited Sandow for 26 violations of the Surface Mining Control and Reclamation Act between 1992 and 1997. Much of the land mined there before the law's 1977 enactment has only been reclaimed under the auspices of the TRC. Hundreds of acres more, left to Alcoa's goodwill, remain a post-mine moonscape.

Massive earth-moving is not the only environmental disruption Alcoa causes at Sandow. The lignite there sits between two branches of the slow-recharging Carrizo-Wilcox aquifer. The deeper the draglines dig the pit, the harder the groundwater presses against the walls of the strip mine. Since 1988, Alcoa has had to pump seeping groundwater out of Sandow to keep it from flooding. Alcoa uses some of this water for dust control and dumps the rest—some 30,000 acre-feet (more than 9.75 billion gallons) annually—into local creeks.

In Texas, although the rules are slowly changing, groundwater is generally governed by right of capture, or the law of the biggest straw: anyone who can put the water to a legally-defined "beneficial use" may extract as much groundwater as their technology allows, and with the state's blessing.

At Sandow, Alcoa has a very big straw. When it began pumping groundwater, the company agreed with the TRC to compensate nearby groundwater users for any damage, such as wells that dried up because the water table dropped out from under them. Of around 600 official complaints Alcoa has received since 1989, the company has addressed less than half to the satisfaction of the party affected.

Most neighbors were willing to put up with the bother, though, because of the jobs and other benefits that Alcoa brings to the area. The facility is the largest unionized employer in central Texas, employing about 1,200 workers. Alcoa also pays royalties to landowners whose property it mines. Others depend indirectly on the mine and smelter for their livelihoods.

Alcoa had long been seen as a livable neighbor—then it decided to get into the water business.

'Til Your Well Runs Dry

Texas' shift from right-of-capture to more formal groundwater regulation began with a 1991 lawsuit against the U.S. Fish and Wildlife Service for failing to protect the wildlife of the Edwards aquifer (located west of the Carrizo-Wilcox) from the effects of excessive drawdown. According to the Sierra Club and area environmentalists, the vast Edwards aquifer, whose three segments span the more than 230 miles from Austin southwest to Del Rio, supports wide ecological diversity in a semi-arid climate.

More to the point, the Edwards passes below and provides water to two of the state's major cities, San Antonio and Austin. San Antonio is entirely dependent on the aquifer for its drinking water and uses about 175,000 acre-feet per year; the city's water use is expected to reach more than 375,000 acre-feet by 2050. In May 1993 the Texas legislature capped all Edwards withdrawals at 450,000 acre-feet per year, a number to be reduced to 400,000 in 2008.

According to San Antonio Water System (SAWS) spokesperson Susan Butler, "our groundwater supply has been severely reduced by regulation," and the city is preparing for the future. In 1997, SAWS started building infrastructure to expand the city's use of treated wastewater. First used in the 1960s to cool area power plants, treated wastewater now irrigates golf courses and has replaced the fresh groundwater that, until the late 1990s, maintained the flow of the San Antonio River through the River Walk. (The San Antonio no longer flows in dry weather without help.) This style of conservation is not for all tourist attractions, though: the log flume rides at

Fiesta Texas, a nearby theme park, are not likely to switch to recycled wastewater. At the same time San Antonio was casting about for ways to reduce its reliance on Edwards aquifer groundwater, the lignite in Alcoa's Sandow mine was beginning to run out. If San Antonio would let Alcoa mine its long-abandoned lignite, the company offered, Alcoa would incidentally mine groundwater for the thirsty city.

The deal was struck in the last days of 1998. Alcoa acquired San Antonio's 14,000 acres of mining rights and began planning to build the Three Oaks mine there, while agreeing to provide SAWS with 40,000 to 60,000 acre-feet of water per year from the Sandow mine. CPS (the municipal utility) signed over to SAWS the water rights to the same land it's leasing to Alcoa for the new mine, rights good for perhaps another 15,000 acre-feet per year. The high-end total is about 40% of San Antonio's current use, and it comes at no small price. In its contracts for water from Sandow and Three Oaks, SAWS agrees to pay Alcoa: for the water itself; a monthly project management fee for the duration of the contract, whether or not any water is delivered; and all the costs of designing, building, and operating the pipeline and other facilities needed to deliver the water, including, "to the extent allowed by law, all taxes, fees, and other costs … incurred … by Alcoa" due to its ownership of any land or facilities. Upon expiration of the contract (set for 2040, but subject to extension), ownership of all land associated with the pipeline is to be transferred to Alcoa by San Antonio. That's water fees, administrative fees that apply whether or not the water is delivered, reimbursement for all infrastructure, eventual ownership of that infrastructure and the land on which it sits, and tax breaks on that land, all accruing to Alcoa at the expense of the citizens of San Antonio.

But San Antonio need not wait so long to see just how short its end of the stick really is. Once Sandow has closed as a lignite mine, very little of the water Alcoa would supply to San Antonio would be directly tied to lignite mining. The point is crucial. Only water extracted for lignite-mining purposes is covered in Alcoa's agreement with the Texas Railroad Commission to compensate other Carrizo-Wilcox users for harm it may cause them by lowering the water table. The 1998 contracts leave SAWS holding the bag for any additional well damage.

It has the potential to be a mighty big bag. The University of Texas Bureau of Economic Geology's model of the effect of the water-export deal on the Carrizo-Wilcox predicts a drop in the water table of as much as 300 feet by 2050. Such a drop is costly when the affected wells must be repaired or their owners compensated. When Lee County resident L. C. Hobbs wanted to sink a well on his property in 1997, Alcoa's records assured him that he would hit water at 80 feet. The water that Hobbs did eventually find, 467 feet down, was so fouled by mineral deposits that it required filtration. Hobbs asked Alcoa for $8,400 to cover the extra drilling and $7,400 for the filtration system. When the company offered to settle at $5,000, Hobbs sued. The area that would be affected by the predicted drawdown is home to tens of thousands of similar small users of the aquifer today, and the local population is increasing rapidly.

But few knew the details of the water deal before the contracts were signed—three months before feasibility studies ordered by SAWS were finished. Why the rush? After a severe drought in 1996, the Texas legislature finally decided to extend the reform of its groundwater policy to aquifers other than the Edwards. Members of the SAWS citizen advisory panel allege that the rush to slide the agreement in under the door of the proposed new groundwater laws kept them ignorant of the deal until it was nearly done. The complex contracts were released to SAWS' citizen advisors just days before the SAWS board voted to approve them.

San Antonians protested the deal once they knew about it, but the ink was already dry. Bob Martin of the Homeowners-Taxpayers Association claimed that a 31% rate increase announced by SAWS in 1999 brought 40 new members to his group, which opposed the Alcoa deal. At a 2000 public hearing, local minister Leslie Ellison declared the cost of the plan "outrageous." Other speakers criticized the Alcoa deal as a "boondoggle" and called Mike Thuss, then head of SAWS, an "imperial parasite."

San Antonio is supposed to take its first delivery of Alcoa water in 2013, although pipeline construction has yet to begin. SAWS has sought other means and more favorable terms on which to fill its water demands, and it has done well enough that Travis Brown, a founder of the local group Neighbors for Neighbors (NFN), speculates that the Sandow deal will eventually be abandoned. Still, the cost to the city for abandoning the deal grows with each passing month, and representatives from both SAWS and Alcoa maintain that the contracts are "current." And even if no Alcoa water ever makes it into San Antonio taps, the city may decide to resell the water. The most likely customers? Growing Austin suburbs, including the very same communities that are to have the water pumped out from under them. Or, if the contracts completely break down, Alcoa may do the selling. After all, they've already laid claim to the water—and as Texas' new groundwater rules emerge, it's clear that prior claims can easily be parlayed into profit (see box "The Longest Straw Lives On").

Unlikely Activists

Cattle ranchers and suburban commuters seem an even more unlikely source of community activism than Sun Belt urbanites, especially on an environmental issue. But Elgin-based Neighbors for Neighbors has organized just such people, give or take a Buddhist nun and a nudist camp, into a vocal and tenacious resistance against the deal. The issue certainly hits closer to home for those who would be losing the water than for those gaining it. And, says Brown, the contracts "kind of blew up this rural versus urban contest." Organizing was the only way for a scattered population to oppose the power of "all these thirsty cities looking to our area."

John Burke, head of Aqua Water, the area's nonprofit water provider, put it more bluntly to reporter Nate Blakeslee: "If you went down to San Antonio and the Edwards Aquifer and said I'm gonna draw down 100 feet over 1,400 square miles, those

The Longest Straw Lives On

In March 1991, when the law of the biggest straw still governed groundwater use across Texas, Ron Pucek opened the Living Waters Artesian Springs catfish farm outside of San Antonio. The farm's raceways were fed by what the owner claimed was the world's largest water well, with a 40,000-gallon per minute capacity. Living Waters' annual water consumption was equal to that of about a quarter of the population of San Antonio at the time. Although Pucek's use of the water was classified as "non-consumptive"—the water still existed when he was done with it—it came out of the raceways with too many impurities, like fish excrement, to be potable. After years of legal wrangling over the wastewater discharge, Pucek packed in Living Waters' fish operations for good.

There was still opportunity in the water business, though, and Pucek took advantage of it. When the Edwards Aquifer Authority asked users to file pumping permit applications in 2000, Pucek was given rights to 17,724 acre-feet annually—far short of his claimed historical maximum usage of 46,483 acre-feet, but still substantial. More legal wrangling followed; in 2001, Pucek gained rights to an additional 4,776 acre-feet per year. In late 2003, the San Antonio Water System, after three years of negotiations, bought the tangible assets of Living Waters Artesian Springs, Ltd., as well as most of its groundwater rights, from Pucek. The deal cost San Antonio $30 million.

people would be coming to your funeral, because someone would hang you."

The announcement of San Antonio's contracts with Alcoa came as a surprise to area residents, according to Brown, and "ignited a firestorm" of protest. Founded in 1999, Neighbors for Neighbors at its peak had 500 dues-paying members and the support of countless other individuals and dozens of community organizations. Brown says, "We would get 200 people to come to [a public hearing] and raise hell."

Neighbors for Neighbors—"one of the most successful grassroots groups" that Brown, in 30 years as an activist, has ever seen—fought the water deal on many fronts, including "raising hell" against Alcoa throughout the complicated process of getting permits for the Three Oaks mine. In 2000, NFN filed an unsuitability petition against the mine before the Texas Railroad Commission. "Most of the area is now a developing suburb of Austin and the area's fortunes are tied to Austin, not Alcoa," says Brown. The mine's proposed location is just 20 miles from the city limits, so "it seemed stupid to ruin this land just to get that dirty lignite out of it." The railroad commission disagreed. Brown counts this as an example of "our state regulatory agencies [being] in the pockets of big corporations."

Brown claims that the "several hundred people" Alcoa says supported the project at public hearings were usually "shipped in by busloads" by Alcoa itself. There were often some "nasty feelings" at such hearings, but, Brown says, "actually we've had some Alcoa employees come to us with good information." Neighbors for Neighbors even has some former Alcoa Rockdale employees among its members. Brown wishes NFN had put more energy into opposing Alcoa's final permits. But NFN's limited resources have been spread thin, protesting the new mine, the water deal—and Alcoa's air pollution.

Burning Dirt

Water is invaluable in Texas' semi-arid climate, but NFN fought its biggest battle with Alcoa over the lignite itself. Lignite is a particularly poor-quality coal; Brown calls it "burning dirt." Sandow lignite produces the more than 104,000 self-reported tons of pollutants that Alcoa's facility dumps into the air over Rockdale each year. Almost all (99.38%) of the pollution enjoys grandfathered exemption from the 1971 Texas Clean Air Act, making Alcoa Rockdale Texas' largest unregulated stationary source of air pollution.

Though NFN's efforts have forced Alcoa to decide how to bring its emissions in line with the Clean Air Act by September, it's already too late for the health of many Rockdale residents. Asks one contractor who occasionally works on refrigeration systems at the plant, "If the air is as safe as they say it is, then why are there so many Alcoa retirees toting around oxygen tanks?" This year, EPA consultant Abt Associates found that every year in Texas, pollution from coal-fired power plants causes 144 deaths from lung cancer, 1,791 nonfatal heart attacks, and almost 34,000 asthma attacks. Most of them could be prevented, according to Abt, if the plants would install available pollution controls.

Alcoa was on the guest list when, in 1997, then-governor George W. Bush invited executives of Texas' largest grandfathered point-source polluters to help him draft a Voluntary Emissions Reduction Permit (VERP) plan. The program's first official review was not scheduled until 2001, a move that ensured VERP a place in Bush's stump speeches in his bid for the presidency. And VERP's corporate co-authors contributed more than their legislation-drafting skills: the same companies donated $250,000 to the Bush campaign. Alcoa itself abstained, but its law firm, Vinson and Elkins, gave $202,850. Bush later tapped Alcoa CEO Paul O'Neill for his cabinet.

Bush would not have gotten nearly as much public relations mileage out of VERP if its first review had come before the 2000 election. In January 2001, the then-Texas Natural Resource Conservation Commission (TNRCC, or "Train Wreck" in local parlance; it later changed its name to the Texas Commission on Environmental Quality) reported that, in its first year and a half, VERP had been responsible for exactly no reductions in grandfathered emissions. None.

To its credit, the Texas Legislature replaced Bush's voluntary reduction plan with a mandatory one in spring 2001. Former state legislators joined citizen organizations in lobbying for the change. Former Representative Sissy Farenthold told the Chronicle that, "Back in 1971, I could have expected that my hair would be white by now, but I certainly did not expect this loophole [of grandfathered emissions] to still be in effect."

The new law was scheduled to take force in September 2001; in another display of impeccable timing, Alcoa finally applied for VERP permits in July, promising to reduce its emissions of smog-forming nitrous oxide by half in one year, and of acid rain-causing sulfur dioxide by 90% by 2006, as long as the reductions proved "economical." Otherwise, Alcoa lamented, pollution reduction would shut the Rockdale smelter down.

Meanwhile, NFN, Public Citizen, and Environmental Defense were gathering dirt on Alcoa's dirt. The groups found evidence that upgrades to the Rockdale facility in the 1980s constituted legally defined "major modifications" that should have nullified its grandfathered status and subjected it to Clean Air Act regulations. Alcoa downplayed the upgrades as "routiwne maintenance." In 1985, however, the Rockdale Reporter quoted Alcoa officials boasting that they had "torn apart as much as [possible] without throwing the whole thing away" and that the facility could "in no way … be called a 30-year-old plant because of the almost constant improvements and construction during the years."

Based on these discoveries, in October 2001 the three groups filed a notice of intent to sue Alcoa in federal court for 15 years of violations of the Texas Clean Air Act. The lawsuit was settled in April 2003. Alcoa would pay $1.5 million in fines and contribute an additional $2.5 million to local land trusts and environmental efforts. By September of this year, Alcoa must decide how to approach long-term reduction of its Rockdale emissions: install pollution control devices in the three existing power plants; shut those plants down and build cleaner ones; or find a cleaner source of energy for the smelter. (Shutting down the power plants would not shut down the mines: Alcoa could still supply lignite to a fourth power plant on site that is owned by another company.)

And there is always the whispered possibility of closing the smelter completely. Since protest against the water deal and the new mine began, Alcoa has complained that the expense of fitting the facilities with pollution controls or switching to a cleaner type of fuel would reduce their profits so much that the smelter would have to be closed.

The Austin American-Statesman has cited the cost of pollution controls at $100 million, resulting in a $40 million drop in profits for the Rockdale facility (no time frame was given for either figure). Alcoa will not reveal numbers for Rockdale alone, but in 1999, the year the Statesman published its figures, the corporation as a whole had $17.46 billion in assets (of which the $100 million would be 0.57%), had profits of $853 million (of which the $40 million would be 4.69%), and employed 92,600 people (of which Rockdale's 1,200 were 1.3%). The lost profits figure in particular makes one wish Alcoa had given the Statesman a time frame. Alcoa could not have meant that improvements at Rockdale would cost it $40 million in a single year; for, if Rockdale accounts for four and a half percent of Alcoa's profits in any given year, then investing one half of one percent of the company's assets in upgrading the site would seem justified. (And what company would give up such workers, who seem to produce three times as much annual profit, on average, as the workforce as a whole?)

It's conceivable that, in September, Alcoa will announce the closure of Rockdale; it already cut capacity by 25% in 2002. If, however, Alcoa continues operating its power plants and smelter, it will spend $4 million in fines and other payments for the Clean Air Act suit, along with the projected $100 million to reduce emissions—where the $100 million by itself was once lamented as too much for the operation to sustain. Perhaps Alcoa hopes that the $104 million cleanup cost (and additional lost profits) at Rockdale will be offset by the cheap coal and the water revenue its new mine nearby is slated to bring.

Everything's Under Control

In 2001, the *Austin Chronicle* declared NFN "Dragon Slayer of the Year," but the group has been forced to retreat while the dragon still lives. Alcoa, with its massive capital assets, can afford to fight such fights indefinitely. (NFN, in contrast, was delighted to get a $14,000 grant from the Ben and Jerry's Foundation in 2000.) Even Alcoa's defeats, as at the hands of the CFO (see box "Alcoa Acts Out Abroad"), are minor, affecting only one part of the corporation and making no change in its usual attitude or behavior.

The mechanical might of the Sandow strip mine can stand as a metaphor for that attitude, which reflects above all a desire to control the environment in which the company operates. The Texas Clean Air Act's requirements inconvenienced Alcoa in Rockdale, so the company blithely ignored the law for more than 30 years. Likewise, the state legislature's proposed groundwater regulations might have impeded Alcoa's ability to trade water for lignite, so Alcoa rushed San Antonio into their 1999 water deal before the legislative session began.

Given the insignificance of the projected cost of alternate fuel for Rockdale relative to the profits and assets of the corporation as a whole, cost may not be the real issue. Perhaps having control over the smelter's energy supply is even more important. Alcoa's bid to build expensive but private energy sources in energy-poor Brazil seems to support the notion, as does its treatment of labor organizers in Mexico.

Alcoa claims that its central Texas deals enjoyed "strong support … from the community," despite the strong, if unsuccessful, resistance they actually encountered. This attempt to revise history may be seen as a reach for control over public perception—keeping up the image of a good corporate neighbor that the company prefers to project. But Alcoa doesn't want to play by the rules set by the communities in which it operates. The company is aided by the complicity of some government officials who make deals that help the company undercut those rules.

"It's the tough stuff, like don't strip mine and don't pollute," that Alcoa can't get straight in Texas, according to former NFN president Billie Woods. When elected officials side with corporations against the public interest, the organized community is perhaps the only effective means for making the public voice heard again. Alcoa, other corporations like it, and the politicians who coddle them cannot claim to be good neighbors, and expect to enjoy the support of the community, until they get the "tough stuff"—including democracy—straight.

Alcoa Acts Out Abroad

Alcoa's disregard for the rules is not limited to Texas. In 1997, members of the Border Workers Committee (known by its Spanish initials, CFO) employed in an Alcoa Fujikura plant in Ciudad Acuña, Mexico, presented Alcoa's shareholders meeting with complaints of undisclosed gas releases that had sickened workers three years before. Then-CEO Paul O'Neill at first denied the claim, saying that the plants were so sanitary that you could "eat off the floors." But by the end of the meeting, where CFO was supported by the Interfaith Committee for Corporate Responsibility, Alcoa agreed to investigate the poisonings. The investigators substantiated CFO's claim, and Alcoa Fujikura's president, Robert Barton, was fired.

In 2002, the company resorted to violence and illegal firings to keep its favored representatives in charge of the state union operating in an Alcoa Fujikura plant in Piedras Negras. The CFO is still demanding that all workers who were illegally dismissed be reinstated, that Alcoa Fujikura recognize an independent union, and that two particularly abusive managers be fired.

And in Brazil in 2001, at a time when individual consumers was suffering electricity shortages, Alcoa proposed three major hydroelectric dams in the Amazon—their power to be used exclusively to fire the company's aluminum smelter in São Luis. The Brazilian government welcomed the project and brushed aside the effect it would have on indigenous settlements and the environment.

Similarly, despite years of intense public protest, the Icelandic government in 2003 gave Alcoa the go-ahead (and promises of subsidized energy) to build a smelter on the north side of the island's largest glacier. The project, which was stalled by a citizens' lawsuit in early 2004, would dam a glacial ice-melt river, divert it into a 25-mile long tunnel, and flood 22 square miles of wild tundra. Supporters point out that the smelter and associated works would employ 600 people; opponents counter that the location is prime for ecotourism, a sector that is growing rapidly in Iceland while aluminum performs erratically on the world market. Neighbors for Neighbors' Travis Brown also intimates that not all of the 600 positions promised would go to Icelanders; some Alcoa Rockdale employees have told Brown that they were offered a choice between early retirement or transfer to Iceland.

Chapter 10

POSITIVE DIRECTIONS

INNOVATIVE LABOR STRATEGIES
10 Campaigns to Learn From
Amy Offner
September/October 2003

Organized labor could use a shot in the arm. Today, the percentage of U.S. workers in unions continues to fall despite massive organizing drives. Public-sector workers have been stripped of basic rights by the most anti-union administration in U.S. history. The hostile political climate and economic downturn have pressured many unions into concessionary bargaining. And immigrant workers—the base of many service sector and light manufacturing unions—are weathering a new nativist crackdown.

But amid all the bad news, there are unions and rank-and-file groups fighting back with innovative campaigns and shop-floor actions. Here are ten recent efforts of note.

Members Organizing Members
In nine months last year, the Laborers Union quadrupled its membership in New Jersey's asbestos abatement industry, organizing 300 workers and raising the percentage of unionized workers in the industry from 15% to 65%. They did it with member organizers. The union hired fifteen of its own members; the new organizers spoke Spanish and Serbo-Croatian, the languages of the largely immigrant workforce, and were led by a worker with 12 years' experience in the asbestos industry. The union backed the member organizers with $600,000 and a sound organizing strategy: instead of targeting one contractor at a time, they simultaneously organized workers at all 60 of the state's asbestos abatement contractors. The result was a surge in the union's numbers and good first contracts, including raises of $5 to $7 per hour, plus contractor-paid health insurance and pensions.

Locking Out the Boss

When shop stewards and members were fired at Toronto's postal station E, workers were angry—but they weren't well organized. Rather than coordinate a large campaign or a strike, they decided to lock out their boss. The action depended on a core of organized members who convinced supporters from other unions and community organizations to arrive at the post office early one morning and link arms to block the boss from entering. Meanwhile, the workers—including many who hadn't known of the action in advance—entered the post office, discussed what was going on, and unanimously passed a resolution firing the bosses for the day. The early-morning action attracted positive TV news coverage and raised the level of activism on the shop floor. The results: the manager was given a new, non-supervisory position and the demonstration of power put a temporary stop to the firings.

Community Contract Campaign

Many unions are working to build and strengthen alliances with community organizations. Teachers' aides and assistants in Ithaca, New York, went so far as to frame their 2001 contract fight as a living wage campaign, launched in cooperation with the local Living Wage Coalition (LWC). NEA and LWC members circulated a community petition in support of the teachers and organized a large number of public events—rallies, marches, vigils, a forum for religious leaders, and a public hearing for the teachers to describe problems at work. After 18 months of union and community pressure, the teachers won raises approaching 50% over three years.

Making the Best of a Bad Reputation

Are movers stupid, violent drunks, or do they just play them on TV? When New York movers in Teamsters Local 814 went on strike in 2000, they made use of their bad reputation to get employers shaking in their boots. Using cell phones, the movers would let each other know where and when scabs were making deliveries throughout Manhattan. Within half an hour, a few dozen movers would be on the scene, acting out a carefully choreographed simulation of a riot. With burly movers shouting at the tops of their lungs, giving scabs the finger, threatening to block traffic, and generally creating scenes all around New York, building managers and clients were begging the employers to stop the strike. The movers shut down 28 deliveries in two days, and after four days, won an improved contract.

Stopping Scabs with Salts

When workers go on strike, employers often turn to day labor firms to provide scabs. But in Chicago, HERE, Teamster, and UE locals have teamed up with the local Day Labor Project to stop them. The key has been to "salt" the day labor firms—get union members or supporters hired as day laborers themselves—and find out the companies' vulnerabilities from the inside. In Chicago, salts have discovered a host of legal violations at day labor firms, from not informing workers that job assignments are scab positions to operating without licenses. Armed with evidence of violations, unions and the Day Labor Project have neutralized day labor firms by threatening them with lawsuits and public demonstrations if they provide scabs during strikes.

Defending Immigrant Rights

One of the labor movement's best innovations is its recent decision to defend the rights of immigrants. Traditionally, U.S. unions have done just the opposite, backing government efforts to deport undocumented workers and colluding with the CIA to undermine trade union movements abroad. Today, with immigrants facing heightened attacks in the guise of "national security," some unions have set important precedents for others to build on.

Challenging No-Match Firings

In San Francisco, HERE has fought employers' use of "no-match" letters to terminate immigrant workers. These letters, sent by the Social Security Administration (SSA) to inform employers when workers' Social Security numbers do not match the SSA database, are increasingly being used to target immigrant workers. But HERE has won an arbitration decision establishing that the letters do not constitute just cause for firing. It has also won a contract provision allowing undocumented workers a year to get documentation without losing their seniority.

Stopping Airport Raids

Last year at the Seattle-Tacoma International Airport, unions faced an employer which called in the INS to arrest and deport workers. In response to the INS raid at Sky Chef, a firm which prepares airline meals, local unions and the Jobs With Justice chapter staged a protest in the airport—an exceptionally difficult location for a rally post-9/11. The coalition used existing laws that designate airports as public spaces, as well as careful logistical planning, to pull off a powerful demonstration. Today, Jobs With Justice is convinced that there will be no more raids at the airport.

Lightning Strikes

There's nothing like a well-timed strike to shift power in the workplace. In many industries, there are times when employers can't afford to lose even an hour of work—and in some sectors, production is structured so that workers are always under time pressure. While these pressure-cooker arrangements burden workers, some unions have turned the tables on employers by staging short but brutal strikes when workers are most needed.

Not-So-Speedy Delivery

The San Francisco Bike Messenger Association (SFBMA, an ILWU affiliate) kicked off a campaign to organize the entire Bay Area urgent-delivery market in 1998-99. In the first year, they staged roughly 10 strikes. With companies guaranteeing deliveries in under an hour, messengers didn't need to park their bikes for long to win concessions: most strikes were just a few hours long. Messengers used the strikes to deliver "death by jabs," rather than knock-out punches to companies: frequent strikes combined with lawsuits and customer, community, and political pressure culminated in contracts and legal victories, including hundreds of thousands of dollars in back pay for wage and hour violations.

Supply Slowdown

More recently, UAW members struck for just two days at Johnson Controls plants in Ohio, Oklahoma, Missouri, and Louisiana, and achieved surprising victories. The June 2002 strikes at the auto parts manufacturer took advantage of the industry's "just-in-time" production strategy, where assembly plants maintain no inventory and depend on a steady flow of parts from suppliers like Johnson Controls. The strike slowed or halted production at five assembly plants and brought Johnson Controls to the table. Workers fighting for first contracts at three of the struck plants won agreements that included $1,500 signing bonuses, wage hikes of $3 or more, a new pension plan, and prohibitions on plant closures. Workers at the fourth plant, who had been fighting for union recognition, won a card-check neutrality agreement—a pledge that Johnson Controls would not fight their organizing drive, and would recognize the union once a majority of workers signed union cards. Not only that, the strike forced Johnson Controls to agree to card-check neutrality at 26 of its other plants.

Rotting Fruit for Rotten Bosses

In 1995, members of Oregon's farmworker union, PCUN, used a series of short, rolling strikes to win a 20% wage increase. The key was to target the strawberry fields, which needed to be harvested quickly. PCUN held two large strikes and a dozen smaller ones organized field by field. Just the publicized threat of rolling strikes at peak harvest time forced some growers to raise wages before the strawberry season began, and by the end of the campaign, farmworkers across the state saw their first wage gains in a decade.

Information on these campaigns is drawn from the *Troublemakers Handboook,* 2nd ed., forthcoming from Labor Notes <www.labornotes.org>. Thanks to authors Dan La Botz and Marsha Niemeijer and to editor Jane Slaughter for sharing draft material. For a key to union names, visit <www.dollarsandsense.org>.

NEXT STEPS FOR THE LIVING-WAGE MOVEMENT

Chris Tilly

September/October 2001

This past May, Harvard University students made national headlines by occupying a university building for three weeks to demand that Harvard and its contractors pay employees a living wage. While Harvard refused to grant the $10.25 wage that the students demanded, they did agree to form a study committee with ample student and union representation. In the days that followed, Harvard also ended a contract negotiation deadlock with food service workers by offering an unprecedented wage increase of over $1 per hour—a surprise move that many attributed to the feisty labor-student alliance built through the living-wage push.

Harvard's living-wage activists represent the tip of a much larger national iceberg, most of which has taken the form of attempts to pass local living-wage ordinances. Over 60 local governments have passed living-wage laws—almost all since a groundbreaking Baltimore ordinance passed in 1994—with more coming on board each month. Such ordinances typically require the local government, along with any businesses that supply it, to pay a wage well above the current federal minimum of $5.15. Living-wage coalitions originally set wage floors at the amount needed by a full-time, year-round worker to keep a family of four above the poverty line (currently about $8.40 per hour), but like the Harvard students, they are increasingly campaigning for higher figures based on area living costs. The community organization ACORN (Alliance of Community Organizations for Reform Now) has spearheaded many of the coalitions, and an up-to-date living-wage scorecard can be found on its web site <www.livingwagecampaign.org>. At the heart of the campaigns are low-wage workers like Celia Talavera, who joined Santa Monica's successful living-wage campaign last May. Referring to her job as a hotel housekeeper, she said, "I am fighting for a living wage because I want to work there for a long time."

The spread of living-wage laws reflects deep public concern about the unfairness of today's economy to those at the bottom of the paid workforce. A recent *USA Today* poll rated "lack of livable wage jobs" as Americans' top worry, even ahead of such perennial favorites as "decline of moral values." This sentiment makes living-wage laws eminently winnable. But it is worth pausing to ask: What, exactly, has the living-wage movement won? And how can we adapt this strategy to win more?

Limited Victories

Opponents of living-wage laws argue that they will increase costs to local taxpayers, and drive business away from the locality. Living-wage boosters have two responses. First, fairness is worth the cost. And second, studies have shown that such ordinances have *not* escalated costs, nor repelled businesses. But why not? After all, economic theory suggests that companies compelled to pay higher costs will either seek to pass them on, or move on to greener pastures.

One reason is that living-wage ordinances typically affect very few workers. At passage, an average of only about 1,000 per locality actually have their wages boosted (in part because many of those covered already earn the mandated wage or more). This number is stunningly small, given that living-wage adopters include Los Angeles, New York, Chicago, and numerous other large cities and counties.

But smallness cannot be the entire explanation. Johns Hopkins University economist Erica Schoenberger and others followed specific contracts to the City of Baltimore, looking at changes from before that city's living-wage law went into effect to two years after. They found that contract costs increased only about 1%, far less than inflation. One possibility, of course, is that the wage floor spurred contractors to find new ways to increase true efficiency—getting the same amount of work done with less labor and less effort. For instance, this can happen if higher wages allow employers to hold on to the same employees longer, shrinking employer expenditures on recruitment, hiring, and training. Or perhaps the businesses have simply accepted lower profit margins.

But there are three less pleasant possibilities as well. Contractors may have sped up their workers, extracting more work in return for the higher pay. They may have reduced the quality of goods or services they delivered. Or, they may simply have failed to comply with the law. The poor track record of many laws that declare labor rights without adequate enforcement mechanisms suggests that this last possibility may be quite real. Even the federal minimum wage is ignored by growing numbers of employers, says economist Howard Wial of the AFL-CIO's Working for America Institute.

Extend the Laws?

How should the living-wage movement respond to this evidence of limited impact? One possibility is to widen and sharpen living-wage laws' bite. Recent living-wage ordinances have set minimums as high as $12 per hour (in Santa Cruz, California). In Santa Monica, California, campaigners extended coverage to tourist-district businesses that had received city subsidies for redevelopment, and elsewhere coalitions aim to expand the law to include any business that receives substantial subsidies or tax abatements from the local government. Activists are also setting their sights on living-wage agreements with large private businesses—starting with those most vulnerable to political and public relations pressure, especially nonprofits such as Harvard. Even more ambitious are the advocates proposing state and federal living-wage laws; legislative proposals are pending in Hawaii, Vermont, and at the federal level. (See box "Vermont's Livable Income Law.")

Others are pursuing area-wide minimum wages set at levels closer to a living wage. Washington, D.C., has long had a minimum wage $1 above the federal minimum. Similar referenda were defeated in Houston and Denver, but New Orleans

Vermont's Livable Income Law

While Vermont politics are famously progressive, its low wages (9% below the national average) and high living expenses (15% above national average) are anything but worker-friendly. Armed with these and other findings detailed in its *Vermont Job Gap Study*, the Burlington-based Peace and Justice Center set out to change those statistics with its Livable Wage Campaign.

The Vermont Livable Wage Campaign has achieved two significant legislative victories. Act 21, passed in 1999, raised the minimum wage by 50 cents, to $5.75 an hour (60 cents above the national minimum, though still a dollar less than in neighboring Massachusetts). The measure also provided funding for the state legislature to form a Study Committee on a Livable Income.

In 2000, the state's General Assembly agreed to some of the Study Committee's recommendations and passed Act 119, which took three more steps on the livable-wage issue:

- an increased minimum wage, now at $6.25 per hour
- a budget of $3.5 million (up 7%) for Vermont's Earned Income Tax Credit
- the publication of four annual reports by the state Joint Fiscal Office of Basic Needs Budgets/ Livable Wage Figures.

Another bill, which would raise the minimum wage to $6.75, passed Vermont's Senate this year. This bill will be taken up in 2002 by the state House of Representatives, where its passage is uncertain. After the 2000 elections, conservatives gained a majority, in a backlash against recent legislation permitting same-sex "civil unions."

The Livable Wage Campaign, however, continues on several fronts, including a multi-year strategy to increase wages for some of Vermont's worst-paid workers—child care staff and public-school support staff at K-12 schools and state colleges.

—*Beth Burgess*

Resources: Vermont's Livable Wage Campaign <www.vtlivablewage.org>; Ellen Kahler, Vermont Peace and Justice Center.

citizens will vote on a local minimum wage this coming February.

These initiatives are important, because there is certainly room for significant wage increases before we can expect negative effects on employment. When adjusted for inflation, hourly wages for the lowest-paid tenth of the workforce jumped by 9% between 1995 and 1999, in large part due to living-wage laws and federal minimum-wage increases. Yet the unemployment rate at the end of the 1990s fell to its lowest level in 30 years. More fine-grained studies of state and federal minimum-wage increases yield the same result: Such increases have caused little or no worker displacement over the last ten years. One reason is that wages for the bottom tenth were beaten so far down over the 1980s and early 1990s—even after the recent wage surge, inflation-adjusted 1999 wages remained 10% below their 1979 level.

But if the movement succeeds in extending and increasing living wages, at some point economic theory is bound to be proven right: costs to taxpayers will climb, employment will decrease, or both. Even in the most positive scenario—that businesses find ways to increase productivity—remember that rising productivity typically means doing the same work with fewer workers. This was the experience of the Congress of Industrial Organizations (now part of the AFL-CIO), which unionized core manufacturing industries in the 1930s and 1940s. The CIO succeeded in hiking pay, and in the decades that followed, U.S. manufacturers avidly hunted for ways to boost productivity. The good news is that U.S. manufacturing became the most productive in the world for several decades. The bad news is that heightened efficiency shrank labor requirements dramatically. In fact, this is the main reason for declining U.S. manufacturing jobs, far overshadowing shifts in the global division of labor. Manufacturing is a slightly larger share of U.S. domestic output today than it was in 1960, but factory employment has dropped from 31% to 14% of the workforce.

If extending the living wage's impact will eventually either raise costs to taxpayers or diminish employment, it may be tempting to adopt the other major argument advocates use: fairness is worth the cost. And this answer makes a great deal of sense. Think for a moment about the federal *minimum* wage's effect. The average person who eats at McDonald's earns more than the average person who works at McDonald's, so if bumping up the minimum wage raises the cost of burgers, cash is shifting in more or less the right direction. By the same token, over the 1980s and 1990s, local and state privatization and tax cuts redistributed income from low-income workers to taxpayers who have higher incomes on average—so if living wages help to reverse this flow, that's a plus for equality.

What about job losses? Few would object to shutting down companies that rely on slavery or child labor. The same logic extends to exploitatively low wages. As with child labor laws, laws that bar low wages will put some workers out of a job. So it is important to view living-wage laws as part of a broader program that includes job creation, training, and income support for those unable to work. To achieve this broader program, we need a powerful movement. And the red-hot living-wage movement offers one of the strongest potential building blocks for such a broader movement.

Build the Movement?

That brings us to another response to the limited impact of living-wage laws to date: using the living wage as a movement-building tool. The living-wage issue encourages labor, community, and religious organizations to coalesce around genuine shared interests, creating an opportunity to open an even broader dialogue on wage fairness and inequality.

The goal should be to build movements that can address some of the weaknesses of current living-wage laws, including non-compliance and the potential for speed-up or job loss. Of course the U.S. institution that has been most effective in monitoring compliance with labor laws, curbing speed-up, and lobbying for job creation is the labor movement—and living-wage laws provide a golden opportunity

Living Wages Overseas

A movement-building perspective helps us think about living wages in an international context. If people in rich countries try to decide the appropriate wage floor for people in poor countries, they run a serious risk of destructive paternalism. Consider the case of Haiti. A few years back, the National Labor Committee (the folks who blew the whistle on the sweatshops behind Kathie Lee Gifford's designer label) and others—me included—made much of the fact that Haiti's export assembly factories paid as little as 11 cents an hour. True enough, but it's also true that in the context of economic collapse, many in the Haitian countryside view this as a sufficiently handsome wage to crowd into shacks in Port-au-Prince for a chance to get one of these jobs. A U.S. trade law that barred goods produced by workers earning less than, say, $1 an hour would effectively shut Haitian goods out of this country, causing job loss in Haiti.

The alternative is to find ways to beef up Haitians' ability to place greater demands on employers, allowing Haitians to decide for themselves what is a living wage. That meant backing President Jean-Bertrand Aristide's adoption of a $2.50 per day minimum wage in 1991. It means supporting Batay Ouvriye (Workers' Struggle) when they help export-sector workers form unions. In general, it means taking a lead from workers, peasants, and pro-people governments in the global South, and conditioning trade privileges on respect for workers' right to organize rather than on any particular wage level. Consistently applying this principle means that goods produced by companies in the United States that flout labor laws—not just such companies in Haiti, Mexico, or China—should likewise be penalized.

for strengthening unions. Baltimore activists who won that city's 1994 living-wage ordinance, considered the spark of the current living-wage prairie fire, sought above all to slow down union-busting privatization. Living-wage laws close off low wages as a competitive strategy, dulling the edge of employer resistance to unions. Some coalitions have also won clauses requiring covered businesses to be neutral in union organizing campaigns or even to immediately recognize any union that signs up a majority of workers, foreclosing employers' usual anti-union tactics. A lower profile way to disarm anti-union employers is to ban retaliation against workers organizing for a living wage—which basically puts a local law against union-busting on the books to supplement weak federal laws.

In addition, living-wage advocates need to pay attention to winning laws that nurture the living-wage movement itself. For instance, some laws give living-wage coalition constituents the first crack at applying for jobs covered by the living wage, in some cases through coalition-controlled hiring halls. Patronage usually gets a bad name, but this kind of community control over hiring can help cement a living-wage movement's strength by giving it the ability to reward its members and supporters. Moreover, although advocates dream of short-cutting the process of passing hundreds of local laws by winning federal legislation, in reality the local mobilizations are the key to success with compliance. Any federal law is likely to remain a dead letter unless we have built those hundreds of robust place-based coalitions ready to monitor the law's implementation and use it as an organizing tool.

The biggest challenge in movement building is reaching beyond wages and jobs to the less obvious issues. For instance, how do we defend the quality of public services? Many nonprofits and community-based organizations have been drawn into the game of privatizing social services. Sometimes these agencies enter unholy alliances with private businesses and city officials to oppose a living-wage law, because they fear it will threaten their job programs for disadvantaged workers. Organizations representing workers, communities, service providers, and clients must search for common ground based on high wages and adequate services. In Massachusetts, for example, unions and service providers have campaigned jointly for a state-funded living wage for human-service workers employed by hundreds of state contractors.

Another tough nut to crack is how to win adequate income for those who are unable to work for pay, or who end up working on a very part-time or part-year basis. Unfortunately, some of the same public attitudes that make it easy to build coalitions around living wages—equating work with virtue, for example—make it hard to defend welfare for people not working for wages. The principals from the living-wage movement—unions, churches, and ACORN itself—have also joined efforts to demand more adequate and less restrictive welfare benefits, but so far with much less success.

More Than Just a Living

The sixty local living-wage laws to date represent a tremendous victory for working people, but one that is, so far, narrow in scope. The challenge now is to extend the reach of the laws, while building and broadening the living-wage movement at the same time. Extending the laws' reach means bringing more cities on board, but even more importantly, boosting the numbers and types of workers covered within each city. To the extent that advocates succeed in passing stronger laws, they will engender fiercer resistance—both direct challenges to the legislation and more covert attempts to flout the laws or shift the costs. To successfully counter this resistance, movement-building efforts must go beyond the boundaries of the current living-wage movement. The end result will look less like a living-wage movement, more like a broad insurgent movement to redistribute income and other resources.

Sources: Robert Pollin and Stephanie Luce, *The Living Wage: Building a Fair Economy* (W.W. Norton, 1998); Lawrence Mishel, Jared Bernstein, and John Schmitt, *The State of Working America 200-2001* (Cornell University Press 2001); David Card and Alan B. Krueger, *Myth and Measurement: The New Economics of the Minimum Wage* (Princeton University Press 1995).

THE COMING ERA OF WEALTH TAXATION
Gar Alperovitz
July/August 2004

Americans concerned with inequality commonly point to huge disparities in the distribution of income, but the ownership of wealth is far, far more concentrated. This fact is certain to bring the question of wealth taxation to the top of the nation's political agenda as the country's fiscal crisis deepens and, with it, the deterioration of public institutions and the pain of all those who rely on them.

Broadly, in any one year the top 20% garners for itself roughly 50% of all income, while the bottom 80% must make due with the rest. The top 1% regularly takes home more income than the bottom 100 million Americans combined.

When it comes to wealth, these numbers appear almost egalitarian. The richest 1% of households owns half of all outstanding stock, financial securities, trust equity, and business equity! A mere 5% at the very top owns more than two-thirds of the wealth in America's gigantic corporate economy, known as financial wealth—mainly stocks and bonds.

This is a medieval concentration of economic power. The only real question is when its scale and implications will surface as a powerful political issue. A wealth tax is "by definition, the most progressive way to raise revenue, since it hits only the very pinnacle of the income distribution," notes economist Robert Kuttner. But conventional wisdom says that it is impossible to deal with wealth head-on. The battle over repeal of the estate tax, in this view, demonstrated that even the most traditional of "wealth taxes" are no longer politically feasible.

Perhaps. However, a longer perspective reminds us that times can change—as, indeed, they often have when economic circumstances demanded it.

Emerging Signs of Change
Indeed, times are already beginning to change. One sign: Although many Democrats were nervous about challenging George W. Bush in the first year after he took office, by early 2004 all the Democrats running for president had come to demand a repeal in some form of his tax giveaways to the elite.

It is instructive to trace the process of change. At the outset, only a few liberals challenged the president. The late Paul Wellstone, for instance, proposed freezing future income tax reductions for the top 1% and retaining the corporate Alternative Minimum Tax (AMT), for an estimated $134 billion in additional revenue over 10 years. Ted Kennedy proposed delaying tax cuts for families with incomes over $130,000 and keeping the estate tax (while gradually raising the value of exempted estates from a then-current $1 million to $4 million by 2010). Kennedy estimated this would generate $350 billion over 10 years.

By May 2002, even centrist Democrat Joseph Lieberman urged postponing both the full repeal of the estate tax and reductions in the top income-tax rates. Lieberman estimated his plan would save a trillion dollars over 20 years. The Bush tax cuts were simply unfair, he said, "giving the biggest benefit to those who needed it the least."

The Democrats failed to stop Bush's 2001 and 2003 rounds of tax cuts. But there are reasons to believe that politicians will ultimately come to accept the validity of maintaining and raising taxes on the wealthiest Americans. Just as many Democrats changed their stand on the Bush tax cuts, a similar progression is likely with regard to wealth taxation more generally over the next few years—and for two very good reasons. First, there is an extraordinary fiscal crisis brewing; and second, wealth taxes—like taxes on very high-income recipients—put 95% to 98% of the people on one side of the line and only 2% to 5% or so on the other.

Go Where the Money Is

The hard truth is that it is now all but impossible to significantly raise taxes on the middle class. This reality flows in part from the ongoing decline of organized labor's political power, and in part from the Republicans' takeover of the South—another long and unpleasant political story. At any rate, it means that the only place to look for significant resources is where the remaining real money is—in the holdings of corporations and the elites who overwhelmingly own them. Put another way: Raising taxes first on the income and ultimately on the wealth of the very top groups is likely to become all but inevitable as, over time, it becomes clear that there is no way to get much more in taxes from the middle-class suburbs.

Moreover, as Democratic politicians have come increasingly to realize, the "logic of small versus large numbers" could potentially neutralize a good part of the suburbs politically, painting conservatives into a corner where they're forced to defend the very unreasonable privileges of the very rich.

The knee-jerk reaction that taxing wealth is impossible is based upon the kind of thinking about politics that "remembers the future"—in other words, thinking that assumes the future is likely to be just like the past, whether accurately remembered or not. Since wealth has not been taxed, it cannot be taxed now, goes the argument (or rather, assumption).

Of course, taxation of wealth has long been central to the American tax system for the kind of wealth most Americans own—their homes. Real estate taxes, moreover, are based on the market value of the home—not the value of a homeowner's equity: An owner of a $200,000 home will be taxed on the full value of the asset, even if her actual ownership position, with a mortgage debt of, say, $190,000, is only a small fraction of this amount. A new, more equitable form of wealth taxation would simply extend this very well established tradition and—at long last!—bring the elites who own most of the nation's financial wealth into the picture.

Many Americans once thought it impossible to tax even income—until the 1913 passage, after long debate and political agitation, of the 16th Amendment to the U.S.

Constitution. Note, however, that for many years, the amendment in practice meant targeting elites: Significant income taxation was largely restricted to roughly the top 2% to 4% until World War II.

Even more important is a rarely discussed truth at the heart of the modern history of taxation. For a very long time now the federal income tax has, in fact, targeted elites—even in the Bush era, and even in a society preoccupied with terrorism and war. In 2000, the top 1% of households paid 36.5% of federal income taxes. The top 5% paid 56.2%. Although detailed calculations are not yet available, the massive Bush tax cuts are not expected to alter the order of magnitude of these figures. Estimates suggest that, ultimately, the tax reductions may modify the figures by no more than two or perhaps three percentage points.

In significant part this results from the rapidly growing incomes of the wealthiest: even at lower rates, they'll still be paying nearly the same share of total income tax. The simple fact is, however, that the record demonstrates it is not impossible to target elites. We need to take this political point seriously and act on it aggressively in the coming period.

Fiscal Crunch Ahead

What makes wealth taxes even more likely in the coming period is the extraordinary dimension of the fiscal crisis, which will force government at all levels to adopt new strategies for producing additional resources. Projections for the coming decade alone suggest a combined federal fiscal deficit of more than $5 trillion—$7.5 trillion if Social Security Trust Fund reserves are left aside.

A worsening fiscal squeeze is coming—and it is not likely to be reversed any time soon. Critically, spending on Social Security benefits and Medicare will continue to rise as the baby-boom generation retires. So will spending on Medicaid. Recent studies project that by 2080 these three programs alone will consume a larger share of GDP than all of the money the federal government collects in taxes. And, of course, the ongoing occupation of Iraq will continue to demand large-scale financial support.

Nor are the trends likely to be altered without dramatic change: The truth is that the Bush tax and spending strategies, though particularly egregious, are by no means unique. Long before the Bush-era reductions, domestic discretionary spending by the federal government was trending down—from 4.7% of GDP a quarter century ago to 3.5% now, a drop during this period alone of roughly 25%.

A radically new context is thus taking shape which will force very difficult choices. Either there will be no solution to many of the nation's problems, or politicians and the public will have to try something new. Suburban middle-class voters, who rely on good schools, affordable health care, assistance for elderly parents, and public infrastructure of all kinds, will begin to feel the effects if the "beast" of government is truly starved. This pain is likely to redirect their politics back toward support for a strong public sector—one which is underwritten by taxes on the wealthiest. Quite simply, it is the only place to go.

Time to Tax Wealth

Ideological conservatives like to argue that all Americans want to get rich and so oppose higher taxes on the upper-income groups they hope to join. In his recent history of taxation, *New York Times* reporter Steven Weisman has shown that this may or may not be so in normal times, but that when social and economic pain increase, politicians and the public have repeatedly moved to tax those who can afford it most. Bill Clinton, for one, raised rates on the top groups when necessity dictated. So did the current president's father! Now, several states—including even conservative Virginia—have seen pragmatic Republicans take the lead in proposing new elite taxation as the local fiscal crisis has deepened.

The likelihood of a political shift on this issue is also suggested by the growing number of people who have proposed direct wealth taxation. A large group of multimillionaires has launched a campaign opposing elimination of taxes on inherited wealth—paid only by the top 2%—as "bad for our democracy, our economy, and our society." Yale law professors Bruce Ackerman and Anne Alstott in their book *The Stakeholder Society* have proposed an annual 2% wealth tax (after exempting the first $80,000). Colgate economist Thomas Michl has urged a net-worth tax, and Hofstra law professor Leon Friedman has proposed a 1% tax on wealth owned by the top 1%. Even Donald Trump has proposed a one time 14.25% net-worth tax on Americans with more than $10 million in assets.

Wealth taxation is common in Europe. Most European wealth taxes have an exemption for low and moderate levels of wealth (especially the value of pensions and annuities). Economist Edward Wolff, who has studied these precedents carefully, suggests that America might begin with a wealth tax based on the very modest Swiss effort, with marginal rates between 0.05% and 0.3% after exempting roughly the first $100,000 of assets for married couples. He estimates that if this were done, only millionaires would pay an additional 1% or more of their income in taxes.

Europe also offers examples of much more aggressive approaches. Wealth taxation rates in 10 other European countries are much higher than Switzerland's—between 1% and 3%—and would yield considerable revenues if applied here. Wolff calculated that a 3% Swedish-style wealth tax in the United States would have produced $545 billion in revenue in 1998. Although an updated estimate is not available, nominal GDP increased about 19% between 1998 and 2002, and wealth taxes would likely produce revenues that roughly tracked that increase.

Some writers have held that wealth taxes are prohibited by the U.S. Constitution. There appear to be two answers to this. The first is legal: Ackerman, a noted constitutional expert, has argued at length in the Columbia Law Review that wealth taxes are not only constitutional, but represent the heart of both original and contemporary legal doctrine on taxation.

The second answer is political. We know that courts have a way of bending to the winds of political-economic reality over time. As the pain deepens, the courts are likely one day to recognize the validity of the legal arguments in favor of wealth taxation. Alternatively, political pressure may ultimately mandate further constitutional change, just as it did in 1913 with regard to income taxation.

There is no way of knowing for sure. But as with all important political change, the real answer will be found only if and when pressure builds up both intellectually and politically for a new course of action. The challenge, as always, is not simply to propose, but to act.

CONTRIBUTORS

Gar Alperovitz is Lionel Bauman Professor of Political Economy at the University of Maryland and President of the National Center for Economic and Security Alternatives.

David Bacon is a journalist and photographer covering labor, immigration, and the impact of the global economy on workers.

Ricky Baldwin is a labor activist and writer. His articles have appeared in *Extra!, Z Magazine, Labor Notes,* and elsewhere.

Phineas Baxandall is a lecturer at the Committee for Degrees in Social Studies at Harvard University and a Dollars & Sense associate.

Ben Boothby is a *Dollars & Sense* collective member.

Heather Boushey is an economist at the Economic Policy Institute in Washington, D.C., where she conducts research on labor markets. She is co-author of *The State of Working America.*

Beth Burgess is a member of the *Dollars & Sense* collective.

Esther Cervantes is a member of the *Dollars & Sense* collective.

Angel Chen is a former *Dollars & Sense* intern.

Chuck Collins, a member of the *Dollars & Sense* collective, is the Program Director at United for a Fair Economy and co-author, with William H. Gates, Sr., of *Wealth and Our Commonwealth: Why America Should Tax Accumulated Fortunes* (Beacon Press, January 2003).

Thatcher Collins is a former *Dollars & Sense* collective member.

Jamie Court, author of *Corporateering: How Corporate Power Steals Your Personal Freedom and What You Can Do About It* (Tarcher/Putnam), is president of the Santa Monica-based Foundation for Taxpayer and Consumer Rights <www.corporateering.org>.

Daniel Fireside is a *Dollars & Sense* co-editor.

Ellen Frank is a member of the *Dollars & Sense* collective, and teaches economics at Emmanuel College.

Ross Gelbspan is a former reporter for the *Boston Globe* and is the author of *Boiling Point* (2004, Basic Books).

Amy Gluckman is a *Dollars & Sense* co-editor.

Elise Gould is an economist at the Economic Policy Institute where she specializes in health and labor issues.

Rosie Hunter is a researcher with United for a Fair Economy in Boston.

David Imbroscio is Associate Professor of Political Science at the University of Louisville.

Betsy Leondar-Wright is the Communications Director at United for a Fair Economy.

Arthur MacEwan, a *Dollars & Sense* associate, is professor of economics at the University of Massachusetts, Boston. His most recent book is *Neoliberalism or Democracy? Economic Strategy, Markets, and Alternatives for the 21st Century* (Zed Books, 1999).

Ann Markusen is a former senior fellow at the Council on Foreign Relations and Professor of Public Policy and Planning at the Humphrey Institute of Public Affairs, University of Minnesota.

John Miller is a member of the *Dollars & Sense* collective, and teaches economics at Wheaton College.

Lorenzo Nencioli is a former *Dollars & Sense* intern.

Amy Offner is a former co-editor of *Dollars & Sense*.

Sarah Olson is a contributing reporter for Free Speech Radio News and the National

Radio Project's "Making Contact."

Doug Orr teaches economics at Eastern Washington University

Nomi Prins is a former investment banker turned journalist, and author of a forth-coming book on corporate corruption, *Money for Nothing* (The New Press).

Alejandro Reuss is a member of the *Dollars & Sense* collective and a board member of Bikes Not Bombs <<www.bikesnotbombs.org>>.

Adria Scharf is co-editor of *Dollars & Sense.*

William E. Spriggs is a senior fellow at the Economic Policy Institute, and was formerly the executive director of the National Urban League Institute for Opportunity and Equality.

Andrew Strom is a lawyer for the Service Employees International Union, Local 32BJ, which represents over 70,000 building service workers in New York, New Jersey, and Connecticut.

Chris Sturr teaches Social Studies at Harvard University and is a member of the *Dollars & Sense* collective.

David Swanson is media coordinator at the International Labor Communications Association.

Todd Tavares is a former *Dollars & Sense* intern.

Chris Tilly, a member of the *Dollars & Sense* collective, teaches at the University of Massachusetts, Lowell.

Rodney Ward is a longtime labor and peace activist, laid-off flight attendant, and staff member at *Dollars & Sense.*

Thad Williamson is a doctoral student in political theory at Harvard and a *Dollars & Sense* collective member.